Faulkner and Material Culture

FAULKNER AND YOKNAPATAWPHA

2004

Faulkner and Material Culture

FAULKNER AND YOKNAPATAWPHA, 2004

EDITED BY
JOSEPH R. URGO
AND
ANN J. ABADIE

UNIVERSITY PRESS OF MISSISSIPPI
JACKSON

www.upress.state.ms.us

The University Press of Mississippi is a member of the Association of
American University Presses.

First edition 2007

Library of Congress Cataloging-in-Publication Data

Faulkner and Yoknapatawpha Conference (31st : 2004 : University of Mississippi)
    Faulkner and material culture : Faulkner and Yoknapatawpha, 2004 / edited by
Joseph R. Urgo and Ann J. Abadie. — 1st ed.
        p. cm.
    Papers originally presented at the 31st Faulkner and Yoknapatawpha
Conference, July 25–29, 2004.
    Includes bibliographical references and index.
    ISBN-13: 978-1-57806-939-2 (alk. paper)
    ISBN-10: 1-57806-939-4 (alk. paper)
    1. Faulkner, William, 1897–1962—Criticism and interpretation—Congresses.
2. Yoknapatawpha County (Imaginary place)—Congresses. 3. Material culture
in literature—Congresses. 4. Southern States—In literature—Congresses.
5. Material culture—Southern States—Congresses. I. Urgo, Joseph R.
II. Abadie, Ann J. III. Title.
    PS3511.A86Z78321176   2004
    813'.52—dc22   2006017776

British Library Cataloging-in-Publication Data available

In Memoriam,
Mary Hartwell Bishop Howorth
May 12, 1920–October 19, 2004

Contents

Introduction

12. *So I made it on the bevel.*
13. *It makes a neater job.*

*They came from some place out in Yoknapatawpha county, trying to
get to Jefferson with it.*
— William Faulkner, As I Lay Dying

1

Readers of the volumes that issue from the annual Faulkner and Yoknapatawpha Conference expect, every year, a new set of perspectives on some
topic arising from or applied to our understanding of Faulkner here in his
home town, at the university he attended and where he was employed
for a while. As you might expect, there is a committee, made up of local
Faulkner scholars and interested professors from Southern, American,
and other literary fields, and this committee meets throughout the year to
talk about topics, potential speakers, the budget, and the various logistical
challenges inherent in hosting a few hundred guests each July from across
the United States, Europe, Latin America, Africa, and Asia. We are hyper-
conscious of the fact that thousands of Faulkner readers on this planet
have as a goal to someday get to Oxford, to see what Faulkner saw, maybe
even to see *as* Faulkner saw, to walk in Yoknapatawpha. Faulkner antici-
pated the day in *Requiem for a Nun,* his one tourist novel, when strangers
would seek out the small Mississippi town that had forfeited any ambitions
of anonymity when it became the town that raised the Nobel Laureate:

> you, a stranger, an outlander say from the East or the North or the Far West,
> passing through the little town by simple accident, or perhaps relation or
> acquaintance or friend of one of the outland families which had moved into
> one of the pristine and recent subdivisions, yourself turning out of your way
> to fumble among road signs and filling stations out of frank curiosity, trying
> to learn, comprehend, understand what had brought your cousin or friend or
> acquaintance to elect to live here.[1]

"Here" is Oxford but it is also not Oxford, but Jefferson—the town of
Faulkner's imagination, the town he built; and "here" is also Lafayette
County but not Lafayette County, rather Yoknapatawpha, the county
he constructed. *The two worlds.* One just happens to be Oxford, and it
belongs to the people of Oxford and to Lafayette County, Mississippi. One

by the labor of a lifetime of writing became Jefferson and is owned by no one, or it is possessed in turn by everyone who can read it and enter, and become what Faulkner called a Yoknapatawphian. I remember moving to this town in 2000 and entering the Lafayette County Courthouse (to me, *The* Courthouse) to get my automobile tags and thinking, when faced with the woman behind the counter (who said yes to the debit card), that this is nothing more than a place for a civil servant to work, and all I am doing is getting my car tag.

Faulkner labeled those people who were here (either as residents or as "you," stranger) and who were aware that they lived in two worlds "the irreconcilable Jeffersonians and Yoknapatawphians." These were people "who had . . . actual personal dealings" with the Courthouse on the Square *quite specifically in Oxford* and with the Courthouse in Jefferson *quite generally everywhere* the books are read and translated and read again. There is a discernible process by which people become "not just Mississippians but Jeffersonians and Yoknapatawphians" (642). In the novel, as you recall, it has to do with being able to read the deeper significance of Cecilia Farmer's name etched into the window pane of the jailhouse window.

> suddenly you would realise that something curious was happening or had happened here: that instead of dying off as they should as time passed, it was as though these old irreconcilables were actually increasing in number; as though with each interment of one, two more shared that vacancy. (642)

And the narrator of *Requiem for a Nun* predicts that one day there will be hundreds—and we can now say thousands, more

> —by now you had already begun to understand why your kin or friend or acquaintance had elected to come to such as this with his family and call it his life, [to become] not just Mississippians but Jeffersonians and Yoknapatawphians: by which time—who knows?—not merely the pane, but the whole window, perhaps the entire wall, may have been removed and embalmed intact into a museum by an historical, or anyway a cultural club of ladies. (642–43)

It is true, something happened here, something so singular in the world of letters and so phenomenally irreconcilable with the material reality of the place that you have to look again and again, and see if you can get it "to move under your eyes," as Faulkner wrote about it, "seeming actually to have entered into another sense than vision," to see the two worlds, to "burn away the rubble-dross of fact and probability, leaving only truth the dream" (648). This is northern Mississippi, after all, not anywhere near urban or cultural centers, not anywhere near where we would have

expected, in the early twentieth century, to see the emergence of an intellectual and literary phenomenon that would redefine narrative, reinvigor-
ate the novel, and forever change the course of literary history. The 2004
conference topic, "Faulkner and Material Culture," grapples with the fact
that the two worlds intersect continuously, they must intersect if either is
to be recognizable. Underwritten by the University Museums, the 2004
conference coincided with the reopening of Rowan Oak, fully renovated
and restored to replicate the way it looked when Faulkner would have last
seen it (which was always a little better than it actually was), before his
death in 1962.

Rowan Oak is emblematic of Faulkner's sense of two worlds, and it also
emerged by the work of his hands and his mind. It was, on the one hand,
"The Bailey Place" when he purchased it in 1930. It was built in the 1840s
by Colonel Robert B. Shegog, who came to Mississippi from Tennessee.
Faulkner renamed the estate Rowan Oak, but not because the property
held either rowan or oak trees—the naming would not come from *that*
world. According to Joseph Blotner, Faulkner knew from Frazer's *The
Golden Bough* that Scottish farmers would place cuttings from the rowan
tree over barn doors to prevent evil spirits from casting spells and stealing
milk. The rowan tree (which is a mountain ash, not an oak) is indigenous
to Scotland and signifies peace and security.[2] Faulkner's impulse was not
unlike Sophonsiba Beauchamp's insistence, in *Go Down, Moses,* that the
Beauchamp house be called Warwick. Nonetheless, Faulkner was more
successful than his vampish (and in his creation of her, self-deprecating)
character in recasting his home as the intersection of two worlds. The difference is significant. Whereas Sophonsiba Beauchamp looked back to
an actual place in England to define her legacy, naming her Mississippi
estate "Warwick after the place in England that she said Mr. Hubert was
probably the true earl of,"[3] Faulkner looked not to what was but to what,
absent his intervention, would never have been. There is, at bottom,
something outrageous about christening a ramshackle, dilapidated, and
abandoned structure "Rowan Oak"—as daring, that is, as renaming an
obscure county in northern Mississippi "Yoknapatawpha." In 1930, both
names issued from Faulkner's pen: *As I Lay Dying*, published in 1930,
is the novel in which the name of the county, "Yoknapatawpha," is introduced for the first time. *As I Lay Dying* was completed in January 1930;
Rowan Oak was purchased in April of the same year, and the newlywed
Faulkners took up residence soon after, although the house was barely
habitable. Even so, "Rowan Oak" stationery was ordered, using Gothic
script,[4] staking the territory of Faulkner's household and domestic vision.
Both represent intellectual excursions: Yoknapatawpha and Rowan Oak

issue from one mind in parallel purpose, and Faulkner worked to make each, in its own media, a real thing.

Neither was not without great labor. William and Estelle Faulkner took possession of the L-shaped, "half two over two" house in May 1930, according to Rowan Oak curator William Griffith.[5] The house had been neglected for some time, long enough for chickens, mice, and other varmints to make a home of it. Faulkner went to work immediately to make the structure habitable, replacing the floors, chunking years of accumulated junk and debris, removing decaying plaster from walls, jacking up the house so that it rested on bricks, above ground, and replacing two main foundation beams. The walls of the house were then replastered. (During this initial reconstruction, from May through July 1930, Estelle did not stay at the house very often.) In July 1930, the couple placed an order for wallpaper. In the summer and fall of 1930, Faulkner built the front porch, placed urn stands on either side of the steps to the front door, and built and installed window screens throughout the house. In all these renovations, Faulkner had assistance from local retired men, whom he would pay by the hour or in whisky. While he wasn't reflooring and replastering Rowan Oak in 1930, Faulkner was revising *Sanctuary*. In December 1930, he sent his publisher, Cape and Smith, the results of his thorough reconstruction of that novel,[6] making, he later said, "a fair job" of the work.[7] Aside from painting and minor repairs, Faulkner was also done, at the end of 1930, with initial renovations to Rowan Oak, and the house remained unchanged until 1931–1932. It had no electricity or plumbing, but in Mississippi in 1930, very few of Faulkner's neighbors enjoyed such luxuries in their homes. Work on the house may have been interrupted as well by the death of Alabama Faulkner, born prematurely on January 11, 1931, and living only a few days.

In August 1931, Faulkner began work on *Light in August,* under the working title "Dark House."[8] That November he traveled to New York, where by his own account he had "created quite a sensation" as the author of *Sanctuary, As I Lay Dying,* and *The Sound and the Fury.* As he wrote to Estelle, "I have learned with astonishment that I am now the most important figure in American letters. That is, I have the best future."[9] Back in Oxford, in the winter of 1931–1932, no doubt buttressed by indications of financial security, Faulkner resumed work on Rowan Oak, adding an "indoor outhouse" to the second floor. The room was installed on the back porch, so that one went outside, on to the porch, and then into the enclosed water closet. (Later, in 1935, Faulkner finished Estelle's room, adjacent to the indoor outhouse, and connected the rooms.) On the first floor he added two French doors to the side porch off the dining room, for privacy, and to extend the downstairs living space. The doors opened to a secluded side yard, which Faulkner enclosed by building a wall extending from the house, further defining and making private the yard outside the dining room. Work was also done to improve the heating system, and Faulkner installed a coal-oil furnace and radiators. This completed the second phase of renovations, and except for minor repairs, painting, and maintenance, the house remained in this condition for twenty years. It was livable, and presentable, but far from luxurious. Turning to the completion of other household matters, Estelle would give birth to Jill Faulkner in June of 1932.

According to Jill Faulkner Summers, after her high school graduation in 1951, Estelle made an extended visit to Victoria and Bill Fielding, sometime in 1952.[10] While Estelle was away for three months, Faulkner went to work on the house, in a third phase of renovations. This phase of renovations coincides with a return to work on *A Fable*, the book on which Faulkner had labored since 1943. While Estelle was away, Faulkner plastered in the first- and second-floor back porches and created a new room downstairs (this they would call the music room, according to Estelle, so-named because it was where the record player was installed). Upstairs, Faulkner enclosed a hallway and built a closet for his hunting equipment. Downstairs, a side hallway was created to provide the house with another entrance (or exit), and off this hallway Faulkner built his office/bedroom, which also included a door to the outside (to the backyard), and a fireplace. On the walls of the new study Faulkner wrote an elaborate outline of *A Fable*, painted over the outline and revised it—the intellectual labor, in effect, indistinguishable from the carpentry. That is to say, the evidence suggests that work on the office and work on the novel proceeded in parallel. The revised and final version of the outline on the walls of the 1952 study is among Rowan Oak's more distinctive and idiosyncratic features, where visitors confront with immediacy the two worlds of Faulkner's creation, standing in the study he built, contemplating the cosmos he created.

Estelle returned home to find this work complete, all of which was planned and executed without consulting her. She was particularly upset because her husband had removed a goldfish pond and flower gardens in the course of the work, landscaping features in which she had taken considerable pride. One cosmetic addition Estelle did like very much. Faulkner hung ceiling-to-floor Swedish wood and glass beads in the new doorways (what a later generation would call hippie curtains). Faulkner liked them also, because they made a good bit of warning noise when someone passed from the front to the back of the house, closing in on his private study.

The house got a face-lift in 1954, when Jill got married. A portion of the five thousand dollars advanced from Random House to pay for the wedding also provided paint, wallpaper, and curtains to Rowan Oak. At the same time, a small interior staircase was added to the upstairs, as well as a large storage closet and a second bathroom, in anticipation of guests. In 1957 Faulkner built a new barn, using money earned from his University of Virginia salary. He kept three horses there; two were his, Tempe and Stonewall, and the third, Lady Go Lightly, was Jill's. Faulkner returned to Charlottesville in 1958 for a second term as writer in residence at the University of Virginia, and in 1959 purchased a house in Charlottesville. In the last years of his life, he would divide his time between Charlottesville and Oxford, until his death in 1962. Estelle Faulkner died in May 1972; that same year Jill Faulkner Summers sold Rowan Oak to the University of Mississippi.

From the moment they mount the steps to the front porch at the entrance to Rowan Oak, visitors embody space envisioned and constructed by William Faulkner. Standing in the study, contemplating the outline to *A Fable*, visitors enter a space where he not only wrote and lived, but which he constructed out of nothing, laying the floors, hammering the nails, plastering the walls, even destroying the work of others in his way if he found it necessary. Rowan Oak is distinctive among the preserved homes of American writers because the greater part of what stands today stands as Faulkner's handiwork. The two barns on the premises are completely his making. And the name Rowan Oak has become immemorial, seemingly organic to the site itself, as if Faulkner simply informed the world of an alternative name belonging to the spot, overlaying Rowan Oak on the Bailey place as Yoknapatawpha overlays Lafayette. It stands today as a refuge, a kind of sanctuary from the increasing sprawl of the town of Oxford and the expansion of the University of Mississippi, a quiet place of contemplation where one may easily do what the fiction of Yoknapatawpha does, sublimate the actual to the apocryphal, and move between the two worlds.

2

We begin on the ground, with a definition of material culture ranging from created objects to "invisible features that produce landscape expressions" and including as well the distinctive odors that define a place to our senses. Charles S. Aiken, "Faulkner and the Passing of the Old Agrarian Culture," surveys Faulkner's representation of terrain and concludes, contrary to much critical interpretation, that to Faulkner, Yoknapatawpha was not "a microcosm of the South but a place in the Lowland South"— a particular and very specifically delineated place. The specificity of Yoknapatawpha County may be sensed, for instance, in the "dusty smell" on Will Falls's "clean faded overalls," a smell brought into the bank because Falls has walked to town "through the dry flour-fine loess soil of the unpaved roads" in the county. Aiken examines the "great alterations" to geography and culture that occurred in Faulkner's lifetime, including the paving of roads, the introduction of such transformative items as tractors and lunch meat, and the "fossils" produced by great alterations, the abandoned "plantation big houses, furnish merchant stores, cotton gins, mule barns, and tenant houses." Tenant dwellings in the era of the New South were scattered across farmlands for proximity to farm sections. Two material changes resulted in the relocation of tenant homes in central locations. The introduction of the tractor altered the farmer's sense of proximity, and the coming of electricity demanded that houses be located centrally so that they would be electrified efficiently. Faulkner lamented some changes, documented many, and embraced others. Aiken reminds us that despite his nostalgia for mules and horses, "Faulkner was one of the first Americans to learn to fly and to own an airplane."

Moving consciously from ground to mind, we go next to Jay Watson, "The Philosophy of Furniture, or *Light in August* and the Material Unconscious." Tracing the etymology of the word "material" to the Latin *materia,* or wood, and linking further back etymologically to the ancient Greek employment of the idea of wood (that is, from forest to idea, and from object to representation) in order to explore the "conceptual under-pinnings for the idea of material itself," Watson works out a comprehensive explication of "the economies of wood in *Light in August*." In Watson's hands the novel emerges as one "extraordinarily overinvested . . . in a material economy involving the production and distribution of timber, lumber, and other wood products and in a signifying economy wherein references to wood and wooden objects are constantly working their way into the language and imagery of the text." Traversing seamlessly across disciplines from literary theory and philosophy to the history of wood-working and furniture-making, social and intellectual history, the material history of forests and lumber, and invoking a wide range Faulkner novels, Watson's analysis of the text's material unconscious reveals an interlocking and progressive building of real things and metaphors, "from the extraction of forest materials, through the production of rough lumber at the sawmill and the value-added process of planing, to the distribution and ultimate consumption of finished wood products at various points along a well-developed transportation network of roads and rails." The essay amounts to nothing less than a revelation of the secret life of *Light in August*, "an integrated economic subplot that shadows, at every moment, the novel's more overt social and political content," grounded at once in organic matter and the everyday materials of human intervention.

Everyday materials emerge, eventually, as everyday's trash, and Patricia Yaeger takes a close look at it in "Dematerializing Culture: Faulkner's Trash Aesthetic" and defines "two opposing narratives of modern detritus." There is "the trash that reeks of the sublime," objects thrown away that may become historical archives, "objects that the captains of capitalism have overlooked" and that may serve the cultural archaeologist like pay dirt. And there is the reading of trash as rubbish, "a sign of everything that's wrong with the outposts of modernity," the litter on roads and in settings of natural wonder that no contemporary mind can manage to sentimentalize. Taking the dichotomy to Faulkner, and juxtaposing Faulkner's trash aesthetic with representations of twentieth-century art as varied as Yoko Ono's *Cut Piece* and various works by Gordon Matta-Clark, Claes Oldenburg, Kiki Smith, and others, Yaeger reveals "how closely Faulkner's characters are allied with detritus, ranging from the body in decay, to matter out of place," to whole worlds turned trash. As a result, we discover a fresh, or perhaps freshly unfresh but entirely unprecedented context for reading Faulkner, the twentieth-century's trash aesthetic, wherein "Faulkner shares with other twentieth-century artists a preoccupation with detritus; it becomes a defining shelter for his character's lives and rebellions."

A materialist perspective offers a new reading as well in Kevin Railey, "*Flags in the Dust* and the Material Culture of Class." Railey finds that what have been considered the novel's critical defects—weak plot, lack of narrative unity—may be reconsidered as "a series of snapshots" in time where figures mark "a distinct moment in history" without necessarily bearing a narrative relationship to one another. Railey centers critical attention not on narrative but on objects of consumption, such as Old Man Falls's pipe, Bayard Sartoris's cigar, Aunt Jenny's glass pane windows, and on the town as consumer location for the distribution of cigarettes and automobiles into the hands of its citizens. Faulkner's attentiveness to objects transfers as well to his understanding of human beings within their material matrix. In Railey's terms, Faulkner's text demonstrates "how the consumption of objects works in two ways: to project subjective identities into things in order to make them valuable and desirable, and to turn certain subjective identities into valuable objects to be consumed." The identities of the novel's major characters, in other words, are tied intimately to the objects they handle and envision possessing, as they themselves become understood as commodities. "Through this lens," Railey argues, "*Flags in the Dust* can be seen to participate in that post-World War I literary generation that explored the alienating and mechanizing effects of the new twentieth-century world on human beings."

A strong material influence on Faulkner's intellectual development was the extensive time he spent in Hollywood, working on movies. Matthew

Ramsey, "'Touch Me While You Look at Her': Stars, Fashion, and Authorship in *Today We Live*," argues that literary scholars have misunderstood Faulkner's Hollywood labor because they do not fully appreciate the material conditions of the work. Ramsey examines the business of the 1930s Hollywood star system, the status of movies as vehicles for the fashion industry, and the complexity of film authorship as a means of presenting a more materially grounded account of what happened to "Turnabout" when it became *Today We Live* in 1931. Bringing Joan Crawford on to the project, for example, saved the film from the obscurity of an all-male production (which, for business reasons, may have never reached completion) and assured a national distribution. Biographically, Faulkner's continued work on the film compelled him to master (or at least, become familiar with) the demands of a film intended to capture a female audience. Howard Hawks, in other words, took up "Turnabout" and gave it back to Faulkner along with the task of "imagining female desire, of finding not just a way to include an important female character but to represent the point of view of a woman sexually alluring, tragic, and noble all at once (in a very Joan Crawford way)." Ramsey invites speculation that Faulkner's intellectual attention to this assignment may have affected the subsequent imagination of Laverne (in *Pylon*) and of Rosa Coldfield, Charlotte Rittenmeyer, Eula Varner, and Linda Snopes Kohl.

As Faulkner always would, we return to Oxford, and Miles Orvell, "Order and Rebellion: Faulkner's Small Town and the Place of Memory," argues that "Faulkner's Jefferson is the place of memory in a culture of change." Focusing on the idea of the Southern town, the local community, and then examining even more closely the Confederate monument at the center of the town, Orvell situates Faulkner's Jefferson within the intellectual currents of the modernist struggle to comprehend and survive place. Faulkner, Orvell reminds us, came of age as a writer "at the height of the anti-village sentiment" in the twentieth century and embodied "the ambivalence of small town life." Periodically escaping Oxford (and in his novels periodically abandoning Jefferson), Faulkner always returned, ultimately finding in the small town the point at which "local events intersect with larger historical forces" and where the individual person moves simultaneously "backward into the past" and forward into a place where "the larger world of mass culture impinges upon small town life." The essay concludes with a particularly revealing study of the Confederate Soldier monuments installed in small towns throughout the South in the era of Faulkner's youth. The monuments embody the memory function of the small town in the face of rapid changes—another cause, nonetheless, defined by its loss. "What we are left with, in Faulkner's evolving representation of Jefferson, is a modernist paean to rootedness . . . brought presciently into the postmodern era of flux and impermanence."

The technology that would arrest change, or preserve what was, is the photograph, and Faulkner seemed especially aware of its effect and its usefulness, according to Katherine Henninger, "Faulkner, Photography, and a Regional Ethics of Form." Henninger studies Faulkner's fictional representation of photographs and the function of "fictional photography" within the visual project of his aesthetics. Finding in Faulkner an "image/text/oral nexus," Henninger sees Faulkner's employment of fictional photographs as a device to interrogate "Southern cultural 'realities'—dynamics, tensions, anxieties, and rewards—of representation, including the ethics of formal division and formal choice." Starting with Faulkner's own fascination with photography (the author, so protective of his privacy, left a lifelong photo-biography of himself), Henninger then surveys major photographs and photographic images in the fiction, particularly in *The Sound and the Fury, Light in August,* and *Absalom, Absalom!* Her most sustained argument centers around the photograph in Judith Sutpen's locket, demonstrating how multiple readings may be generated depending on the identification of that famously ambiguous photographic image. Concluding that Faulkner's text demonstrates how "the meaning of a photograph lies in its use, its narration," Henninger probes further to show "that there is also something important about what is represented, or not represented, by the photograph's inscrutability." Calling upon a stranger—Shreve, the outsider, the newcomer—for the second look, the revisionist gaze, Faulkner's project depends upon what Henninger calls "a radically unforeseeable stranger, a reader, to interact with and enact his text," and this function is often filled, in the text, by the interactions between Faulkner fictional characters and their fictional photography.

The volume closes with Jackson Lears, "True and False Things: Faulkner and the World of Goods," a personal reminiscence of "professional Southerners" and a coda on Faulkner's antimodern modernism. Classifying the author with writers such as Willa Cather, Ralph Ellison, and Gabriel García Márquez, Lears sees in Faulkner the use of modernist forms "to produce a critique of bourgeois modernity." A widespread and persistent phenomenon, antimodern modernism "focused on the meretriciousness, the inauthenticity, of mass consumerable goods and exalted preindustrial craft as an authentic alternative." In Faulkner's hands, the phenomenon is complicated due to his own conviction that "appearances, surfaces mattered," and because of his own interest in such consumer goods as airplanes and sailboats. Lears surveys Faulkner's incidents of craftsmanship and commodities for the conflict they embody, revealing himself to be the rival of Henry James and Edith Wharton as "anthropologist of American material life," implicitly recognizing the ways in which "artificial materials could be used to fashion an authentic self." At the same time, Faulkner's own "longing for lost things re-enchanted the disenchanted world of modernity, endowing even the most banal objects with power and significance." Having it both ways is one way the fiction draws us back, again and again, to see which way we've got it, and which world we inhabit, when we look.

Joseph R. Urgo
The University of Mississippi
Oxford, Mississippi

NOTES

1. William Faulkner, *Requiem for a Nun*, in *Novels 1942–1954* (New York: Library of America,1994), 642. Subsequent references cited parenthetically.

2. Joseph Blotner, *Faulkner: A Biography*, One-Volume Edition (New York: Random House, 1984), 262

3. William Faulkner, *Go Down, Moses*, in *Novels 1942–1954* (New York: Library of America, 1994), 6–7.

4. Blotner, 262.

5. Much of the information concerning Faulkner's renovations comes from an interview with Rowan Oak Curator William Griffith in December 2004.

6. Michel Gresset, *A Faulkner Chronology* (Jackson: University Press of Mississippi, 1985), 30. Much of the chronological detail in this and subsequent paragraphs is indebted to Gresset's helpful work.

7. William Faulkner, *Sanctuary* (New York: Modern Library, 1932), vii. The comment appears in the introduction to this later edition of the 1931 novel.

8. See Jay Watson's essay in this volume for evidence of how much Faulkner had learned about the lumber industry while working on Rowan Oak, knowledge put to extensive use in *Light in August*.

9. William Faulkner, *The Selected Letters of William Faulkner*, ed. Joseph Blotner (New York: Random House, 1977), 53.

10. As told by Mrs. Summers to William Griffith.

A Note on the Conference

The Thirty-first Annual Faulkner and Yoknapatawpha Conference sponsored by the University of Mississippi in Oxford took place July 25–29, 2004, with more than two hundred of the author's admirers from around the world in attendance. Eight presentations at the conference are collected as essays in this volume. Brief mention is made here of other conference activities.

Activities began on Sunday with a reception at the University Museums and two lectures, followed by a buffet supper at historic Memory House. That evening, Oxford Mayor Richard Howorth welcomed participants to the conference, as did Joseph R. Urgo, chair of the University English Department, who also presented the Frances Bell McCool Faulkner Dissertation Fellowship to the first recipient, Taylor Hagood, a doctoral candidate in English from Ripley, Mississippi. The fellowship, donated by alumnus Campbell McCool in memory of his mother, will be awarded biennially to a promising young Faulkner scholar at the University. Charles Reagan Wilson, director of the Center for the Study of Southern Culture, presented the eighteenth annual Eudora Welty Awards in Creative Writing. Nyssa Perryman, Emma Richardson's student at the Mississippi School of Math and Science in Columbus, won first prize, $500, for her story "Dixon Gray." Joseph Noel, Mary Thompson's student at Lee Academy in Clarksdale, won second prize, $250, for his poem "Triumph." Frances Patterson of Tupelo, a member of the Center Advisory Committee, established and endowed the awards, which are selected through a competition held in high schools throughout Mississippi. Donald M. Kartiganer, director of the conference, introduced David Sheffield, who read the winning entry—"As I Lay Kvetching"—of the fifteenth annual Faux Faulkner Contest, sponsored by *Hemispheres* magazine of United Airlines, the University of Mississippi, and the Yoknapatawpha Press. Then, the singer/songwriter group Reckon Crew performed its adaptation of Faulkner's *As I Lay Dying*.

Monday's program included two lectures, Seth Berner's talk on collecting Faulkner, and "Teaching Faulkner" sessions conducted by James B. Carothers, Charles A. Peek, Terrell L. Tebbetts, and Theresa M. Towner. Ted Atkinson, Jeffrey Carroll, and Brannon Costello were panelists for the first of three sessions sponsored by an anonymous gift made in honor of Joseph Blotner, Faulkner biographer and longtime friend of the University of Mississippi and the Faulkner and Yoknapatawpha Conference. Colby

Kullman moderated the fourth Faulkner Fringe Festival, an open-mike evening at Southside Gallery on the Oxford Square.

Guided tours of North Mississippi and the Delta took place on Tuesday, as did an afternoon party at Tyler Place, hosted by Charles Noyes, Sarah and Allie Smith, and Colby Kullman. The day ended with Miles Orvell's lecture and a party at Square Books. After three lectures and a panel with presentations by Brandon Kempner, Caleb Smith, and Eileen O'Brien, attendees gathered for the annual picnic at Faulkner's home, Rowan Oak, and afterward enjoyed John Maxwell's performance of his acclaimed monologue *"Oh, Mr. Faulkner, Do You Write?"* Among the events that took place on Thursday were a "Teaching Faulkner" session and panel presentations by Barbara Ensrud, Jennifer Middlesworth, and Sharon Desmond Paradiso. The conference ended with a party at the home of Dr. and Mrs. Beckett Howorth Jr.

The William Faulkner Exhibition and Museum Design Proposal and Bruce Newman's photographs were on display at the University Museums. Two other photographers exhibited their work during the conference: Jane Rule Burdine, in the Gammill Gallery at Barnard Observatory, and Thomas S. Hines, at the Southside Gallery. The University's John Davis Williams Library displayed Faulkner books, manuscripts, photographs, and memorabilia; and the University Press of Mississippi exhibited Faulkner books published by university presses throughout the United States.

The 2004 conference was supported in part with congressionally directed funds through the Institute of Museums and Library Services, a federal agency; a grant from the Yoknapatawpha Arts Council helped fund the Reckon Crew performance. Gifts from the William Faulkner Society and the *Faulkner Journal* as well as donations in memory of John W. Hunt, Faulkner scholar and Emeritus Professor of Literature at Lehigh University, were made in support of two William Faulkner Society Fellows at this year's conference. The conference planners are grateful to these groups and to all the individuals and organizations who support the Faulkner and Yoknapatawpha Conference annually. In addition to those mentioned above, we wish to thank Square Books, St. Peter's Episcopal Church, the City of Oxford, the Oxford Tourism Council, and the Mississippi Congressional Delegation: Senator Thad Cochran, Senator Trent Lott, and Congressman Roger Wicker.

Faulkner and Material Culture
FAULKNER AND YOKNAPATAWPHA,
2004

Faulkner and the Passing of the Old Agrarian Culture

Charles S. Aiken

Geographers define *material culture* as "all physical, material objects made
and used by a culture group, including clothing, buildings, tools, instruments, furniture, and artwork."[1] However, material culture also includes
invisible features that produce landscape expressions. Because people
and material objects have distinct aromas, many geographers believe
that odors are products of material culture. Material culture is significant
because it distinguishes places and culture groups. Geographers have
developed a considerable literature on economic regions of the United
States but have given little attention to the anatomy and physiology of culture regions. The nation's cultural geography is viewed in the context of
distinct realms. Wilbur Zelinsky identifies five major ones: New England,
the Midland, the South, the Middle West, and the West. Each of the culture realms has regions within it. The two primary regions of the southern
realm are the Upland South and the Lowland South.[2]

The Lowland South has a plantation tradition, which differs from the
white, yeoman farmer heritage of the Upland South. The Lowland South
emphasizes four great staple crops—rice, sugarcane, tobacco, and cotton.
Agriculture of the Upland South is based on grains, primarily corn and
wheat, and on livestock—hogs, cattle, poultry. Previously, mules, horses,
and sheep were important. Because slavery was associated primarily with
plantation agriculture, most of the nation's blacks traditionally resided
in plantation regions of the Lowland South. William Faulkner did not
view his fictional Yoknapatawpha County, which occupies the location of
Lafayette County, Mississippi, as a microcosm of the South but a place in
the Lowland South.[3]

A beginning to evaluation of material culture in the works of Faulkner
is Eudora Welty's essay on place in fiction. Welty wrote, "Place is one of
the lesser angels that watch over the racing hand of fiction, perhaps the
one that gazes ... from off to the side, while the others, like character,
plot, symbolic meaning, ... are doing a good deal of wing-beating about
her chair; and feeling, who in my eyes carries the crown, soars highest of
them all and rightly relegates place into the shade."[4] What Welty wrote of
place also can be said of material culture. In most fiction, material culture

3

is critical to the setting, to the definition of characters, and even to the theme, but cultural objects usually are not the foci of the narrative.

Faulkner's Yoknapatawpha chronicles commence with a scene in *Sartoris* that uses material culture to define quickly two characters and to reveal the grip of the dead past. *Sartoris* begins with the elderly Will Falls entering a bank in Jefferson to visit aged Bayard Sartoris. Falls has walked three miles from the county Poor Farm. He is dressed in clean faded overalls.[5] Falls's dress is hardly the focus of the scene, but it succinctly conveys much. Overalls are the uniform of poor whites and blacks. That Falls's overalls are worn, but clean, indicates he is destitute, apparently well cared for at the Poor Farm, and knows to dress in his best clothes to visit a bank on the courthouse square in Jefferson. The "dusty smell" is from his walk through the dry flour-fine loess soil of the unpaved roads along which he has trudged. Falls brings into the bank the long-deceased John Sartoris, under whom he served in the Confederate army more than sixty years ago. Falls fetches "like an odor, like the clean dusty smell of his faded overalls," the spirit of Colonel Sartoris "into that room where the dead man's son sat." The hold of the dead Confederacy is also conveyed in the form of a pipe, which Colonel Sartoris gave to Falls, and Falls now presents to Bayard because "a po'house ain't no fitten place for anything of his'n." On the pipe bit are the "prints of his father's teeth, where he had left the very print of his . . . bones as though in enduring stone" (1–2).

Bayard is a member of the gentry. Faulkner conveys the Sartoris image, not by clothing, but by the way Bayard departs from the bank. He is called for by Simon, a black servant, who arrives in a carriage pulled by a pair of matched geldings. The departure is so outdated by motor vehicles that onlookers stop to savor a scene which they know is vanishing. Bayard condescendingly calls owners of motor vehicles "paupers," Faulkner's subtle reference to "that gesture of haughty pride which repeated itself generation after generation" among the Sartorises (3–4, 375). In the scene, Faulkner emphasizes what by 1900 perceptive scholars of the South, including Walter Hines Page, John Spencer Bassett, and Edgar Garner Murphy, had identified as keeping the South backward, the ghost of the Confederacy.[6]

When *Sartoris* appeared in 1929, the South was on the verge of transformation by a series of inventions, innovations, and national and world events that would destroy the grip of the dead past and produce significant changes in material culture. Although Faulkner treats the Old South era and the Civil War, most of his stories are set during the New South and the period of rapid change that led toward the Modern South. That Faulkner wrote much of his Yoknapatawpha chronicle during an era of great upheaval is fortuitous. Economic misfortune of the Great Depression, the Second World War, and deep domestic social unrest and great economic growth that followed the war created dramatic changes.[7]

Between 1935 and 1970 great alterations occurred in the material culture of the plantation South. The methods of cotton production were reorganized. During the New South era cotton was grown by white yeomen on small, hard scrabble farms and on plantations that employed black and white tenant farmers. The transformation that began in the mid-1930s used machines and chemicals to plant and harvest a crop and to keep it free of grass and weeds. The numbers of sharecroppers and share tenants began to decline during the Great Depression, and decreases accelerated after the Second World War. All-purpose tractors began to appear in cotton fields during the mid-1930s, and they were followed by mechanical cotton harvesters in the late 1940s. Chemicals that controlled grass and weeds in fields, eliminating the back breaking work of chopping the grass from between the plants with hoes, were introduced in the mid-1950s.[8] Alterations occurred in Southern lifestyles with introduction of inexpensive motor vehicles, improved roads, and electric power. Many material culture objects from the Old and New South eras were abandoned or discarded. Some objects ended up in junk yards, flea markets, and, eventually, antique shops. The sweeping changes were experienced most by the three generations of Southerners who were born between approximately 1870 and 1945. Included are Faulkner's generation, his parents', and his daughter's.

The sudden departure of Faulkner from the literary scene near the end of the period of dramatic change is unfortunate. His unexpected death at age sixty-five in 1962 occurred during the confrontational phase of the civil rights movement and the culmination of mechanization of cotton production. *The Reivers*, published a few weeks prior to Faulkner's death, is a backward glancing novel that serves as an affectionate farewell.[9] However, the Yoknapatawpha story is unfinished within the context of the rapidly changing South during which Faulkner wrote much of the chronicle.

The agrarian material culture of the New South era was expressed on the landscape in buildings, field patterns, farm machinery, and labor practices. My purpose is to discuss five types of New South buildings in Faulkner's stories and to demonstrate that he learned that objects rendered obsolete by change could be preserved by him in a special way. The five important buildings are plantation big houses, furnish merchant stores, cotton gins, mule barns, and tenant houses. A few of the buildings survive as *relics*, objects from the past that continue to be occupied or used, and as *fossils*, abandoned historic objects.[10]

Among the relics and fossils of the Southern landscape that captivated Faulkner and his readers are large dwellings, often called big houses. Although large old dwellings in the Lowland South are thought to be associated with plantations, most large two-story houses in towns were owned by merchants, attorneys, physicians, and other professional persons.

Miss Habersham is a seventy-year-old Jefferson spinster, who sells produce and poultry for a meager income. But her ancestor was among the
founders of Jefferson, and her home is a "columned colonial house on the
edge of town."[11] The Old Frenchman place, Compson's Mile, Sutpen's
Hundred, and the McCaslin-Edmonds plantation have sent Faulkner
enthusiasts scouting north Mississippi for counterparts. By the first decade of the twentieth century, the seventy-year-old big house on what had
been Sutpen's Hundred was a relic. It is seen by Quentin Compson on a
gray, cold day in drizzling rain. Quentin "looked up the slope before them
where the wet yellow sedge died . . . like melting gold and saw the grove,
the clump of cedars on the crest of the hill . . . beyond which, beyond the
ruined fields beyond which would be the oak grove and the gray huge
rotting deserted house half a mile away." In 1931, the Old Frenchman
place was a fossil, "a gutted ruin rising gaunt and stark out of a grove of
unpruned cedar trees."[12]

The big house of Compson's Mile is an occupied relic as the land is sold
bit by bit. "What was left of the old square mile was now known merely as
the Compson place—the weedchoked traces of the old ruined lawns and
promenades, the house which had needed painting too long already, the
scaling columns of the portico."[13] To Faulkner, decaying big houses symbolize decline of planter leadership. The vacuum left is filled by aggressive poor whites, many of whom are rogues the likes of Will Varner and
Flem Snopes. With his large land holdings, furnish store, cotton gin, and
numerous farm tenants, Varner meets the definition of *planter*. But he is
not identified as such by Faulkner, nor does Varner want to be so labeled.
Varner owns the decaying ruin of the old Frenchman place, but he has no
desire to restore the dwelling or to occupy it.[14]

Old big houses are abandoned for reasons other than the demise of the
families who own them. They are expensive and, sometimes, unpleasant
places in which to live. W. J. Cash's description of the typical four-
over-four big house is incisive:

> It was not, to be truthful, a very grand house really. Built of lumber sawed on
> the place, it was a little crude and had not cost above a thousand dollars. . . .
> Essentially, it was just a box, with four rooms, bisected by a hallway, set on four
> more rooms bisected by another hallway, and a detached kitchen at the back.
> Wind-swept in winter, it was difficult to keep clean of vermin in summer. But
> it was huge, it had great columns in front, and it was eventually painted white,
> and so, in this land of wide fields and pinewoods it seemed very imposing.[15]

The kitchen of a big house was a separate building at the rear. Some
kitchens were connected to the big house by a breezeway, an open passage with a roof. The detached kitchen lessened the danger of the big

house catching fire and kept cooking odors out of it. Some kitchens were brick, even if the big houses were wood. Occasionally, the kitchen was a single- or double-pen log structure, which was a plantation's first main dwelling. Bedrooms were on the second floor of a two-story big house. The rooms on the first floor included a parlor on one side and a dining room across the hall. In four-over-fours, the dining room usually was directly behind the parlor, separated by double doors. The fourth first floor room was an office, a bedroom, a women's parlor, or an early version of a bathroom with bathing facilities and chamber pots. The parlor, the most formal room, was for receiving guests and for entertaining. A piano was often the most unique and expensive piece of furniture in the parlor. The piano in Levi Harmon's Lafayette County estate was valued at $475 in 1854, about the price of a new Steinway in today's money.[16]

In an effort to preserve the furniture and rugs, doors and windows of parlors often remained closed, draped, and shuttered. In a land of high humidity and oppressive summer temperatures, closed parlors became musty rooms associated with death, for the bodies of family members lay in state in the formal rooms. McGehee's Gate plantation on the Tate-Panola county boundary, a few miles northwest of Lafayette County, was owned by Miss Caroline McGehee, a cousin of Stark Young, who used the plantation for the setting of his novel, *Heaven Trees*. In 1938 the four-over-four big house was much as it had been at the end of the Civil War. A visitor described its contents. "Treasures of a cultured family are housed in rooms whose size is reminiscent of another age. A rosewood piano inlaid with mother-of-pearl, a gift of Colonel McGehee to his bride in 1857, is the central piece of a collection of heirlooms. . . . An unusual piece is a bathing machine, a shower and tub arrangement."[17] By 1961 McGehee's Gate had passed to the Nelsons, a family with young children. A modern kitchen and den had been added to the rear of the house. But a musty odor hung in the air of the vintage parlor and dining room, which were closed and rarely used.

A similar fate befell the parlor of the Sartoris big house. The parlor

> fell less and less into use. . . . Miss Jenny bothered with formal callers but little and with the parlor not at all. She said it gave her the creeps.
>
> And so it stayed closed nearly all the time, and slowly acquired an atmosphere of solemn and macabre fustiness. . . . the room was associated with death, an idea which even the holly and tinsel of Christmastide could not completely obscure.[18]

The Shegog-Bailey house at the southeast edge of Oxford was purchased by Faulkner, together with four acres, for $6,000 in 1930. He named the place Rowan Oak. It was not wired for electric power nor did it have indoor plumbing. The house needed a new roof, new wallpaper, and window and door screens to keep out mosquitoes and other insects. Both the interior and the exterior needed to be painted. Most critical was the deteriorated condition of the foundation beams, which had to be replaced.[19] Despite its charm, Rowan Oak was a constant challenge for Faulkner to keep in livable condition. Snakes never ceased wintering in the walls. And Faulkner was never able to stop water from leaking into the interior around the internal chimneys during rain storms.

Regardless of the house's condition, the property was a good buy for Faulkner. The dwelling was close to Oxford's courthouse square but was secluded from the street by trees and a fence. Also, Faulkner purchased additional property that served as a buffer between Rowan Oak and the university and the developed part of Oxford. The house was officially on Garfield, but the street was never extended past the Rowan Oak property. Garfield made a ninety degree turn in front of Rowan Oak's gate and became the Taylor Road leading southward from Oxford. As Faulkner's stature as a writer grew, Rowan Oak became a prop in creating his legend. People who were drawn to Oxford because it was the home of William Faulkner, without intruding past the front gate, could see his home, a large white two-story mansion, the type of house that most expected.

As the twentieth century progressed, some of the more affluent families who lived in big houses built new dwellings, usually one-story bungalows and ranch houses that incorporated new wonders of material culture, including plumbing and gas furnaces and hot water heaters. Building a new dwelling was often less expensive than refitting an old one. Although planter families gained more livable dwellings with modern conveniences, they lost the instant superficial authority conveyed by the large imposing dwellings that they so readily forsook.

Stores operated by furnish merchants were a second type of building on the New South landscape.[20] Under the tenant system of agriculture that developed after the Civil War, merchants furnished basic clothing and foods to poor landless blacks and whites and took liens on crops as security. Larger plantations had commissaries that supplied their tenants. When the debts were paid after harvest of the crops in autumn, most merchants and plantation commissaries added 10 percent interest. Furnish stores were strategically located in towns and at hamlets in the countryside. Stores stocked a range of items that included basic foods to a few luxury items, such as coffee and cheese; essential clothing for men, women, and children; and patent medicines for a variety of ailments, including constipation, malaria, and tuberculosis. The larger stores were literally cradle-to-the-grave businesses. Baby clothes were sold at the front counters and coffins were built out back.

The Galloway store at College Hill was Faulkner's source for Garroway's Store at Seminary Hill. The Galloway store was the surrogate Fraser's Store in the 1949 Metro-Goldwyn-Mayer film of *Intruder in the Dust*. Galloway's store, which stands as a cultural fossil, is rather small. Most rural furnish merchant stores were wider and higher with double doors and two windows at the front and a door and a window or two at the rear. The windows were covered with heavy wicker wire or bars. The towering walls permitted goods to be stocked so high that they had to be retrieved with ladders. The large high attics provided additional storage space and made the main floor cooler in summer.

The largest and most comprehensive furnish merchant stores were in towns. The farmers' supply store in Jefferson, where Jason Compson is a cotton buyer, is "a cavern cluttered and walled and stalagmite-hung with plows and discs and loops of tracechain and singletrees and mulecollars and sidemeat and cheap shoes and horse linament and flour and molasses." The store is "rank with the blended smell of cheese and kerosene and harness oil and the tremendous iron stove against which chewed tobacco had been spat for almost a hundred years."[21] The larger town stores were parts of agribusinesses that included a cotton gin, ice plant, coal yard, fertilizer sales, and cotton grading and purchase. Stores in small towns and the north Mississippi countryside were supplied by Memphis wholesale companies. Salesmen for W. B. Mallory, Malone and Hyde, Orgill Brothers, and other companies plied the towns of the rural countryside weekly.

Stores are often viewed as businesses of last resort. With a modest stock of goods a person can open a store in almost any type of building. Following the Civil War, Thomas Sutpen is destitute. Of the 100 sections that were Sutpen's Hundred, all that remains in his possession is one section, 640 acres. It contains the big house, former slave quarters, and the Sutpen family cemetery. Sutpen opens a little crossroads store under the delusion of regaining his 64,000 acre plantation. The store is stocked with goods for former slaves and poor whites. Its merchandise includes plowshares, calico, kerosene (known colloquially as coal oil), and cheap beads, ribbons, and candy.[22] Because Sutpen died in August 1869, he would have had to have opened his store immediately after the war. The dates 1865–1869 seem too early for the development of a furnish merchant store. Financial conditions were in turmoil in Mississippi immediately after the war.[23] Also, the infrastructure for Memphis wholesale companies to serve stores remote from railroads and navigable rivers was not fully developed.

A description of a rural store at the apex of the New South era is Varner's in Frenchman's Bend about 1932. Persons traveling across the rural South or working away from home for a day usually had to rely on rural stores for their meals. Over time a modest cuisine of foods developed. Some of the foods may be surprising in their availability to the rural poor in the South. The foods included cheddar cheese, which came in large wax-coated hoops. Black rind, New York sharp was considered to be the best cheese, and some stores used it as a loss leader. To go with the cheese were crackers, which originally came in wooden boxes and barrels. Also, there was pickled sausage, the cheapest of which was made from lips, tongues, stomachs, udders, and other undesirable parts of cows and hogs. With refrigeration, bologna sausage and liver cheese became popular items that largely replaced pickled meats. Canned and potted meat, canned sardines, oysters, mackerel, and pork and beans were also favorites. Desserts included cheap candy and cakes, especially Moon Pies and Powerhouse and Baby Ruth bars. In *Light in August* Lena Grove travels through Frenchman's Bend to Jefferson. She stops at Varner's store, where she buys cheese and crackers. She also treats herself to a can of sardines and asks for "a nickel box." Jody Varner replies, "Sardines is fifteen cents."[24] Some stores stocked two grades of canned meat and sardines. Small smoked sardines were imported from Norway, and tins of larger cheaper fish were canned in Maine.

One of the most graphic descriptions of the foods sold in country stores is a meal purchased by Mink Snopes in *The Mansion*. After serving thirty-eight years in the Mississippi state prison at Parchman for killing Jack Houston over impoundment of a cow, Mink hitchhikes to Memphis to buy a pistol with which to kill Flem Snopes, his kinsman who did not help him at his trial. Mink is let out of one of his rides at "a small tight neatly cluttered store plastered with placards" off U. S. Highway 61 at the hamlet of Lake Cormorant. Mink asks for a tin of sardines, but sardines are twenty-six cents. He buys a can of "lunch meat" for eleven cents and a loaf of bread. Mink asks the proprietor, "What is lunch meat?" The reply is, "Dont ask. . . . Just eat it." Then Mink sees a stack of soft-drink cases. He has not had a soft-drink in thirty-eight years. He thinks of "a spring of a thin liquid like fire or the myriad stinging of ants all the way down to his stomach." Before he can stop from spending more of his $13.85, which he is hoarding to buy the pistol, he has downed two of the drinks.[25] Soft drinks include not only Coca-Cola and Dr. Pepper, but a group of large bottles of sweet and brightly colored grape, orange, strawberry, and peach sodas sold by Royal Crown.

Most important are the books of stores, the ledgers. All businesses kept day books on sales and charges. The daily charges usually were transferred to ledgers containing personal accounts. On the McCaslin plantation the books that record the annual furnish to black tenant farmers and the cotton grown and ginned by them are merely a continuation of books kept about slaves, their purchase, lives, and productivity. Actual day books and ledgers, like those in the McCaslin plantation commissary, often are annotated with comments about people, their accounts, and random bits of information: the price of a new automobile, the amount to pay a tenant farmer for chopping stove wood, a recipe for permanent whitewash, the formula for a spring tonic for mules.[26]

Ledgers in the McCaslin plantation commissary are "in their scarred cracked leather bindings . . . in their fading sequence . . . the yellowed pages scrawled in fading ink by the hand first of . . . [Isaac McCaslin's] grandfather and then of his father and uncle." From the Old South era into the New South era the short misspelled passages of the history of the McCaslin family and its plantation continue without interruption:

> in the small cramped and cluttered twilit room not only the ledgers but the whole plantation in its mazed and intricate entirety—the land, the fields and what they represented in terms of cotton ginned and sold, the men and women whom they fed and clothed and even paid a little cash money at Christmas-time in return for the labor which planted and raised and picked and ginned the cotton, the machinery and mules and gear with which they raised it and their cost and upkeep and replacement—that whole edifice intricate and complex and founded upon injustice and erected by ruthless rapacity and carried on even yet with at times downright savagery not only to the human beings but the valuable animals too, yet solvent and efficient and, more than that: not only still intact but enlarged, increased.[27]

Although Faulkner wrote vivid descriptions of big houses and furnish merchant stores, he does not include much about cotton gins in his stories. Because the Falkners did not own or manage gins, the writer probably knew little about the complex machinery. Cotton gins are among the more obscure large material culture items in Faulkner's fiction. The term *gin* is used for the machine that separates cotton fiber from the seed, what technically is the *gin stand*. The term *gin* also refers to the building that houses the gin stands and the auxiliary machinery that conveys cotton through the process of drying, cleaning, and baling the lint and channeling the seed to a temporary storage building. The "cotton gin on the edge of town" mentioned in a section of *The Unvanquished* that is set immediately after the Civil War would have been a mule powered gin stand in a two-story wooden building with an external buzzard wing cotton press.[28]

A technological revolution occurred in cotton ginning after the Civil War. The gin on the Sartoris plantation about 1929 was a "metal-roofed cotton gin on the railroad siding" near the railroad flag station.[29] Faulkner does not give any additional description, but the metal roof implies that the building is wood. A number of New South era gins were housed in two-story wooden buildings. The structure contained an automated ginning system developed during the 1880s and sold by several firms, including the Continental Gin Company in Birmingham, Alabama, and the Gullet Gin Company in Amite, Louisiana. Continental and Gullet were among the popular brands of ginning systems in north Mississippi. A ginning system had two or more gin stands and was powered by a steam engine.

Sartoris gin is part of a complex that includes a sorghum mill. Other mills often found on plantations included a saw mill and a grist mill. The mills, together with a commissary, church and school for blacks, and the houses of the owner and tenants comprised a hamlet. The Delta has more of its land area in plantations than any other region of the South, and the plantations and gins are larger than those in Lafayette County and the Loess Plains. In "Delta Autumn," the annual party from Yoknapatawpha County travels into the Delta about 1940 to find wilderness and game. To the elderly Isaac McCaslin "the only permanent mark of man's occupation seemed to be the tremendous gins, constructed in sections of sheet iron."[30]

Mule barns were among the most important material culture objects on both the Old South as well as the New South landscape because they housed the realm's preferred draft animal. The mule is a sterile cross between a male donkey and a female horse. Historically, most of the mules in the United States were in the South.[31] Most were bred in the Upland South and exported to the plantation regions of the Lowland South. Little Dixie in Missouri and the Nashville and Bluegrass Basins in Tennessee and Kentucky were the principal areas of origin. Mules were bred in various sizes, from large animals that pulled heavy loads to small creatures, known as cotton mules, that dexterously drew plows down rows without stepping on plants. Faulkner described the cotton mule as an animal with "delicate mule-legs and narrow deer-like feet."[32] In *Sartoris* he paid the mule a tribute with what, probably, was originally a separate essay. The mule

> was, more than any other one creature or thing, who, steadfast to the land when all else faltered before the hopeless juggernaut of circumstance, impervious to conditions that broke men's hearts because of his venomous and patient preoccupation with the immediate present, won the prone South from beneath the iron heel of Reconstruction and taught it pride again through humility, and courage through adversity overcome; who accomplished the well-nigh impossible despite hopeless odds, by sheer and vindictive patience.[33]

Mule barns ranged from small sheds to great structures, which were among the largest buildings on the cotton landscape. The most common mule barn in north Mississippi was a long building with a gabled roof. Stalls were along both sides of a central aisle, which had doors at each end. The roof sloped and covered rooms that ran the length of the barn on each side where wagons, planters, plows, and other types of farm equipment were stored. A corn crib, with one or more compartments, was constructed several feet above the ground. The crib held unshucked corn, the primary feed for farm animals. Access to the cribs was through locked doors. A room off the entry was used to store cotton seed meal and other types of supplementary feed. House cats were sometimes used to control mice and rats, but snakes were the most dependable and efficient predators. Some snakes became pets to the extent of greeting the person who came for corn. Hay was stored in the barn loft, which had large doors at each end. In addition to mules, horses were usually housed in the mule barn. Milk cows were housed in a separate shed or small barn or in one or two stalls of the mule barn. Calvin Brown, Jr., compares barns to Gothic cathedrals. The central hallway was the nave, and stalls and cribs corresponded to chapels.[34]

Faulkner did not compose lengthy descriptions of mule barns, but the blunt title of his 1938 short story "Barn Burning" implies the buildings' importance and vulnerability. Loss of a barn and feed was a disaster; loss of mules and horses was a catastrophe. In "Barn Burning," set in the 1890s, Abner (Ab) Snopes burns the barns of landlords who offend him. "Barn Burning" won the 1938 O. Henry Memorial Award for the year's best short story. But the story, which was published by *Harper's*, was rejected by several magazines, including *Red Book* and *American Magazine*, because it was too depressing.[35]

At the opposite extreme of big houses were the humble shacks of tenant farmers. The classification of farm tenants by the Bureau of the Census changed over the years between 1870 and 1959, but defined by the way and the amount they paid for use of land, there were three basic types: sharecroppers (or croppers), share tenants, and cash tenants. All tenants were furnished with a house and had the right to cut trees for cooking and heating from a forest or a wood lot. Most had the right to plant a garden and to pasture a milk cow. A sharecropper had nothing with which to grow cotton and corn crops except family labor. The landlord furnished land, mules, equipment, and cash with which to buy food and clothing or credit at the plantation commissary. A sharecropper paid 50 percent of the cotton and corn crops as rent. A share tenant owned mules and farm implements. The landlord furnished land and was paid one-third or one-fourth of the crops as rent. A cash tenant had mules and farm implements but differed from the share tenant in that he paid a preagreed amount in cash or in part of the crops, such as one bale of cotton and thirty bushels of corn.[36]

Although share and cash tenants who remained on a plantation for a number of years may have made modest improvements in their houses, the basic dwelling did not vary by tenant class. Even the best tenant houses were in abysmal condition by today's standards. They typically were one to four room dwellings. Many did not have any outbuildings, even a toilet. People simply went behind a bush, a practice that spread hookworm and other parasites and diseases. Walls and floors of houses usually were one plank thick, and the dwellings were heated by fireplaces. To make them warmer in winter and to decorate them, walls were covered with cardboard, newspaper and magazine pages, and cheap garish wallpaper. Many tenant houses sat unpainted decade after decade, but some were whitewashed and others coated with cheap red and green lead paint. Following the Second World War, a number of planters tried to improve the houses and make them less expensive to maintain by covering them with heavy tar paper that had the appearance of red or brown brick.

The dwelling on Major de Spain's land, to which Abner (Ab) Snopes moves his family following eviction from a tenant farm on Mr. Harris's place because he burned the barn, is "a paintless two-room house identical almost with the dozen others . . . [the wagon] had stopped before . . . in . . . ten years." After Ab is evicted by Major de Spain, he rents a farm on land owned by Will Varner. The yard of the shack is overgrown and littered with rubbish. Ab tells Varner, "The house aint fitten for hogs. But I reckon I can make out with it." The worldly possessions in a tenant house were used and broken castoffs of affluent whites and a few cheap new items, which were purchased but not cared for. The household goods of the Ab Snopes family are "the battered stove, the broken beds and chairs, the clock inlaid with mother-of-pearl, which would not run."[37]

During the New South era, houses were scattered across the landscape because tenants wanted to be close to their farms and away from the watchful eyes of landlords and plantation managers. The introduction of tractors during the 1930s caused some landlords to move tenant houses into lines along roads. This new arrangement not only facilitated the use of tractors in fields, but made it easier to extend power to the dwellings when electricity reached a farm or plantation.

Faulkner had a complex relationship with material culture and change. He was among the vanguards in adopting certain new material wonders. Faulkner was one of the first Americans to learn to fly and to own an airplane. He earned part of his income from selling his novels and short stories to motion picture studios and to television production companies. Writing scripts for movies was among his most lucrative sources of income. Rowan Oak was kept up-to-date in select new innovations for the home. Gas heaters were installed as soon as gas for homes became available in Oxford. On the other hand, Faulkner refused to own a radio, television, or phonograph and for a time forbade his daughter to have any in the house.[38] The owner of one of Oxford's popular restaurants unplugged the jukebox when the Faulkners entered to dine.

Although Faulkner hardly resented and resisted all types of change, he lamented particular kinds of landscape alteration, from destruction of the Mississippi wilderness to the demolition of old buildings, which he admired. He actively participated in preservation. When Miss Ellen Bailey died in 1923, Sallie Bailey Bryant inherited the Shegog-Bailey house and the adjoining acreage. The dwelling began to fall into disrepair. Several persons approached Mrs. Bryant about purchasing the property. In 1930 she sold the house and four acres to Faulkner because he was the only one who wished to restore the dwelling. In 1947, Faulkner wrote a letter to the *Oxford Eagle* supporting the newspaper's efforts to preserve the Lafayette County courthouse, which was saved.[39]

During the 1930s, from his experiences with Rowan Oak, Faulkner discovered that preservation requires continual work and money. He learned a sterner lesson about conservancy in his efforts to preserve wilderness. By the mid-1930s, only a few tracts of virgin wilderness remained in the Delta close to Oxford. One tract a few miles west of Batesville surrounded the hunting camp of "General" James Stone. As he grew older and the game scarcer, Stone lost interest in his camp and the annual November hunts that he sponsored. In a sentimental effort to preserve wilderness, game, and the annual hunts, Faulkner and two other members of the annual November hunting party chartered the Okatoba Hunting and Fishing Club, which was to be managed by a game warden. The scheme failed for lack of money and interest in the club by other hunters. In November 1936, "General" Stone died at the camp, and the following year the Stones, who were in serious financial trouble, lost the land surrounding the hunting lodge. The timber rights were sold, and the wilderness was logged.[40]

Faulkner drew on his preservation experiences in writing hunting stories and "The Bear" section of *Go Down, Moses*, which deals with obsolescence and the futility of attempting to arrest change and to preserve things as they are. A young Isaac McCaslin witnesses the slaying of Old Ben, the bear; the sale of Major de Spain's hunting camp; and the cutting of the doomed wilderness. Isaac comprehends that the forces which altered the landscape were initiated years before. The small innocent log train, the machine the hunting party rode to de Spain's hunting lodge, is a major agent in destruction of the wilderness. General Compson and Walter Ewell propose a plan to incorporate the group of hunters into a club that would lease hunting rights on de Spain's land. Faulkner terms the scheme "an invention doubtless of the somewhat childish old General but actually worthy of Boon Hogganbeck himself." Even the boy . . . recognized it for the subterfuge it was.[41]

In 1938, Faulkner purchased a 320 acre farm northeast of Oxford, borrowing $2,000 from the New Orleans Land Bank. He named the farm Greenfield. He bought mules and recruited four black tenant families.

Faulkner also stocked a small commissary. John (Johncy) Falkner, his brother, was appointed the manager and lived in a cottage on Greenfield. If Faulkner had had a fifth tenant, Greenfield would have met the 1940 United States Census definition of a plantation.[42]

Faulkner also purchased a Fordson, one of the first agricultural tractors. The Fordson, manufactured by the Ford Motor Company, was a popular tractor in the 1920s. However, by 1938, the Fordson had been rendered obsolete by the innovative International Harvester Farmall and other brands of tricycle tractors. Despite obsolescence, Faulkner's Fordson was among the first tractors in Lafayette County. Symbolically, Faulkner participated in the introduction of the machine into American cotton production. The tractor replaced mules and made mule barns obsolete. It also destroyed New South farm tenancy, setting in motion the migration of tenants from the land, desertion of furnish merchant stores, and abandonment of tenant houses. The first mechanical cotton pickers, which began to be manufactured in 1948, were mounted on tricycle tractors, which were driven backward down the rows. Mechanically picked cotton required machinery to dry seed cotton and to clean excessive trash from the lint. The new gins were considerably larger, faster, and more expensive than ones built before the impact of the mechanical cotton picker. By the end of the twentieth century, four- and six-row mechanical cotton pickers were replacing two-row machines and seed cotton was compacted into large modules that were hauled to cotton gins on large trailer trucks. In 2001, none of the 100 cotton gins operating in Mississippi were in Lafayette County.[43]

To accept change and the possibility of the destruction of anything on the landscape, Faulkner came to a rather simple, but for him profound, answer, which he reiterated several times before his death in 1962. In his important 1956 interview with Jean Stein, Faulkner stated, "The aim of every artist is to arrest motion, which is life, by artificial means and hold it fixed so that 100 years later when a stranger looks at it, it moves again since it is life. Since man is mortal, the only immortality possible for him is to leave something behind him that is immortal since it will always move." Faulkner stated the same about change in answer to a question about wilderness and Old Ben, the bear, in a graduate literature course at the University of Virginia in May 1958. "What the writer's asking is compassion, understanding, that change must alter, must happen, and change is going to alter what was. That no matter how fine anything seems, it can't endure, because once it stops, abandons motion, it is dead. It's to have compassion for the anguish that the wilderness itself may have felt by being ruthlessly destroyed by axes, by men who simply wanted to make that earth grow something they could sell for a profit, which brought into it a condition based on an evil like human bondage." In the preface to *The Mansion*, the third volume of the Snopes trilogy, Faulkner wrote, "the author likes to believe, hopes that his entire life's work is part of a living literature, and . . . 'living' is motion, and 'motion' is change and alteration."[44]

Faulkner's belief that life is motion and motion is change and an artist, a writer, arrested motion by artificial means reassured him in two ways. First, it provides an alternative for preservation of material culture other than the saving of actual objects. A house, a barn, a store, and any other landscape object can be accurately preserved by intense creative description. Furnish merchant stores are gone, but Faulkner left a record of what they were like, even to the diverse aromas in them. Second, Faulkner's idea that an author could arrest motion by artificial means also explains and vindicates his rage to write. The older Faulkner was more at peace with himself than the younger Faulkner, in part, because he could justify a life largely lived in words on paper. Critics, not Faulkner, are concerned about lack of consistency in his complex Yoknapatawpha saga. Although Faulkner was justly proud of his literary accomplishments, he wrote for the moment, which gave him peace from his passion.

NOTES

1. Terry G. Jordan-Bychkov and Mona Domosh, *The Human Mosaic: A Thematic Introduction to Cultural Geography* (New York: Longman, 1999), 259–91, 534.

2. Wilbur Zelinksy, *The Cultural Geography of the United States*, rev. ed. (Englewood Cliffs, N.J.: Prentice Hall, 1992), 117–40. Zelinsky, an innovative American geographer, identifies the southeast coast of the United States as the "early British colonial South" culture region. All geographers do not accept this area as a distinct region. I include the coastal area as part of the Lowland South.

3. Charles S. Aiken, "Faulkner's Yoknapatawpha County: A Place in the American South," *Geographical Review* 69 (1979): 332–48.

4. Eudora Welty, *Place in Fiction* (New York: House of Books, 1957), 1.

5. William Faulkner, *Sartoris* (New York: Harcourt, Brace, 1929), 1. Subsequent references cited parenthetically.

6. John B. Boles, *The South through Time: A History of an American Region* (Englewood Cliffs, N.J.: Prentice Hall, 1995), 428–29.

7. Charles S. Aiken, *The Cotton Plantation South since the Civil War* (Baltimore: Johns Hopkins University Press, 1998), 10.

8. Ibid., 97–132.

9. William Faulkner, *The Reivers* (New York: Random House, 1962).

10. Carl Sauer, "Forward to Historical Geography," *Annals of the Association of American Geographers* 31 (1941): 1–24.

11. William Faulkner, *Intruder in the Dust* (New York: Random House, 1948), 75–77.

12. William Faulkner, *Absalom, Absalom!* (New York: Random House, 1936), 187; *Sanctuary* (New York: Jonathan Cape & Harrison Smith, 1931), 6.

13. William Faulkner, "1699–1945 The Compsons," in *The Portable Faulkner*, ed. Malcolm Cowley (New York: Viking Press, 1946), 735–56.

14. William Faulkner, *The Hamlet* (New York: Random House, 1940), 5–7.

15. W. J. Cash, *The Mind of the South* (1941; New York: Vintage Books, 1991), 16.

16. Yancy Wiley et al., "Appraisement of Personal Property of Levi Harmon," 1854. Harmon Family Papers, possession of Charles S. Aiken.

17. Federal Writers Project of the Works Progress Administration, *Mississippi: A Guide to the Magnolia State* (New York: Viking Press, 1938), 381.

18. Faulkner, *Sartoris*, 59–60.

19. Joseph Blotner, *Faulkner: A Biography*, 2 vols. (New York: Random House, 1974), 1: 651–58.

20. An authoritative reference on the country store is Thomas D. Clark, *Pills, Petticoats, and Plows: The Southern Country Store* (New York: Bobbs-Merrill, 1944).

21. Faulkner, "1699–1945 The Compsons," 746.

22. Faulkner, *Absalom, Absalom!*, 180–81, 188.

23. James Wilford Gardner, *Reconstruction in Mississippi* (1901; Baton Rouge, Louisiana State University Press, 1968), 122–24.

24. William Faulkner, *Light in August* (New York: Harrison Smith & Robert Hass, 1932), 23–24.

25. William Faulkner, *The Mansion* (New York: Random House, 1959), 259–61.

26. Day Books and Ledgers of William Thorne, 1933–1949, passim. Possession of Charles S. Aiken.

27. William Faulkner, *Go Down, Moses* (New York: Modern Library, 1942), 261 and 298.

28. Charles S. Aiken, "The Evolution of Cotton Ginning in the Southeastern United States," *Geographical Review* 63 (1973): 196–224; William Faulkner, *The Unvanquished* (New York: Random House, 1938), 234.

29. Aiken, "The Evolution of Cotton Ginning in the Southeastern United States"; Faulkner, *Sartoris*, 147.

30. Faulkner, *Go Down, Moses*, 341.

31. Robert B. Lamb, *The Mule in Southern Agriculture*, Publications in Geography 15 (Berkeley: University of California Press, 1963).

32. Faulkner, *The Hamlet*, 55.

33. Faulkner, *Sartoris*, 278–79.

34. Calvin S. Brown Jr., *A Glossary of Faulkner's South* (New Haven: Yale University Press, 1976), 24–25.

35. William Faulkner, *Collected Stories of William Faulkner* (New York: Vintage Books, 1977), 3–25; Blotner, *Faulkner: A Biography*, 2: 1005–31.

36. Aiken, *The Cotton Plantation South since the Civil War*, 29–35.

37. Faulkner, *Collected Stories*, 3–25; *The Hamlet*, 8–10, 22–23.

38. Faulkner enjoyed an undistinguished television situation comedy, *Car 54, Where Are You?*, which he watched every week at James Silver's house. Blotner, *Faulkner: A Biography*, 2: 1812.

39. Blotner, *Faulkner: A Biography*, 1: 652 -61; William Faulkner, letter to the editor of the *Oxford Eagle*, in *Essays, Speeches, and Public Letters by William Faulkner*, ed. James B. Meriwether (New York: Random House, 1965), 202–3.

40. Aiken, *The Cotton Plantation South since the Civil War*, 449–53; Susan Snell, *Phil Stone of Oxford: A Vicarious Life* (Athens: University of Georgia Press, 1991), 236.

41. Faulkner, *Go Down, Moses*, 315–21; Aiken, *The Cotton Plantation South since the Civil War*, 449–52.

42. Blotner, *Faulkner: A Biography*, 2: 986–91; U.S. Bureau of the Census, *Special Study: Plantations Based on Tabulations from the Sixteenth Census* 1940 (Washington, D.C.: Government Printing office, [1948]).

43. Blotner, *Faulkner: A Biography*, 2: 986–88, 991, 1004,1026; Aiken, "The Evolution of Cotton Ginning in the Southeastern United States"; Aiken, *The Cotton Plantation South since the Civil War*, 104–32. Staple Cotton Cooperative Association, "2002 Newsletter" (Greenwood, Miss.), 2 pages.

44. William Faulkner interview by Jean Stein Vanden Heuvel, New York, 1956, in James B. Meriwether and Michael Millgate, eds., *Lion in the Garden: Interviews with William Faulkner* (New York: Random House), 237–56, reference on 253; originally published in Jean Stein Vanden Heuvel, "The Art of Fiction," *Paris Review*, Spring 1956; Frederick L. Gwynn and Joseph L. Blotner, *Faulkner in the University: Class Conferences at the University of Virginia, 1957–1958* (Charlottesville: University of Virginia Press, 1959), 276–77; Faulkner, "Preface," *The Mansion.*

The Philosophy of Furniture, or *Light in August* and the Material Unconscious

JAY WATSON

If you take one of the key words for this year's conference, "material," and trace its etymological roots back far enough, you will arrive, first, at the Latin word for matter, *materia*, but then at an even older meaning for *materia*: wood, or more specifically, "the usable wood of a tree as opposed to its bark, fruit, sap, etc."[1] The Greek term for "primary matter" or "material cause," *hyle*, contains a similar prehistory; before Aristotle brought it into a specifically philosophical discourse, the word originally meant forest. In this way wood, which already supplied the classical world with its principal source of fuel and building material,[2] came to supply the classical mind with its conceptual underpinnings for the idea of the material itself. Taking my cue from this embedded history lesson, I want to explore the comprehensive links between material culture and what I will call the economies of wood in *Light in August*, a novel noted in the Faulkner oeuvre for its dense, realistic presentations of the north Mississippi landscape and object world. As I hope to show, *Light in August* is extraordinarily overinvested, from nearly its first page to its last, in a material economy involving the production and distribution of timber, lumber, and other wood products and in a signifying economy wherein references to wood and wooden objects are constantly working their way into the language and imagery of the text, often in quite conspicuous ways but just as often in subtle or offhand ones. In this curious aspect of the novel we can see the workings of what the critic Bill Brown, in his important study of Stephen Crane and the American 1890s, calls the material unconscious.

According to Brown, "the 'material unconscious' names literature's repository of disparate and fragmentary, unevenly developed, even contradictory images of the material everyday."[3] It manifests itself in what Brown calls "referential excess" (4) or "surplus materiality" (171), "a kind of excess signification, undermotivated by manifest theme or plot," that gives the literary text "the capacity to preserve (however marginally) residues of phenomena that remain in some sense unrecognizable (if not unrepresentable)" in the conventional narrative forms we use to make sense of history (3–4). The "archival task" of the materialist critic, according to Brown, "consists of developing a chain of associations that seem, retrospectively, to have converged already in the literary work. The analytical task," he continues, "consists in representing that convergence as an image that freshly eluci-dates the signifying structures and material changes of everyday life—the task, in other words, of producing the history that lingers within neglected images, institutions, and objects" (4–5). In this way, the "undernarrated, 'subhistorical' fragments" and "inconspicuous surface-level expressions" of history (15), or what Brown elsewhere calls the "ephemera that have yet to attain historicity" (5), can shed light on the cultural logic (or illogic) of their place and time. Brown calls for a "new materialism that does not just recognize the materiality of everyday life unconsciously registered by the literary, but also recognizes how literature develops what we might call the unconscious of material objects themselves" (250). In *Light in August* the story unconsciously told by such objects—a story told *by* and *through* the material everyday—is also ultimately a story *about* the every-day, the terrible cost of upholding its façade of normality.

Here a few points need clarification. First is the difference between Brown's idea of the material unconscious and Fredric Jameson's now canonical concept of the political unconscious. In the preface to his study, Jameson describes "two distinct paths" that the "historicizing" brand of criticism he favors can follow: "the path of the object and the path of the subject, the historical origins of the things themselves and that more intangible historicity of the concepts and categories by which we attempt to understand those things."[4] "For better or worse," he continues, "it is this second path we have chosen to follow here," a path that ultimately takes Jameson deep into what he calls the ideology of form, into the constitu-tive repressions and constraints that attend an author's choice of narrative genre (see for instance 76, 98). If I understand Brown correctly, the study of the material unconscious concerns itself more with Jameson's first path, with teasing out the historicity and ideology that lie within material objects themselves, as those objects find literary representation in the realist text. Accordingly, my analysis of *Light in August* will zero in on physical things and economic processes as it were "uttered" by the text, rather than on the generic or stylistic modes in which it "utters" them.[5]

Second, it is important to distinguish the kind of analysis Brown pro-poses from theme criticism. Key here is Brown's insistence on "referential excess," on a surplus that marks the material unconscious at work. Brown stresses how often this reference is incongruous, gratuitous, unorganized, in contrast to the implied sense of organization and coherence at work in the very concept of a text's "thematic" dimension. Moreover, while the examples, references, and associations that establish a theme can range indiscriminately across history, myth, and psyche, for Brown the contents

of the material unconscious are typically limited to products of the history
and economy of a specific era, the era of the text's own production. One
example of what it means to observe this difference is that my analysis of
the economies of wood in *Light in August* will not capitalize on the fact
that a major character is named Grove or that the text refers on numerous
occasions to the Christian Cross, whereas a theme-based study of the general motif of "wood" would certainly permit both moves. It is true that allusions to the Cross allow Faulkner to implicate fundamentalist Christianity
in the South's racial violence, and that wooden crosses were in fact burned
across twentieth-century Mississippi in the attempt to intimidate African
Americans and other enemies of white supremacy. It is also true that
there is a well-known grove on the University of Mississippi campus in
Faulkner's hometown of Oxford. These signifiers, however, function more
on a mythic or symbolic level in *Light in August* than as concrete images
or traces of "the material everyday" in Depression-era Mississippi. For this
reason I will have much more to say about sawmills, boards, and benches
than about groves and crosses in the pages ahead.

Third, I should point out that Brown's study of the material unconscious
in Crane does *not* revolve around economies of wood but around economies of play, the material and social practices attending the growth of the
mass amusement industry in late nineteenth-century America: the rise of
spectator sports such as football and boxing; the popularity of mechanical
toys; the emergence of photojournalism and its commodification of war,
athletics, and deviance; the birth of the motion picture industry; the rise
of amusement parks, with their roller coasters and ferris wheels; and the
growing popularity of freak shows and other outlets for the spectacular
display of human oddities. Brown in fact confesses that his book began
in his need to make sense of an anachronistic reference to football in *The
Red Badge of Courage*, a novel set years before the sport achieved national
prominence. In *Light in August*, by contrast, "the unconscious of material objects themselves" primarily involves wooden objects and the sites
at which they are produced. Before delving further into the significance
of this "referential excess," however, we need a better sense of the many
levels at which it operates in the novel.

We can start with seemingly gratuitous comments by characters such
as the mill foreman in chapter 2, who suggests running Joe Christmas
through the planing machine as a way to take the look of arrogant indiffer-
ence off his face.[6] The narrator makes similarly offhand remarks, noting,
for instance, that as five-year-old Joe awaits what he is certain will be a
beating from the dietitian, "the muscles of his backside were becoming flat
and rigid and tense as boards" (124), and that when Joe receives a dollar
instead of the expected punishment, he has a nauseating vision of "ranked
tubes of toothpaste like corded wood, endless and terrifying" (125). Years

later, Joe endures a strapping from his foster father, McEachern, with such rigid self-control that the narrator observes, "[t]he boy's body might have been wood or stone" (159–60). Still later, one of Joe's black lovers is compared to an ebony carving (225). From such incidental bits of language and dialogue we can move on to basic elements of characterization. Lena Grove's introduction, for instance, is simultaneous with that of the Alabama sawmill town where she lives with her brother until becoming pregnant (3–6). Before he is even named, Lucas Burch is identified as a "sawdust Casanova" (6) who works cutting lumber in Doane's Mill. Burch's first appearance in Jefferson, like Lena's, is at the local planing mill, where he finds a job shoveling sawdust (36); Christmas, in fact, enters the text at this same mill (31), as does Byron Bunch, who runs the planer and loads the surfaced lumber onto railroad cars (47). And on the fateful night the circus comes to town to lure his daughter into bitchery and abomination, Doc Hines, the former railroad brakeman, is employed as a sawmill foreman (373). It is as if the "surplus materiality" set in motion by the novel's economies of wood reaches into the realm of character itself, calling human figures into being. Even Hightower is announced by the neatly carpentered sign in the corner of his yard (57–58), and Joanna Burden by the "tall yellow column" of woodsmoke that rises from her burning home to greet Lena as she approaches Jefferson by wagon at the close of chapter 1 (30). Indeed, if we follow the lead of the many critics who have approached the small-town community of Jefferson itself as a kind of character, monolithic in its collective suspicion and intolerance of outsiders, that character, too, leaves its first material trace in the novel in that same spire of yellow smoke. The neighboring community of Mottstown, Jefferson's partner in racial anxiety and violence, announces itself in much the same way, in woodsmoke viewed from a distance, as Christmas approaches the village, also by wagon, after a week on the run from the law (339). In each case, smoke becomes an indexical sign of civilization—but a civilization characterized by a consuming, constitutive violence.

The economies of wood, then, leave their mark on setting as well as on language and characterization. At times this mark is no more than a quick, passing reference: at the age of fourteen, for instance, Joe Christmas has his first sexual encounter in "a deserted sawmill shed" near the farm of his foster family, the McEacherns (156). Elsewhere, however, the lumber and woods products industries play a fundamental role in defining setting. The novel opens, for instance, on a scene of extractive industry that sets character and event in motion, the wholesale clearing of the land in Doane's Mill:

> All the men in the village worked in the mill or for it. It was cutting pine. It had been there seven years and in seven years more it would destroy all the

timber within its reach. Then some of the machinery and most of the men
who ran it and existed because of and for it would be loaded onto freight cars
and moved away. But some of the machinery would be left, since new pieces
could always be bought on the installment plan—gaunt, staring, motionless
wheels rising from mounds of brick rubble and ragged weeds with a quality
profoundly astonishing, and gutted boilers lifting their rusting and unsmoking
stacks with an air stubborn, baffled and bemused upon a stumppocked scene of
profound and peaceful desolation, unplowed, untilled, gutting slowly into red
and choked ravines beneath the long quiet rains of autumn and the galloping
fury of vernal equinoxes. Then the hamlet which at its best day had borne no
name listed on Postoffice Department annals would not now even be remembered by the hookwormridden heirs at large who pulled the buildings down
and burned them in cookstoves and winter grates. (4–5)

By the end of this passage—which owes not a little to the deserted, decrepit
Michigan mill site that opens Hemingway's "The End of Something"—
wooden dwellings are yielding, in a kind of domino effect, to the same
hungry human onslaught that felled the trees from which they were presumably made.[7]

From here we quickly move on to the pivotal role played by the planing mill as social and economic setting in the novel's middle world of
Jefferson. As we have seen, the mill is the insertion point for four of
the novel's half-dozen primary characters, the site and vehicle of their
entrance into "community," however ambivalent that process may look
in retrospect. It is also the occasion for much of their direct interaction
with each other—where Byron meets Lena, for instance, and Christmas
finds a bootlegging partner in the coworker he knows as Joe Brown. In
this respect, Byron couldn't have picked a less apt site for the general-
ized stance of nonengagement he seems, like his friend Hightower, to
favor in life. As its location on a rail artery suggests, the planing mill is
not peripheral to Jefferson life but central to it, at once participating in
and, on a more abstract level, symbolizing its most characteristic functions and processes.[8] And finally, the principal setting for the novel's concluding episode, which is recounted by a traveling furniture dealer to his
wife in the comfort and quiet of the marriage bed, is the truck in which
he picks up and delivers his wares for his customers in north Mississippi
and southwestern Tennessee. On his way "to get some old pieces of furniture which he had bought by correspondence" (494), he delivers the
hitch-hiking Byron and Lena (and baby) at least as far as Saulsbury,
Tennessee, where they leave Mississippi and the novel behind.

At this point I should admit that the "surplus materiality" I have been
tracing might also be seen as characteristic of other Faulkner novels that
deal in a sustained way with the economies and material culture of wood.

There is *As I Lay Dying*, for instance, where Jewel Bundren is likened by his brother Darl to "a cigar store Indian," "pale eyes like wood set into his wooden face," where the two brothers avoid directly confronting their mother's death by delivering a wagonload of lumber, where a third brother, Cash, chips meticulously away at the supreme wooden fetish object in all of Faulkner, Addie Bundren's near-unnameable coffin, and where Darl is eventually sent away for burning down a man's barn, a cultural spectacle that also haunts *The Hamlet* and, of course, Faulkner's great 1939 story, "Barn Burning."[9] There is also *Go Down, Moses*, which documents the coming of the lumber industry to the Big Woods of late nineteenth-century Yoknapatawpha and the conversion of wilderness spaces into timber plantations, where the totem bear falls beneath the hunter's knife "as a tree falls" and trees fall like matchsticks beneath the mechanized rapacity of railroad and sawmill.[10] And there is *Intruder in the Dust*, where the man found in Vinson Gowrie's grave turns out to be "a shoestring timber-buyer" named Montgomery "from over in Crossman County."[11]

What singles out *Light in August* is the depth and scope with which its "referential excess" comes to signify. We can begin to get at this depth by returning for a moment to Doane's Mill. Lawrence Buell has suggested that the "concise history of the cut-and-get-out phase of the timber indus-try in the Deep South" that Faulkner provides in his prose portrait of Doane's Mill offers a social as well as environmental framework for the understanding of character at the outset of the novel.[12] Characters like Lucas and Lena "are what they are," writes Buell, "not just because of who they are but because of where they fit in the history of Mississippi lumbering" (3). Certainly the sense of restlessness and displacement that first brings Lena and Lucas together and later drives them apart is more than the product of adolescent desire followed by masculine ambiva-lence. It is also the direct social result of the predatory, irresponsible, and mobile economy and culture of large-scale logging operations in the South. Contemporary scholars noted the "necessarily nomadic," "transi-tory" character of production and labor in the lumber industry.[13] Writing in 1931, the year Faulkner composed *Light in August*, labor historian Charlotte Todes characterized the industry as "'sick' from overdevelop-ment, chaotic production and fierce competition" and refused to condemn its large caste of "migratory workers" for their understandably casual atti-tudes toward the on-again, off-again terms of their employment.[14] At the other end of the Depression, Vernon H. Jensen echoed Todes, describing the industry as "an aggressive, ingenious, unstable migrant" that "turned many of its workers into migratory laborers."[15] In this context it may make sense to believe Lucas when he tells Lena that the foreman in Doane's Mill is "down on him" (19) and that his hasty departure is necessary if he

Fig. 1. Planing machine, 1940s. Reprinted from *Establishing and Operating a Small Sawmill Business*, Industrial Series No. 20 (Washington: U.S. Department of Commerce, 1945), 88.

is to better his unstable economic situation. To see Lucas and ultimately Lena as "uprooted" by the logging operation only underscores their resemblance to the logs themselves, whose path in the timber economy they in fact follow from the forests to the mill towns.

The parallels between industrial and social processes continue in Jefferson, where rough-cut lumber arrives from the sawmills to be fed into the planer, which a recent reference work on the furniture industry describes as "a machine with a rapidly turning, horizontal cylinder inlaid with very sharp knives used to smooth the tops and bottoms of boards."[16] (See figure 1.) The machine's function seems only too emblematic in a community itself fanatically bent on smoothing out, or shearing off, the rough spots in Joe Christmas, Gail Hightower, Joanna Burden, Lena Grove, and other characters whose subversive, destabilizing perform-ances of racial, gender, and sexual identity threaten small-town values. Indeed, we need only recall how Percy Grimm attempts to solve the social and cultural riddle of Joe Christmas, to whittle his frighteningly excessive and contradictory identity down to socially intelligible proportions, with a rapidly moving, very sharp knife.[17] Byron's foreman, then, has turned out to be a prophet. Through its agent Grimm, Jefferson does in effect run

Joe Christmas through the planer, in a hideous "surfacing" operation that exposes the brutal logic of small-town social norms.

From the planer, the surfaced boards would ordinarily move on to be graded, assigned a specific category and value on the basis of visible imperfections such as checks, skips, splits, knots, warps, or signs of rot remaining on the surface of the wood.[18] Softwoods such as pine (Byron's mill almost certainly cuts softwood, since customers of the time usually preferred to buy hardwood lumber unsurfaced) would be graded anywhere from "A," the highest of the "select" grades, to "No. 5," the lowest of the "common" grades.[19] *Light in August* never alludes to the grading process directly, but it is likely that the boards Byron loads onto railroad cars each Saturday have been sorted by grade, perhaps by Byron himself. Grading, of course, is another lumbering practice that finds a social equivalent in Jefferson, a community nearly fanatical in its recourse to numerous interlocking classification schemes to assign value to individuals and award or withhold social privileges accordingly. And not just in Jefferson generally but at the planing mill specifically, where first Joe Christmas and then Joe Brown are assigned to the "negro's job" of shoveling sawdust (36), indicating that the same racial division of labor is in place at the mill that contemporary experts noted at work throughout Southern lumbering: white men like Byron ran the machines, while menial labor fell to African Americans (when they got mill work at all).[20] Surely it is no coincidence that Christmas and Brown, the two most racially ambiguous characters in the novel, form the sawdust detail at the mill. Critics of *Light in August* have for the most part neglected to attend to the racial and racializing dimensions of these work assignments—whether, for instance, they reflect preexisting racial suspicion directed against Christmas and Brown from the beginning of their tenure under Jefferson's communal gaze, or whether, more intriguingly, the economic positioning of the two men in "negro's jobs," like their living situation in a "negro cabin" on the Burden place, contributes actively to the racial uncertainty that increasingly surrounds them.

There is a deeper inevitability at work here that is worth a closer look. Robert Pogue Harrison's study of the role of forests in the Western imagination takes as one of its central themes the dependence of civilizations that "literally cleared [their] space[s] in the midst of forests" on those forests not only as resource bases but as culturally encoded spaces made to signify everything human civilization is not (Harrison, ix). In the history of the West, he writes, "forests represent an outlying realm of opacity which has allowed . . . civilization to estrange itself, enchant itself, terrify itself, ironize itself, in short to project into the forest's shadows its secret and innermost anxieties" (xi). Forest spaces are imagined as outside law, reason, and order, where "the law of identity and the principle of noncontradiction go astray" and "conventional distinctions" threaten to "collapse" into chaos (63). This is one major reason why, throughout the history of Western civilization, a battery of rational, technical, and representational strategies has been brought to bear against the forest in order to reduce (or at least accommodate) its anarchy, savagery, and irrationality to the order and reason of human community.

Now one way to look at a sawmill is as a concrete, compact embodiment of this comprehensive cultural process, the material and conceptual conversion of forest into *polis*. Indeed, beyond its participation in the general work of deforestation, the sawmill from its origins in fourteenth-century Germany[21] has served as perhaps the definitive social site at which the raw materials of the forest are physically transformed into the raw materials of the city: floors, ceilings, walls, doors, windows.[22] In this context, it seems perversely fitting that Joe Christmas, a living incarnation of the same "opacity" and contradiction that get projected onto forests, should turn up at a mill, the place where forest meets city only to be stripped of its native character and bent to the demands of human living—and that, within moments of his arrival at the mill, he would be compared to the rough lumber that is brought there to be run through the planer.[23] By the same token, it makes sense that when Christmas tries to evade the forces of cultural containment that would bend him into Joanna Burden's "negro" lover and murderer, he flees to the forests surrounding Jefferson and Mottstown, where he manages to avoid legal capture and racial classification for seven long days in chapter 14. In the end, though, the normalizing force of the *polis* and the planer proves too strong for him.

Finally, the concluding chapter of the novel finds Byron and Lena riding around together and separately in the "housedin" (494) back of the furniture dealer's truck, almost as if they have become specimens of the wood products that are his stock-in-trade. Moreover, *Light in August* ends with the strong suggestion that Lena will never find Lucas Burch—that, indeed, she isn't really even looking for him!—and that, eventually, she will settle down with Byron ("likely . . . for the rest of her life," according to the salesman [506]) to create a stable home for her infant son. In this context, the conspicuously absent furniture of chapter 21—everywhere evoked yet nowhere to be found, just up the road from Saulsbury, just over the text's own horizon—might be seen as a key ingredient *and signifier* of the domestic life on which the couple seems destined to embark. It has long been a truism in the furniture business that newlyweds are among the industry's best customers: "A considerable amount is spent on furniture in the months before and after a wedding," writes one industry expert. "When two people are starting their lives together, furniture is likely to be one of their major expenditures."[24] What awaits the salesman on each leg of his journey, then—the load of furniture in Tennessee, the marriage bed in Mississippi—is presumably what will await Byron and Lena when their long, roundabout journey toward domesticity reaches its end.

By now it should be clear that the three sites I have been describing—Doane's Mill, Jefferson, the furniture truck—represent the progressive stages of a comprehensive and thoroughly modern economy of wood that takes us from the extraction of forest materials, through the production of rough lumber at the sawmill and the value-added process of planing, to the distribution and ultimate consumption of finished wood products at various points along a well-developed transportation network of roads and rails.[25] By mapping these economic spaces directly onto the narrative structure of beginning, middle, and end, the material unconscious of *Light in August* works to transform and organize elements of space into elements of time, creating an integrated economic subplot that shadows, at every moment, the novel's more overt social and political content, which of course revolves around the dynamic between small-town conformity and individual acts of resistance, deviance, and transgression. In this respect it makes little sense to see Lena Grove, the only character to traverse all three economic and narrative phases, in the timeless mythic terms of "something moving forever and without progress across an urn" (7). Better, perhaps, to see her movement through the novel as a slow but steady historical progress across the clock face of Southern economic time, a forward movement the text seems unconsciously to render at once in cartographic and chronometric terms, with an implicit bird's-eye view in which the chronotopes[26] of western Alabama, north central Mississippi, and southwestern Tennessee all take their places on the larger "dial" of what we now call the Mid-South. (See figure 2.)

I want to suggest that what ultimately links *Light in August*'s manifest social plot and its latent economic subplot is the way each plot comes to foreground the production of the ordinary, the everyday, the unremarkable—that sense of the uneventful that is so crucial to the felt experience of small-town social life. I have suggested that the planing mill offers, from within the economy of wood, one oblique image of this process. But it also contributes to it directly, as a disciplinary institution that, like Foucault's factories and prisons, actively reshapes laboring bodies and their unruly energies into a docile work force that arrives punctually and decorously each Monday, no matter how wild the weekend may have been.[27]

> Some of the . . . workers were family men and some were bachelors and they were of different ages and they led a catholic variety of lives, yet on Monday morning they all came to work with a kind of gravity, almost decorum. Some of them were young, and they drank and gambled on Saturday night, and even

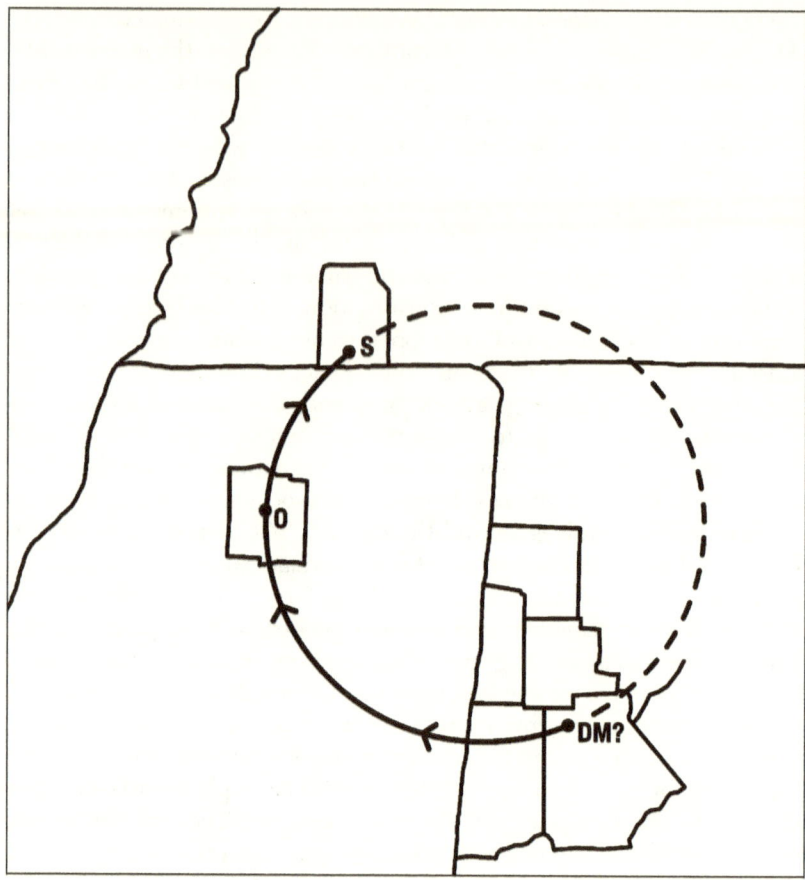

Fig. 2. The clockwise path of Lena Grove's peregrinations. In posing an approximate location for Doane's Mill (DM), I have followed Roland M. Harper's 1943 forest census of Alabama and assigned the town to Harper's region 6, "the central pine belt," and in particular to region 6A therein, "the short-leaf pine belt," where, "[o]n account of the abundance of three species of pine, and the comparative smooth topography, lumbering has long been an important indus-try. . . . In 1913 [region 6A] contained about 20% of the sawmills and 15% of the other wood-working industries of the state, though its area was less than 10% of the total." It could however be argued that region 6B, "the central long-leaf pine hills," which Harper designates as "a chain of seven islands" within the short-leaf belt, is equally plausible as a site for Doane's Mill, since the area was home to the highest-capacity sawmills, on average, in the state. If so, the town should lie more to the southeast of the spot I have designated on the map. See Harper, *Forests of Alabama* (University, Ala.: Geological Survey of Alabama, 1943), 64–65, 128–143. Calvin Brown's *Glossary of Faulkner's South* (New Haven: Yale University Press, 1976), ordinarily so useful on questions of actual and fictional geography in the Faulknerian cosmos, contains no entry for Doane's Mill and fails to mention the town in its lengthy appendix on geography and topography. Saulsbury (S) is an actual town, approximately six miles east of Grand Junction in Hardeman County, Tennessee. For the location of the fictional Jefferson, I have substituted the location of the actual Oxford (O), in Lafayette County, Mississippi.

went to Memphis now and then. Yet on Monday morning they came quietly and soberly to work, in clean overalls and clean shirts, waiting quietly until the whistle blew and then going quietly to work, as though there were still something of sabbath in the overlingering air which established a tenet that, no matter what a man had done with his sabbath, to come quiet and clean to work on Monday morning was no more than seemly and right to do. (41)

Call it yet another planing operation: with all transgressive impulses successfully vented off over the weekend, what is left is the smooth, finished surface of orderly social relations. In much the same way, as the conscious plot of *Light in August* arrives at the near-banality of chapter 21, a heaping helping of the mundane laid on perhaps a little too thick, so the economy of wood arrives at the distribution of furniture, a commodity whose utilitarian function is precisely to assist in the production of the ordinary, the stable, uneventful realm of the domestic—or, we might say, to provide the material infrastructure of the unremarkable.

Now there is a tradition of writing and talking about furniture, both in the academic study of the decorative arts and in the discourse of the industry itself, that approaches the subject in exactly the opposite way. In this tradition, which stresses the ornamental function over the utilitarian, furniture is seen as extraordinary, unique, an expression of the distinctive character and personality of a customer, a society, or an age.[28] The purpose of furniture, to this way of thinking, is to be remarkable, to call attention to itself and thereby to reflect meaning and value onto someone or something else. We see this expressivist discourse at work in scholarly accounts of period style and in advertisements for furniture dealers and manufacturers. One book-length study of furniture design, for instance, opens with the observation that furniture "provides an intimate, personal record of habits, postures, manners, fashions and follies."[29] Similarly, an advertisement for a New York-area furniture company that is roughly contemporary with *Light in August* stresses the role of "Personality" "in making 'buyers' out of 'shoppers'": indeed, its products are arranged for display in "PERSONALITY SALESROOMS" such as the one pictured in the ad, where they wait patiently for their chance to express—or enhance—the individual taste of some lucky consumer.[30] (See figure 3.)

Edgar Allan Poe approached the decorative arts as a field for the expression of national identity and temperament in his 1840 essay, "The Philosophy of Furniture," which ends with a call for a distinctively or at least competently American style of furnishing worthy of comparison with the decorative genius of the English. It's a little like what we'd have if Ralph Waldo Emerson's famous address to the Phi Beta Kappa Society at Harvard three years before Poe published his essay had been called "The American Decorator" instead of "The American Scholar." Here is Poe,

Fig. 3. Reprinted from Marta
K. Sironen, *A History of
American Furniture* (East
Stroudsburg, Penn.: Towse
Publishing Co., 1936), n.p.

for instance, throwing down the gauntlet as he compiles an international census of furnishing foibles from which only the English are exempt:

> The Italians have but little sentiment beyond marbles and colors. In France . . . the people are too much a race of gadabouts to maintain those household proprieties of which, indeed, they have a delicate appreciation, or at least the elements of a proper sense. The Chinese and most of the Eastern races have a warm but inappropriate fancy. The Scotch are *poor* decorists. The Dutch have, perhaps, an indeterminate idea that a curtain is not a cabbage. In Spain they are *all* curtains—a nation of hangmen. The Russians do not furnish. The Hottentots and Kickapoos are very well in their way. The Yankees alone are preposterous.[31]

As we would expect from the author of "The Fall of the House of Usher," rooms and their contents do not so much express *"character"* as exude it (390), and in America, that character is above all "harsh" (388), "inartistical" (386), and ostentatious. Poe is at his most elitist in linking these flaws with the nation's "republican institutions," which he blames for a general "corruption of taste" in U.S. society (389).

Against this expressivist tradition, however, there is also a long history of philosophical discourse about furniture that treats tables, chairs, beds, and other such items as exemplary theoretical objects, and exemplary precisely because of their absolute ordinariness as material artifacts.[32] Unlike Poe's "philosophy of furniture," the furniture of philosophy that I refer to here can anchor theoretical speculation and ground important thought problems because it is so intrinsically unremarkable.

When Aristotle, for instance, turns in book 2 of the *Physics* to the crucial question of the primacy of matter or form in the nature of a thing, he remembers that the Sophist philosopher Antiphon, a contemporary of Socrates, has visited the question before him, and Antiphon's choice of philosophical object could hardly be more homely or familiar:

> Some people take the nature and substance of any natural thing to be its primary component, something which is unformed in itself. They say, for instance, that wood is the "nature" of a bed, bronze the "nature" of a statue. Antiphon cites as evidence the fact that if you bury a bed and, as it rots, it manages to send up a shoot, the result is wood, not a bed. He concludes from this that the arrangement and design of the bed, which are due merely to human convention, are coincidental attributes, and that the substance is that which persists throughout, however it is affected.[33]

Antiphon, then, is a materialist, whereas Aristotle goes on to argue the opposite view: though it is true that "beds do not come from beds," it is nonetheless also true that "men come from men," the father reproducing his human form, and not just his organic material, in the son, allowing Aristotle to conclude "that form too is nature" (35).

Plato may well have had Antiphon's philosophical parable in mind when, in book 10 of the *Republic*, Socrates and Glaucon come to discuss the nature of human making, in an exchange that lays the groundwork for the famous argument to exclude poets from the ideal state. In an attempt to differentiate the products of genuine creation from those of mere imitation, Socrates invites Glaucon to consider the quotidian example of a bed.[34] According to Socrates, beds "are of three kinds": an unchanging idea or what we would now call a Platonic form, authored by God; the wooden bed constructed by the carpenter in accordance with the Platonic model, or the idea given particular material form; and the bed as rendered by the painter, a second-order imitation modeled not on the Platonic concept but on the carpenter's interpretation of it. Thus poets, who like painters imitate other imitations, are "third in the descent from nature" and thus "thrice removed . . . from the truth," dangerously susceptible to illusion and error. This is why the Republic is ultimately better off without them—though not, we should note, without carpenters and beds. What I would call your attention to here and in the previous episode is the exemplary way in which furniture is held by both Antiphon and Socrates to incarnate the relationship between matter and form—whichever side of the question the philosopher happens to be arguing! Were there anything idiosyncratic or extraordinary about the nature or function of beds, they could not serve in this heuristic capacity.

Aristotle returns to this exemplary item in book 5 of his *Nicomachean Ethics*, where the possibility of exchanging five beds for a house, or a single bed for enough money to pay one-fifth of the cost of a house—the possibility in other words of finding equivalent values for otherwise incommensurable objects—offers a material analogy for the ethical concept of distributive justice, also characterized by relations of reciprocal exchange.[35] Karl Marx in turn cites this passage from Aristotle while developing his labor theory of value in the opening chapter of *Capital*.[36] There, we may recall, Marx's discussion of the commodity form initially takes as its exemplary object not an item of furniture but a linen coat (see 132–63). But when Marx turns to his brilliant analysis of commodity fetishism, his theoretical object changes, and we witness the return of the furniture of philosophy:

> It is absolutely clear that, by his activity, man changes the forms of the materials of nature in such a way as to make them useful to him. The form of wood, for instance, is altered if a table is made out of it. Nevertheless the table continues to be wood, an ordinary, sensuous thing. But as soon as it emerges as a commodity, it changes into a thing which transcends sensuousness. It not only stands with its feet on the ground, but, in relation to all other commodities, it stands on its head, and evolves out of its wooden brain grotesque ideas, far more wonderful than if it were to begin dancing of its own free will. (163–64)

There is a method in Marx's rhetorical madness here. His allusion to the tipping tables of contemporary European spiritualism is a vivid and accessible way to evoke the "metaphysical subtleties and theological niceties" (163) that result when value is expropriated from its true sources in human labor and reassigned to the commodified object.[37] Even more significant, though, is the way Marx's exemplary piece of furniture suddenly stops being an ordinary sensuous object and becomes remarkable, grotesquely animated by unseen forces as it dances its way across the page.[38] This exceptional moment, however, only proves my general rule: for when the furniture of philosophy so uncharacteristically plunges into the extraordinary, the event marks a breach in the structure of the normative itself. It is a sign that an ethical boundary has been violated: when tables and other material objects are endowed with properties that rightfully belong to their human makers, the result is a fundamental, structural injustice.

More recently, Elaine Scarry's study *The Body in Pain* has attempted to take this critique a step farther. For Scarry, perhaps the most original philosopher of material culture since Marx, the value of the artifact ultimately lies not in its ability to absorb and objectify human labor but in its potential to relieve—indeed, to preempt—the burdens of embodiment by channeling the shock and friction of the external environment away from sentient human tissue. In this sense, what Scarry calls "the interior structure of the artifact" amounts to the realization in material form of a wish: let there not be pain.[39] Scarry's analysis ranges across a wide spectrum of artifacts, from clothespins and light bulbs to novels, symphonies, and constitutions, but she reserves a central place in her discussion for tables, beds, and especially chairs. Here, for instance, is the sentence that perhaps comes closest to condensing the book's entire argument about material making: "The shape of the chair is not the shape of the skeleton, the shape of body weight, nor even the shape of pain-perceived, but the shape of perceived-pain-wished-gone" (290). Once again, it is only when this process goes wrong, when the ethical work of material artifacts is short-circuited, that furniture becomes remarkable, as in Scarry's extraordinary analysis of the structure of torture (27–59). There she documents how tables, chairs, bathtubs, benches, stools, refrigerators, bedsteads, and other objects, along with the walls, floors, and ceilings that delimit the boundaries of the domestic as "the ground of all making" (45), are deconstructed into weapons, made to inflict agonizing pain rather than to relieve it (see especially 40–41). The furniture of torture becomes the point-by-point negation of the furniture of philosophy, the epitome of everything ordinary artifacts must not be and do.

Finally, near the end of his little book *Theory of Religion*, Georges Bataille surveys the familiar landscape of his room in an effort to fathom the deep meaning of human existence among material artifacts. What he sees there—"my table, my chair, my bed"—are products of labor that moreover, because he writes for a living, become sites and vehicles of labor, shackling him to a stultifying regime of work.[40] Table, chair, and bed are thus doubly inscribed in an economy of production and accumulation that, for Bataille, insures "man's reduction to thinghood" and blocks access to the sacred, that anguished ecstasy of the subject in crisis states of eroticism, mysticism, sacrifice, and the throes of artistic inspiration. This same film of thinghood prevents us from seeing the deeper beauty and radiance of objects themselves, a radiance that is released when they are sacrificed, wastefully consumed. Thus Bataille calls for a "general destruction of things," a creative deconstruction that at once emancipates human beings from enslavement to objects and liberates the inner glory of the objects themselves.

How might such a destruction be brought about? Bataille's parable continues with the act of placing "a large glass of alcohol" on his table (102). Now, he claims, the table is no longer "a means of labor: it helps me to drink alcohol," to destabilize the borders of selfhood in that pursuit of lost intimacy that, for Bataille, defines the religious impulse. "In setting my drinking glass on the table, to that extent *I have destroyed the table....* At least this table in this room, heavy with the chains of labor, for a time had no other purpose than my breaking loose." As such, the table "ceases to form a distinct and opaque screen between the world and me," and new ways of seeing self and world alike become possible (103). Once again, the heuristic value of furniture lies in its ability to evoke the ordinariness that, for Bataille, at least, hangs like a pall over human artifacts and human consciousness.

Light in August's key insights into the production of the ordinary, on the economic level as well as the social, are, first, that this phenomenon is attended at nearly every moment by a constitutive violence that it, in turn, works to mask, and, second, that it brings in its wake a fundamental poverty of means and spirit. These processes are perhaps most visible in the novel's final chapter, where a rarely commented on series of substitutions works to "produce" examples of relatively unremarkable social identities and relations out of transgressive ones. I refer here to the way Byron and Lena emerge *as a couple* in the closing pages to replace the more troubling and unpredictable combination of Lucas and Lena that presides over chapter one—but also, more pointedly, to replace the even odder odd couples that dominate the novel's middle: Byron and Hightower, Christmas and Lucas, and of course Christmas and Joanna Burden, *Light in August*'s poster children for transgression. This ascendancy of Byron and Lena as exemplary comedic couple demands, even as it mystifies and compensates for, the excision of more threatening figures like Lucas, Joe, and Joanna from the social landscape, and the violence of these excisions is explicitly marked by the bloodshed that accompanies each one: Joanna's throat is slit with a razor, Joe is shot and castrated, and Lucas gets into a bloody fistfight with Byron just before hopping a freight car out of Yoknapatawpha and the novel. This physical violence, as I have argued elsewhere, is accompanied by a rhetorical violence that works to stabilize and even normalize the uncanny hybridity of both Joe and Joanna through oversimplification and cliché, as when Jefferson belatedly reconstructs the former "nigger-lover" and nonentity Joanna as a paradigmatic white female victim of black rape and murder (291–92), or when, to return to chapter 21, the furniture salesman reduces the novel's consummate border crosser to the hopelessly inadequate stereotype of a "nigger" who was "lynched" in Jefferson (497).[41] In this respect, the salesman's crude but efficient formula represents the logical continuation and culmination of Gavin Stevens's more fumbling attempt in chapter 19 to tilt Joe's contradictory racial identity over into blackness by invoking an atavistic rhetoric of white and black "blood" at war—a struggle whose outcome is predetermined by the framing presence of the one-drop rule (448–49).

If the salesman's words thus replace Stevens's, smoothing out their rough spots and eliding their telltale ironies and vacillations, this in turn prepares us to confront a final substitution in chapter 21, as even the modestly unorthodox Byron and Lena yield their place in the narrative to the working-class couple whose pillow talk simultaneously frames and expels them. So unremarkable is this final couple, so enveloped in the aura of the routine and the normative, of marriage, work, and domesticity, that they are never even distinguished by means of proper names. (Here we might compare them to the Armstids, the not-so-anonymous couple who witness and comment on Lena's journey in chapter 1.) Here, then, the production of the ordinary reaches a kind of apex that is simultaneously a kind of impoverishment, as if, for all his amiable garrulousness, the salesman reaches center stage with his wife only to drain the novel of the sense of eventfulness, the capacity for surprise, that ultimately drives narrative. For what can there be to say about a world emptied of Byron and Lena, Joe and Joanna, Lucas Burch and Doc Hines—the world over which this utterly quotidian couple now presides? The salesman may drive on, and chatter on, but the text stalls and falls silent, as if his world—the triumph of the ordinary—is literally beneath mention.

The material culture of wood in *Light in August* mirrors this dynamic of violence and poverty. It is the violence that in the novel's economic subplot uproots trees and people, clears forests and villages, erodes the land and fouls watersheds, rips away bark and whittles away rough edges, sorts out mill hands into white and "negro" jobs, all in order to supply an anxious Southern citizenry with the artifacts of a reassuring domestic stability: tables, chairs, floorboards, window frames. It is the iconic poverty of dilapidated Doane's Mill, the simple pine headstone on Lena's father's grave, and the hoboes who drift in and out of the mill towns: Lena and Byron hitching rides, Lucas jumping a train, Christmas living on cigarettes until his first payday in Jefferson. Moreover, so complete is the entanglement of the economic and the social in *Light in August* that when furniture arrives in chapter 21 to take center stage in the novel's material unconscious, the items in question are, once again, simultaneously a triumph of the ordinary and somehow beneath or beyond mention. I refer of course to the salesman's never-specified merchandise in Tennessee, anonymous pieces not so unlike characters who fail to achieve names of their own.[42]

The silence and anonymity I am describing here bring to mind Alfred Kazin's influential account of "the stillness of *Light in August*," in an essay published almost half a century ago. With this phrase Kazin attempts to evoke the novel's framing atmosphere of social tranquility, its stately narrative pace and luminous mythic sheen, along with an "intense sense of the earth" lost to Joe Christmas but literally second nature to Lena Grove.[43] What the student of the material unconscious is perhaps in a better position to see than Kazin is that Yoknapatawpha's stillness is not so much the antithesis of its endemic violence as grounded in it, that throughout the text the quiet façade of the ordinary harbors subterranean rumblings. And this brings me to a final element of referential excess in the novel's depiction of the material everyday. *Light in August* responds, from within its economy of wood, to the illogic of a communal and textual "stillness" founded in violence, with a group of brief but intense scenes in which these subterranean rumblings surface, as wooden objects—or to be more precise, wooden furniture—becomes remarkable, intervening directly and incongruously in the narrative action.[44]

On at least two occasions furniture reverses the function of pre-empting human pain assigned to it by Scarry and instead directly inflicts injury. First a chair and then a bench become weapons, instruments of violence, in the hands of Joe Christmas, who breaks the chair over the head of his foster father, McEachern, when the older man catches him with his lover Bobbie Allen at a country dance (205) and clubs a young black man with a bench leg after invading an African American church service while on the run from the sheriff (325).[45] Elsewhere we have seen furniture assist in the creation of a sense of the uneventful; here it assists in the shattering of that very sense. I can think of no better illustration of Brown's point that the contents of the material unconscious are not only "disparate and fragmentary" but "contradictory" (4). Indeed, I would go farther to suggest that the contradictory functions of furniture in the text express the more basic contradiction that governs the economic world of Yoknapatawpha, a regime of useful objects founded in the systematic misuse of people and nature.

A third example is easily overlooked amidst the racial theatrics of chapter 19, where Joe Christmas has his fatal collision with Percy Grimm in Hightower's kitchen:

> It was as though [Grimm] had merely been waiting for the Player to move him again, because with that unfailing certitude he ran straight to the kitchen and into the doorway, already firing, almost before he could have seen the table overturned and standing on its edge across the corner of the room, and the bright and glittering hands of the man who crouched behind it, resting upon the upper edge. Grimm emptied the automatic's magazine into the table; later someone covered all five shots with a folded handkerchief. (464)

Several years ago at this conference, I described the way "words [turn] into unspeakable acts and things" as this harrowing scene unfolds.[46] Here however I would add that things themselves are subject to strange and sudden transformations as the horror escalates. Take for instance Hightower's table. The language of the passage above, in which, like Grimm, the reader comes upon the table already "overturned and standing on its edge" without ever seeing who turned and stood it, is just ambiguous enough to impute a kind of agency to the table itself, as if, sensing the violence about to erupt around it, it has leapt into motion and raced across the room to interpose itself between assailant and victim.[47]

What are we to make of this extraordinary metamorphosis? We might follow Marx in seeing the "metaphysical subtleties" displayed by a table standing grotesquely on its head as its way of announcing itself as a commodity, one whose sudden animation, after all, coincides with the deanimation, the final alienation, of Joe Christmas—a former worker in the wood products industry. For that matter, we could follow Marx back to *his* source and read the scene for its complicated mimicry of spiritualist table-tipping, as if mysterious forces are at work in the room to draw the table toward the abyss in the rational opened up by Joe's uncanny performances of race and gender and sexuality—the same breach that ineluctably draws in Grimm, who attempts to repair it by force. Or we might see the table as an example of Bataille's radiant artifact, freed from immurement in the utilitarian order of production and accumulation to assist in a general destruction of things that elides into the destruction of the human subject—a destruction, moreover, that seems to release a kind of radiant glory in Joe Christmas himself, whose dying moments are narrated as a liberation, in a Bataillean language of anguish, ecstasy, eroticism, and sacrifice:

> For a long moment he looked up at them with peaceful and unfathomable and unbearable eyes. Then his face, body, all, seemed to collapse, to fall in upon itself, and from out the slashed garments about his hips and loins the pent black blood seemed to rush like a released breath. It seemed to rush out of his pale body like the rush of sparks from a rising rocket; upon that black blast the man seemed to rise soaring into their memories forever and ever. (464–65)

Viewed this way, Hightower's table becomes part of what Bataille would call Joe's "breaking loose" into a sacred apotheosis.

In the end, though, I would suggest reading the scene as an almost surreal exaggeration and defamiliarization of Elaine Scarry's philosophy of furniture. In writing of the artifact as "the structure of a perception," Scarry notes the seemingly universal human habit of attributing "object-awareness" to our material creations, of presuming them to be "as knowledgeable about human pain as if [they] were [themselves] animate and in

pain" (289; italics removed). Indeed, Scarry continues, they "must know
a great deal more about their human makers than the particular needs
they accommodate" (302). So with Hightower's table. From the quintes-
sential domestic space of the kitchen, it *remembers* its purpose of protect-
ing human tissue from injury, shielding human sentience from pain, then
forces itself into the scene to absorb the shots, the five martyr wounds,
from Grimm's pistol, yet still spectacularly fails in its self-appointed role
as second skin, as Christmas collapses to the floor behind it. And then it
fails again, "flung aside" in the next paragraph as Grimm stalks Joe with
the butcher knife (464). In this way it disappears from the novel, but not
before managing to gather to itself the semantic resonance of the Cross
and the lynching tree[48] all at once. The table's failure to carry out its ethical task should not be read as an indictment of the object but as an indictment of the human world in which it attempts to function, a world of such
excessive violence and risk that not even material culture, with its in-built
charge of compassion and charity,[49] can shelter the human subject from
its blows. This is the world that, in a colossal irony, the shell-shocked citizens of Jefferson ponder as they sit around *their* "suppertables" on the
night of Joe's death, trying to make sense of what has happened (443).
Here in the regime of the unremarkable, these tables are assisting, in
their homely, obscene way, in the framing of a collective alibi, one that will
shift blame for the communal violence mobilized against Joe's otherness
to the other himself: "It was as though he had set out and made his plans
to passively commit suicide."[50] Only Hightower's extraordinary table, by
contrast, attempts to come to Joe's aid. Had "someone" not been so quick
to lower the veil of his handkerchief over the bullet holes in Hightower's
tabletop, the town folk might have gained, in the "surplus materiality" of
that anomalous image, a brief, demystifying glimpse of the danger and
contradiction that lurk beneath the stillness of *Light in August*, waiting to
erupt through the veneer of the ordinary.

It is a mark of *Light in August*'s realism that the novel deals so extensively with the wood economy. Though King Cotton may still rule our
imagination of turn-of-the-century life in Mississippi, the truth is that
timber and lumber were perhaps the dominant facts of economic life
in Faulkner's part of the state, and certainly in most points south and
east of Oxford and Lafayette County.[51] It is also true that the strange
career of Joe Christmas encompasses, with uncanny symmetry, the quar-
ter-century when the South led the nation in lumber production, with
Mississippi playing a major role in that effort.[52] In this context it is surely
significant that the cotton economy receives only the most cursory attention in *Light in August*, far less, for instance, than in *The Sound and
the Fury*, where, despite the novel's preference for town settings over

rural ones, the cotton market becomes a subject of obsessive concern for Jason Compson—and far less than in *As I Lay Dying*, whose signifying economy of wood does not obscure our many views of the agricultural activities and rhythms that govern the lives of the Bundrens. (It is enough simply to remind oneself how the novel gets under way, with Darl and Jewel marching up out of the fields to Addie's bedside, or to recall how Lafe gets Dewey Dell pregnant.) I am not suggesting, though, that the significance of the wood economy in *Light in August* is merely a matter of background or realistic setting. Indeed, my account of the novel's material unconscious suggests quite the opposite. For as we have seen, the impact of the text's "referential excess" is often to shatter the "referential illusion" that, according to Roland Barthes, is the defining stylistic feature of realism's representational code.[53] When that happens, when the turbulence and contradiction that structure the social order break through the still surface of the everyday, the novel's realism flirts with surrealism, and the material unconscious of *Light in August* leads us, though by a different route, to much the same destination as Jameson's political unconscious: to an awareness of history as "what hurts," "what refuses desire and sets inexorable limits" to human endeavor.[54] In *Light in August*, that history is not only inscribed, indelibly, on the human form, it is chopped, carved, burned, and blasted into wood as well.

NOTES

An early version of this essay was presented to the Research Seminar in Literature at the University of Turku, Finland, in March 2004. I am grateful to the organizers of the seminar, Professor Pirjo Ahokas and Professor Liisa Saariluoma, for the opportunity to share my work with their group, and to the graduate and undergraduate participants in the seminar whose questions and other responses helped me sharpen my argument. I also want to thank my Mississippi colleagues, Don Kartiganer and Joe Urgo, for reading the first draft of the written version and offering a number of useful comments and suggestions, especially concerning opportunities to cut material from the conference talk! Finally, I want to recognize two undergraduate students, Candice Casey and Zachary Jex, who explored some of the same problems that inform this essay in critical papers for English 466, the senior-level Faulkner survey at the University of Mississippi. Candice and Zach would no doubt disagree with some of the conclusions I have come to here, but their often provocative ideas helped jump-start my thinking, and for that I am grateful indeed.

1. Robert Pogue Harrison, *Forests: The Shadow of Civilization* (Chicago: University of Chicago Press, 1992), 28. See also John Perlin, *A Forest Journey: The Role of Wood in the Development of Civilization* (Cambridge: Harvard University Press, 1989), 31.

2. For a fascinating social history of wood as a strategic resource in the classical age, see Perlin, 9–93.

3. Bill Brown, *The Material Unconscious: American Amusement, Stephen Crane, and the Economies of Play* (Cambridge: Harvard University Press, 1996), 4.

4. Fredric Jameson, *The Political Unconscious: Narrative as a Socially Symbolic Act* (Ithaca: Cornell University Press, 1981), 9.

5. Brown's 2003 study, *A Sense of Things*, extends his engagement with material culture, but in a slightly different direction than *The Material Unconscious*. Brown himself probably explains his differing approaches best: *The Material Unconscious* "tried to show how the material culture of the American 1890s impressed itself on the literary imagination, how it remains subliminally present no matter how underdetermined the apparent references to it. I tried to show how the material everyday . . . had left textual residues that help us to reconstruct cultural history even as they test what we mean by 'culture' and 'history.' In *A Sense of Things* I want rather to explore the imaginative technologies for lifting and redeeming that substratum. . . . The question I am asking is no longer about an unconscious logic that can explain a peculiar, barely perceptible cultural reference. . . . It is more about the logic of reference as such within one period of literary history," about "the rhetorical strategies by which fiction works to convince us not just of the visual and tactile physicality of the world it depicts but also of that world's significance[.]" With this shift of emphasis from the material everyday to the "rhetorical strategies" by which it acquires significance, *A Sense of Things* appears to take at least a small step in the direction of Jameson's ideology of form. See Brown, *A Sense of Things: The Object Matter of American Literature* (Chicago: University of Chicago Press, 2003), 16–17.

6. William Faulkner, *Light in August*. The Corrected Text (1932; New York: Vintage International, 1990), 32. All subsequent textual references are to this edition.

7. See Ernest Hemingway, "The End of Something" (1925), *In Our Time* (1930; New York: Charles Scribner's Sons, 1970), 31.

8. On the entangled histories of railroading and lumbering in America, see John Ise, *The United States Forest Policy* (1920; New Haven: Yale University Press, 1924), especially 53–55, 83; and Sherry H. Olson, *The Depletion Myth: A History of Railroad Use of Timber* (Cambridge: Harvard University Press, 1971).

9. See William Faulkner, *As I Lay Dying*, The Corrected Text (1930; New York: Vintage International, 1990), 4, 49, 4–5.

10. See William Faulkner, *Go Down, Moses,* The Corrected Text (1942; New York: Vintage International, 1990), 231, 303–6.

11. William Faulkner, *Intruder in the Dust* (1948; New York: Vintage, 1972), 104.

12. Lawrence Buell, "Faulkner and the Claims of the Natural World," *Faulkner and the Natural World: Faulkner and Yoknapatawpha 1996*, ed. Donald M. Kartiganer and Ann J. Abadie (Jackson: University Press of Mississippi, 1999), 2. See 1–3 generally for Buell's account of *Light in August*.

13. K. W. Woodward, *The Valuation of American Timberlands* (New York: John Wiley and Sons, Inc., 1921), 198; Nelson Courtlandt Brown, *Timber Products and Industries: The Harvesting, Conversion, and Marketing of Materials Other than Lumber, including the Principal Derivatives and Extracts* (New York: John Wiley & Sons, Inc., 1937), 2. See also I. F. Eldredge, *The Four Forests and the Future of the South* (Washington: Charles Lathrop Pack Forestry Foundation, 1947), 5.

14. Charlotte Todes, *Labor and Lumber* (New York: International Publishers, 1931), 9, 76.

15. Vernon H. Jensen, *Lumber and Labor* (New York: Farrar & Rinehart, Inc., 1945), 3, 21. Jensen argues that Southern forest labor was somewhat exempt from the industry's chronic nomadism because "[t]he fast-growing trees of the South reclothed the stump fields left by the exploiters of the original forests" and thus allowed the industry to "h[a]ng on in small units" (21), and because the "close association of workers with agriculture" there meant that displaced or downsized woods workers could always flow back onto the farms rather than leave the area or region entirely (22). In *Light in August*, however, the example of Lucas Burch would appear to suggest otherwise.

16. Richard H. Bennington, *Furniture Marketing: From Product Development to Distribution* (New York: Fairchild Publications, 1985), 84. For a fuller account of the invention and operation of the planing mill—and one from Faulkner's own era—see Stanley F. Horn, *This Fascinating Lumber Business* (Indianapolis: Bobbs-Merrill Co., 1943), 151–52.

17. I have explored this scene at greater length in a pair of earlier essays on *Light in August*. See Jay Watson, "Overdoing Masculinity in *Light in August*; or, Joe Christmas and

the Gender Guard," *Faulkner Journal* 9.1–2 (Fall 1993/Spring 1994): 166–72, and "Writing Blood: The Art of the Literal in *Light in August*," *Faulkner and the Natural World: Faulkner and Yoknapatawpha 1996*, ed. Donald M. Kartiganer and Ann J. Abadie (Jackson: University Press of Mississippi, 1996), 86–89.

18. "Planed lumber is always graded and tallied before loading on trucks or railroad cars for shipment to market. There is considerable degrade (reduction in grade) from the rough-fresh-sawed lumber to the dry, planed lumber, as a result of checking and cupping." Joseph L. Muller, *Establishing and Owning a Small Sawmill Business* (Washington: U.S. Department of Commerce, 1945), 68–69.

19. See Phillips A. Hayward, *Wood: Lumber and Timbers*, Chandler Cyclopedia for the Scientific Selection, Purchase, and Use of Commodities, vol. 1 (New York: W. L. Chandler, 1930), 68–69.

20. See Eldredge, 42, Jensen, 76–77, and Todes, 83.

21. See Eric Mercer, *The Social History of the Decorative Arts: Furniture 700–1700* (New York: Meredith Press, 1969), 84.

22. John Perlin's social history of wood offers an account of this process at work in early America that is almost allegorical in its concision: "Mills played an important role in the settlement and growth of America. As Robert Sears explained in his *New and Popular Pictorial Description of the United States*, 'For the occupation of a new [locale] in the wilderness . . . one of the first points secured is a mill site.' . . . Many villages and towns grew around such mills. In southern Maine, a village commonly began at a waterfall on a river or on a watercourse capable of running a water mill, Edward Kendall explained. Kendall, the author of *Travels through the Northern Parts of the United States in the Years 1808–1809*, noted that the first building to go up in the wilderness was usually a sawmill. Lumberjacks either sold their logs to the mill owner or had them sawed into boards or planks, giving the mill owner some logs in exchange for the service. The owner of the mill accumulated wealth through his business and, according to Kendall, with his money 'builds a large wooden house,' opens a store, and 'erects a still and barters rum' and other goods for more logs. The woodsmen eventually clear a good portion of the surrounding countryside. Farmers settle on the deforested land and they soon need a gristmill, Kendall observed, which goes up near the sawmill. Sheep are also raised on the farms, requiring a mill to prepare woolen fibers for spinning. More farmers move to the vicinity to take advantage of living near such mills" (Perlin, 334–35). For Perlin, as for Sears and Kendall before him, the sawmill becomes the leading edge of civilization on the North American continent.

23. Thoreau once developed a similar comparison, though for different purposes. In *The Maine Woods* (1864), he argues that "the pine is no more lumber than man is, and to be made into boards and houses is no more its true and highest use than the truest use of a man is to be cut down and made into manure" (quoted in Max Oelschlaeger, *The Idea of Wilderness* [New Haven: Yale University Press, 1991], 150). Thoreau, of course, is making a primarily ecological point about environmental exploitation. Faulkner, by contrast, cites the violence of lumbering in order to make a primarily social point about the destructive objectification of human beings. In this respect, *Light in August*'s planing mill scenes and comments perhaps deliberately recall Charles Chesnutt's terrible allegory of slave objectification, "Po' Sandy," whose title character, in an attempt to evade the slave's legal condition as movable property, is magically transformed into a pine tree, only to be chopped down and cut up into lumber for his master's new kitchen. Sandy and his wife, Tenie, thus learn the hard way that there is no escape, not even in conjure, from the slave's peculiar liquidity as chattel. See Chesnutt, "Po' Sandy," *The Conjure Woman and Other Conjure Tales*, ed. Richard H. Brodhead (Durham: Duke University Press, 1993), 44–54.

24. Bennington, 112.

25. Given Faulkner's famous suggestion that the figure of Percy Grimm was a prophetic image of a "Nazi Storm Trooper" (see *Faulkner in the University: Class Conferences at the University of Virginia, 1957–1958*, ed. Frederick L. Gwynn and Joseph L. Blotner [1959; Charlottesville: University Press of Virginia, 1977], 41), it is tempting to see the furniture dealer, who hails from "the eastern part of the state" (494), as another prophetic figure, who presages the coming of the furniture industry to the constellation of communities in

the vicinity of Lee County and its seat of Tupelo—an event that got under way roughly
a generation after the novel's publication. See Albert Benson Nylander III, "The Growth
of the Furniture Industry in Northeast Mississippi from 1948 to 1994: A Social Structural
Analysis," M.A. thesis, University of Mississippi, 1994. Nylander traces the migration of the
U.S. furniture industry "from the Atlantic Coast" of Boston, Buffalo, and Philadelphia "to
the upper Midwest" of Cincinnati, Columbus, Grand Rapids, and Chicago "and then to the
South" of High Point, North Carolina, and eventually northeast Mississippi (19–21). The
most important production centers seem to have sprung up in areas recently vacated or in
the process of being vacated by the timber industry, as the great forests of the Northeast, the
Lakes region, and the Appalachians were progressively logged out and the industry turned
its eye toward the massive stands of the Northwest.

26. In Mikhail Bakhtin's sense of spaces that embed specific forms of historical and
human temporality, where "[t]ime, as it were, thickens, takes on flesh, becomes artistically visible" as "space becomes charged and responsive to the movements of time, plot
and history." See Bakhtin, "Forms of Time and Chronotope in the Novel" (1937–1938),
The Dialogic Imagination: Four Essays, ed. Michael Holquist, trans. Caryl Emerson and
Holquist (Austin: University of Texas Press, 1981), 84. As Bakhtin's American translators
usefully put it, "The chronotope is an optic for reading texts as x-rays of the forces at work in
the culture system from which they spring" (see the Glossary to *The Dialogical Imagination*,
425–26). Just so with Doane's Mill, Jefferson, and what Bakhtin would call the chronotope
of "the road" at work in the closing pages of *Light in August* (and indeed throughout the
novel). For Bakhtin's comments on the "road" chronotope and the important role it has
played in the history of novelistic discourse see 243–45.

27. See Michel Foucault, *Discipline and Punish: The Birth of the Prison* (1975), trans.
Alan Sheridan (New York: Vintage, 1979), especially 135–69.

28. Or as Miles Orvell has written of turn-of-the-century realist fiction, "decorative
style could be used as a code for character." See Orvell, *The Real Thing: Imitation and
Authenticity in American Culture, 1880–1940* (Chapel Hill: University of North Carolina
Press, 1989), 58. Orvell's analyses of works by Abraham Canan, Theodore Dreiser, and
Frank Norris, however, make it clear that if furniture often functioned in turn-of-the-
century America as an indicator of class status, it was a troublingly unstable indicator at best
(see 53–58 passim).

29. John Gloag, *A Social History of Furniture Design, from B.C. 1300 to A.D. 1960*
(New York: Bonanza Books, 1966), 1. Another scholar adds definitively, "Decoration and
display have always played a far more important role than comfort in the history of furniture." See Sir Francis Watson, "Introduction," *The History of Furniture*, Watson et al. (1976;
New York: Crescent Books, 1982), 9.

30. Such as, perhaps, Flem Snopes? In *The Town* we learn that on the day before he is
named vice-president of the local bank in Jefferson, Flem makes a furniture purchase from
a dealer in Memphis. Clearly the purchase is motivated by social insecurity and an expressivist agenda; as an announcement of Flem's newly won status and respectability, it parallels
the announcement of his new position at the bank. When, four years later, Gavin Stevens
enters the Snopes home to discuss Linda Snopes's future with Eula, he remarks of "the low
table, the two intimate chairs," "suddenly I knew where I had seen the room and hallway
before. In a photograph, the photograph from say *Town and Country* labelled *American
Interior*, reproduced in color in a wholesale furniture catalogue, with the added legend:
*This is neither a Copy nor a Reproduction. It is our own Model scaled to your individual
Requirements*." This is personality salesmanship with a vengeance, perfectly engineered to
capitalize on the uncertainties of an arriviste like Flem. See Faulkner, *The Town* (1957; New
York: Vintage, 1961), 220–21. My thanks to Joe Urgo for reminding me about this scene.

31. Edgar Allan Poe, "The Philosophy of Furniture" (1840), *Selected Prose, Poetry, and
"Eureka,"* ed. W. H. Auden (New York: Holt, Rinehart and Winston, Inc., 1950), 385.

32. There is also the long historical climb of furniture toward the kind of social visibility
that allowed it to express taste and status. Indeed, though some historians, as we have seen,
draw on an expressivist vocabulary to analyze the decorative function of furniture, others cite
evidence of the low esteem in which furniture was generally held in the centuries leading

up to the late medieval and early modern periods. At this time, explains John Morley, textiles were considered far more valuable—and thus, in wills, inventories, and other written documents, far more noteworthy—than furniture: to "the restlessly mobile rich" who "had to travel to eat and maintain their authority," textiles "were versatile, gave rich effects, and could be easily stored, protected, and transported." See Morley, *The History of Furniture: Twenty-Five Centuries of Style and Design in the Western Tradition* (Boston: Bulfinch Press, 1999), 71. By contrast, early medieval furniture was used for the display of such valuables: the tables, chairs, and benches of the period were typically too bulky and crudely made to assume a genuinely decorative function, so they were relegated to invisibility beneath the cloths, carpets and cushions routinely draped over them (Mercer, 28). As a result, while "one cannot cite any [medieval] document which positively singles furniture out for denigration," there are nonetheless "many in which textile furnishings are minutely described and highly praised while furniture in contrast is ignored or passed over in a word or two" (Mercer, 27; see also Wheeler, 20–21). Interestingly, it was only with the late medieval advent of the sawmill and other "technical advances which enabled joiners to work in wood with a skill and artistry which had previously been attained only by masons and by the craftsmen who worked in precious materials" that wooden furniture crossed the threshold of visibility and acquired a "new standing" in European society (Mercer, 86, 83). So lately (and literally) beneath mention, it became less unremarkable, more ornamental and less strictly functional, and as such was "no longer ignored" by "legal documents" and "travellers' accounts" (Mercer, 83).

33. Aristotle, *Physics*, trans. Robin Waterfield (New York: Oxford University Press, 1996), 34. I first ran across the reference in Harrison (see 27).

34. Plato, *Republic*, trans. B. Jowett (New York: Modern Library, n.d.), 361–65.

35. Aristotle, *Nicomachean Ethics*, trans. Christopher Rowe (Oxford: Oxford University Press, 2002), 167.

36. Karl Marx, *Capital*, 1 (1867), trans. Ben Fowkes (1976; New York: Penguin, 1990), 151.

37. For an excellent analysis of spiritualist table-tipping and the breach it introduced into the structure of nineteenth-century reason, see Daniel Cottom, *Abyss of Reason: Cultural Movements, Revelations, and Betrayals* (New York: Oxford University Press, 1991), 22–48.

38. In *A Sense of Things*, Brown argues that the liveliness of Marx's "deranged table" actually works against Marx's argument, "violat[ing] the very dynamic it is meant to illustrate" (28) and dramatizing instead an even more fundamental, aesthetic form of fetishism at work behind the general "human fascination with objects" (30). Marx's initial illustrations of the commodity form—linen, coffee, corn, and so on—"could hardly be more banal," Brown observes (29). (Indeed, "Marx even makes gold uninteresting.") In chapter 1 of *Capital*, "only the unruly table can be said to captivate our pictorial imagination, and indeed to frustrate that imagination as we try to picture a table not upside down but, rather, standing on its head. Only the table emerges . . . as an object worth imagining or an object worth having, as an object personified while remaining very much an object." This marks the moment, Brown argues, where Marx inadvertently "intimates not the fetishism he theorizes but the more pedestrian, not to say less powerful, fetishism through which objects captivate us, fascinate us, compel us to have a relation to them, which seems too have little to do with their relation to other commodities. This is a social relation neither between men nor between things, but something like a social relation between human subject and inanimate object, wherein modernity's ontological distinction between human beings and nonhumans makes no sense. This relation, hardly describable in the context of use or exchange, can be overwhelmingly aesthetic, deeply affective—it involves desire, pleasure, frustration, a kind of pain" (29–30). As such, Marx's table ultimately "illustrate[s] something in excess of his structural point" about the ontological distortion introduced by the commodity form (30).

39. See Elaine Scarry, *The Body in Pain: The Making and Unmaking of the World* (New York: Oxford University Press, 1985), 299.

40. Georges Bataille, *Theory of Religion* (1973), trans. Robert Hurley (New York: Zone Books, 1992), 101.

41. A nervous Cleanth Brooks may have been the first to argue for the inadequacy of the term "lynching" as a description of the murder and mutilation of Joe Christmas. See Brooks,

William Faulkner: The Yoknapatawpha Country (1963; New Haven: Yale University Press, 1966), 51–52. Brooks, of course, is eager to individualize the pathology responsible for Christmas's death, to attribute it to Grimm alone rather than to the community he (Brooks) prefers to see as normative and organic.

42. It could be argued that the salesman's unnamed merchandise is the literary descendant of the never-quite-specified "spoils of Poynton," in Henry James's 1896 novel of that name. In an interpretive tour de force, Brown explores James's "narratological device" of "withholding things" (*A Sense of Things*, 149), "effectively effac[ing] [them] from the descriptive register" of his novel (141), where the furnishings of an English manor play a pivotal role in the plot—coveted, quarreled over, shuttled from place to place, and finally burned up along with Poynton itself in a climactic conflagration—without ever quite achieving material specificity. In this way, argues Brown, James manages to make "the mise-en-scène at Poynton . . . a matter of aura, not artifacts" (147; and see 140–55 generally).

43. Alfred Kazin, "The Stillness of *Light in August*," in *Faulkner: A Collection of Critical Essays*, ed. Robert Penn Warren (1958; Englewood Cliffs, N.J.: Prentice-Hall Inc., 1966), 149.

44. These scenes would not be out of place in Patricia Yaeger's account of the strangeness and violence of Southern object relations in writings by Southern women. See Yaeger, *Dirt and Desire: Reconstructing Southern Women's Writing, 1930–1990* (Chicago: University of Chicago Press, 2000), 186–217.

45. Christmas also breaks a broom handle over the back of his exhausted horse while hurrying to town to meet Bobbie in the aftermath of the violence at the dance (see 209–11).

46. Watson, "Writing Blood," 89.

47. Nor does Gavin Stevens's subsequent reconstruction of the scene help with this ambiguity. In his account, too, the table is simply "overturned," with no agent being specified (449).

Hightower's frenetic table is perhaps the immediate descendant of Addie Bundren's dynamic coffin, which over the course of *As I Lay Dying* not only stands, leaps, swims, and even speaks but also becomes riddled with holes (Vardaman's drill anticipating Grimm's pistol) and fails to prevent bodily damage to the human form it shelters. The connections are suggestive but must remain undeveloped here.

48. Ecocritic Michael Bennett has recently noted that "[t]he historical memory of slavery and its aftermath includes a forest of trees that were used to enforce southern lynch law, as we are reminded in cultural images from Billie Holliday singing 'Strange Fruit' to Speech, of Arrested Development, rapping about 'trees my forefathers hung from' in Tennessee." See "Anti-Pastoralism, Frederick Douglass, and the Nature of Slavery," *Beyond Nature Writing: Exploring the Boundaries of Ecocriticism*, ed. Karla Armbruster and Kathleen R. Wallace (Charlottesville: University Press of Virginia, 2001), 207.

49. "It is almost universally the case in everyday life that the most cherished object is one that has been hand-made by a friend: there is no mystery about this, for the object's material attributes themselves record and memorialize the intensely personal, extraordinary because exclusive, interior feelings of the maker for just this person—This is for you. But anonymous, mass-produced objects contain a collective and equally extraordinary message: Whoever you are, and whether or not I personally like or even know you, in at least this small way, be well. Thus, within the realm of objects, objects-made-for-anyone bear the same relation to objects-made-for-someone that, within the human realm, caritas bears to eros. Whether they reach someone in the extreme conditions of imprisonment or in the benign and ordinary conditions of everyday life, the handkerchief, blanket, and bucket of white paint contain within them the wish for well-being: 'Don't cry; be warm; watch now, in a few minutes even these constricting walls will look more spacious'" (Scarry, 292). Likewise, "material culture . . . holds within itself the universal salutation of Amnesty [International]'s whispered 'Corragio!' It passes on the password of Isaiah's ancient artisans—'Take Courage!' " (326).

50. As the locals swap theories about Joe's escape attempt and its grisly aftermath, it might as well be the suppertables themselves talking: "There were many reasons, opinions, as to why he had fled to Hightower's house at the last. 'Like to like,' the easy, the immediate,

ones said, remembering the old tales about the minister. Some believed it to have been sheer chance; others said that the man had shown wisdom" (443).

51. Historian Thomas D. Clark, for instance, writes that "sawmills and planing mills were more prominent" in turn-of-the-century central Mississippi "than were cotton gins, and they produced a far greater volume of heavy freight." See Clark, *The Greening of the South: The Recovery of Land and Forest* (Lexington: University Press of Kentucky, 1984), 18. And on the central role of the timber and lumber industries in the economic and social history of southern Mississippi, see Nollie Hickman, *Mississippi Harvest: Lumbering in the Longleaf Pine Belt, 1840–1915* (University: University of Mississippi, 1962).

52. According to Horn, the South "held first rank in regional production" of lumber from 1899, when it eclipsed the Lake states, through 1925, after which it was eclipsed in turn by the West (30–32). If we take 1931, the year of *Light in August*'s composition, as the year in which its "present-time" events are set—following the precedents set by *The Sound and the Fury*, written and set in 1928, and *Sanctuary*, drafted and set in 1929—then Joe Christmas's dates would appear to be 1895–1931.

53. See Roland Barthes, "The Reality Effect" (1968), *The Rustle of Language*, trans. Richard Howard (1986; Berkeley: University of California Press, 1989), 148. For Barthes the reality effect consists above all in strategically artless allusions to the "insignificant gestures, transitory attitudes, insignificant objects," and "redundant words" that convey an aura of "what is ordinarily called 'concrete reality'" (146). And as a literary example of those insignificant objects, Barthes cites a passage from Flaubert's "Simple Heart" describing—what else?—home furnishings: an "old piano," "a barometer," and "a pyramidal heap of boxes and cartons" (quoted in Barthes, 141). Once again the furniture of philosophy, furniture as theoretical object, grounds the philosophy of the ordinary.

Incidentally, it is much the same bric-a-brac linked by Barthes with the realism of realistic fiction that Willa Cather would banish from the modernist novel in her 1922 essay "The Novel Démeublé," a manifesto on behalf of a more austere, oblique "unfurnished" prose in keeping with the general cultural reaction against Victorian/bourgeois clutter and ornament. The historian Jackson Lears has described a more lowbrow example of this general attitude: "Beginning in the 1890s, mainstream decorating magazines like *House Beautiful* took up the growing outcry against 'the tyranny of things' and 'the bric-a-brac habit.' Often their arguments were hygienic and therapeutic," complementing Cather's aesthetic discussion. See Cather, "The Novel Démeublé," *Stories, Poems, and Other Writings* (New York: Library of America, 1992), 834–37; and Lears, *Fables of Abundance: A Cultural History of Advertising in America* (New York: Basic Books, 1994), 381. See also Brown, *A Sense of Things*, 143–44.

54. Jameson, 102. Jameson continues that the "ruses" of this intractable history turn "individual as well as collective praxis . . . into grisly and ironic reversals of their overt intention." Is there a better way to describe how Percy Grimm's intent to protect Joe Christmas from mob violence morphs into its opposite, at just the moment Hightower's table begins its *danse macabre*?

Dematerializing Culture: Faulkner's Trash Aesthetic

Patricia Yaeger

Rubbish, trash, garbage, detritus: why make these the subjects of high art? But objects just as peculiar have become the stuff of aesthetic ecstasy. Ruins—those monumental buildings beset with decay—have been the source of artistic and metaphysical contemplation for centuries. In the Renaissance their crumpled facades gained altitude, signaled the triumphs of the Greco-Roman world. In the Romantic era ruined abbeys and temples became rich signs of decay defying Enlightenment precepts. Similarly, still life, a genre focused on the daily or quotidian, gained aesthetic resonance in the sixteenth and seventeenth centuries. Still-life paintings offered, at first, a form of meditation permitting a measured withdrawal from epic Christianity, and then a way to celebrate the vigor of a growing Dutch bourgeoisie.[1] But it is not until the twentieth century that a fascination with formlessness, with the random shapes of object-decay embodied in trash, waste, or detritus, gained a wide-ranging aesthetic stature. In 1939 Yeats insisted that even though his poems depended on "pure mind," his images still found their origin in "a mound of refuse or the sweepings of a street, / Old kettles, old bottles, and a broken can, / Old iron, old bones, old rags." If his poems were secretly founded in dirt, then the aging poet must flounder there as well: "I must lie down where all the ladders start, / In the foul rag-and-bone shop of the heart."[2]

Why does trash assume such a vigorous life in modernist/postmodernist art? In the 1940s Jackson Pollack not only painted horizontally, he also tossed trash onto his canvasses. Careless, fickle, these specks of spent desire—cigarette butts, floor crud—freckle thick ropes of paint. In 1955 Elizabeth Bishop took decaying fish scales and gave them the smell of sublimity. In "At the Fishhouses" an old man "sits netting, / his net," the odor of codfish so prickly in the air "it makes one's nose run and one's eyes water." And yet the smelly bits that cover dock and storehouse, gangplank and wheelbarrow, turn these workaday objects to silver:

> The big fish tubs are completely lined
> with layers of beautiful herring scales
> and the wheelbarrows are similarly plastered

Fig. 1. Walter Robinson, photograph of young man looking at Damien Hirst's *Armageddon*. Courtesy *Artnet Magazine*.

with creamy iridescent coats of mails,
with small iridescent flies crawling on them.[3]

These beautiful flies come to life again in the twenty-first century. (Figure 1) In 2004 the "Minimalism" exhibit at the New York Guggenheim began with a work by Damien Hirst called *Armageddon*. Brown-black amber, a massive canvas brimming with organic bumps and rills: everyone wants to get closer, to see what this black amber is made of. And Hirst does not disappoint: "Houseflies on canvas," the legend reads, and on the floor beneath, one finds random wings and little dried-up bodies. Hirst's canvas depicts these flies' final battle with the exterminator, their magnificent, detritusy death.

This ethos of rubbish sublimity, of repeated encounters with a trashy sublime, extends to film as well as poetry and painting. *Citizen Kane*, the most archetypal of twentieth-century American movies, gives us a dose of rubbish American style. After Kane dies in his mansion (beset by a solitude that outflanks even his most ponderous objects), his collections are gathered for inspection: some as treasure, some as trash; some for the auction house, some for the incinerator. A group of reporters gossip: "'How much do you think this is worth?' 'Millions—' 'If anyone wants it.'"[4] Pegged as detritus, Kane's random objects assemble themselves into a miniature city: his great hall so filled with crates and castaways that it becomes its own landscape. And then everything speeds up as the camera swings in for a close-up of a child's sled, just as it is tossed into an incinerator. What does it mean for Welles, as director, that this longed-for, forgotten sled turns to ash?

Like the detritus in Bishops's "Fishhouses" and Hirsts's *Armegeddon*, the sled gleams as it goes, the letters winking in revelatory flames. The audience learns Kane's brightest secret—hidden even from himself—that his loss of mother, snow, and home—here the accoutrements of lower-class dailiness—costs him a world of love and ritual. His old plaything offers the audience an archive for reading not just the past, but its meaning—and just when all traces of this meaning are being obliterated. Why does this movie create, as its climax and epiphany, a moment when "trash" has such weight? *Citizen Kane* is, in part, a meditation on the wages of capitalism. How do we retain our love objects in a commodified world where everything seems replaceable, interchangeable? There is still room for longing in Kane's economy, but the endless objects meant to fulfill it only attain this meaning the moment they are destroyed. In an age of increasingly serialized commodification, the myth of replaceability, the way the new is instantly out of date, old, means that the object goes missing the minute one acquires it. *Citizen Kane* shows us the poignancy of one object that cannot be traded in, but also makes this uniqueness trebly poignant as the sled turns to ash—a fiery archive of a world gone missing. If mourning for the transformational object is the base note, the foundation of capitalism, then to see this object trashed is to bear witness to capitalism as witlessness: the throwaway offers an archive of longing, at once dirge and annal.

Even though detritus shines at the center of twentieth- and twenty-first-century aesthetics, this sense of its gleams or archival residue is variable. "Sublime rubbish" is not a constant across either century. In T. S. Eliot's "Waste Land" the modern Thames bears "empty bottles, sandwich papers/Silk handkerchiefs, cardboard boxes, cigarette ends," echoing a permanent melancholia in the narrator: "By the waters of Leman I sat down and wept."[5] Fishing in the dull canal the narrator is so rattled he can barely hear the snatches of mythopoesis that fly past him. For Eliot, the everyday trash that fascinates Welles, Yeats, or Bishop elicits contempt. His nausea can only be assuaged by a return—not to daily detritus, but to the elegance of ruin: "These fragments I have shored against my ruins"—in this poem, tidbits from an archaic world put modern dross to shame (line 431).

In contrast to Eliot's scorn for the trash of the present and his nostalgia for the pastoral residue, the rubbish in F. Scott Fitzgerald's *The Great Gatsby* stimulates a different loathing. In Gatsby's world of steak and women a la mode, only the latest fashion will do. But as Nick Caraway and Tom Buchanan sweep toward the furious pace of twenties capitalism, their train grinds to a halt when it reaches the valley of ashes. On this "fantastic," ashy "farm," detritus grows like a perverse New World hybrid. "Where ashes grow like wheat into ridges and hills and grotesque gardens," everything is covered with grime, and even the "transcendent" efforts "of men who move dimly and already crumbling through the powdery air" seem wasted. A line of grey, ghastly cars comes down the track, "and immediately the ash-grey men swarm up with leaden spades and stir up an impenetrable cloud which screens their obscure operations from your sight."[6]

While these men covered in ash crumble, above them, "above the grey land and the spasms of bleak dust which drift endlessly over it, you perceive . . . the eyes of Doctor T. J. Eckleburg, . . . some wild wag of an occulist" who set up his advertisement and then forgot it (27). It is the captains of advertisement who preside over incinerators that yield so much ash, making fashion a prime source of detritus and connecting the novel's disconnected realms of wealth and penury. As Michael Breitweiser says, for those who lack access to the world of commodities and luxury that Gatsby represents, "the thing is a mere thing, a dispirited outcome . . . figured as 'foul dust' or ashes—devitalized remainder. These symbols of nonsymbolicity are extremely interesting . . . because they are the valleys where Fitzgerald . . . confines social life that fails to express the ideal (revulsion marking that place where insight will later appear). Insofar as a person is a living seismograph of the ideal, a pure register of abstract national content, he is truly vital, alive . . . insofar as he is particular—a person with projects, worries . . . inflected by ethnicity, region . . . and so on—he is a failure, merely particular, an outpost in which the rhythms of capital have long since been forgotten."[7] And in fact, the workplace of the poor, struggling garage owner, Mr. Wilson, is covered with ash: "a white ashen dust veiled his dark suit and pale hair as it veiled everything on the vicinity" (30).

Contrasting Yeats's and Orson Welles's reproductions of rubbish with Eliot's and Fitzgerald's, we see the emergence of *two opposing narratives of modern detritus*. First, we have encountered trash that reeks of the sublime. As the daily grind of garbage disposals, recycling, and shifting modes of production replaces the rhythms of weather or seasons, trash becomes modernity's quick fix on mortality, its symbolic site for accessing the rhythms of death or decay. The thrownaway object offers an archive for the histories—the tenderness and trauma—nestled in objects that the captains of capitalism have overlooked. But if detritus can be filled with gleams, if it becomes a vital remainder, it also represents—for Eliot, Fitzgerald, and countless others—a devitalized remnant, a sign of everything that's wrong with the outposts of modernity. Although not as sexy, this pessimistic view of rubbish seems the most commonsensical. Martin Luther King was assassinated in Memphis at a Sanitation Workers' strike (protesting black garbage men's unjust wages and working conditions), while Lady Bird Johnson mounted a highway campaign to clean up the mountains of litter on America's roads. Thinking of ozone days, of the gargantuan size of New York's Fresh Kills Landfill (the only man-made object visible from outer space), of environmental racism, the toxic trash produced by systematic overpackaging and a score of industrial pollutants, why should rubbish give off transcendent gleams, why should it be the beloved of modern/postmodern aesthetes?

I want to take this question home to that most loss-inspired of American modernists, William Faulkner. What role does detritus play in Faulkner's narratives about loss, about wasted social practices? At minimum, both *Gatsby* and *Absalom, Absalom!* feature men covered in waste—in ash or in mud. When Gatsby's ashen men work with incinerated household matter, coal dust, the ash so obliterates their bodies that they lose themselves to disintegration. Their labor is swallowed by lung-clogging clouds. In contrast, Sutpen's Afro-Haitians slaves are men not of ash, but of dirt. Often covered in mud, they are nearly as invisible as Gatsby's workers—emerging from the background of the story only to give Miss Rosa's or Mr. Compson's tale the urgency of nightmare. While Gatsby's ash-men work with remainders, with throwaways, what these mud-covered Afro-Haitians make is Sutpen's Hundred—something with both monumental stature and use value, but only for the book's white denizens, and only for a short span of years. The mud on their bodies creates a practical mosquito barrier and evokes, for the narrator, an insulting affiliation with animals and earth. And yet it also gleams. Chasing the French architect through forests and swamps, these slaves light pine knobs against the dark, and when the horses' eyes shine in the torch light, the black men's bodies gleam as well: "the dogs and the niggers (the niggers mostly still naked except for a pair of pants here and there) with the pine torches smoking and flaring above them and the red light on their round heads and arms and the mud they wore in the swamp to keep the mosquitoes off dried hard and shiny, glinting like glass or china and the shadows they cast taller than they were at one moment and then gone the next."[8] How do we read these gleams? Faulkner translates them instantly into "glass or china," suggesting their triviality, as Sutpen's Hundred will one day fill with the minor accoutrements of wealth and power. These gleams are, then, ambiguous—suggesting at once the sublime aura worn by men who are always more than mud but also invoking, even in the midst of implacable wilderness, Ellen's shopping and Sutpen's man-obliterating, commodity-driven dream.

Elsewhere in *Absalom* Faulkner teases us; his characters promise a world free of detritus. When Sutpen first meets Charles Bon, (Quentin muses) "he stood there at his own door, just as he had imagined, planned, designed . . . and after fifty years the forlorn nameless and homeless lost child came to knock at it and no monkey-dressed nigger anywhere under the sun to come to the door and order the child away." At that moment, even before Judith and Bon have met, "he must have felt and heard the design—house, position, posterity and all—come down like it had been built out of smoke, making no sound, creating no rush of displaced air and not even leaving any debris" (rather like Citizen Kane's sled) (267). This is a teaser because, by the novel's end, the house goes down in a riot, an orgy, of rot and decay.

How, then, does detritus or bodily waste function in Faulkner's fiction—does it qualify as vitalized or devitalized remainder? Is Faulkner of the party of Yeats or T. S. Eliot? In Elizabeth Bishop's camp, or F. Scott Fitzgerald's? To give a framework for answering these questions, I want to look at Faulkner's fiction askance, in the context of several contemporary visual artists who are preoccupied with trash or trashing. Their art will offer a heuristic site for thinking about the aesthetics of detritus and labor and how we handle the totemic fact of bodily decay.

Let's begin with the most detritus-driven story in Faulkner's canon— with Ab Snopes's mischief in "Barn Burning." Snopes is a barn burner—a man who is angry about a past strewn with his own violence and with social inequity. A sharecropper, he takes vengeance on the men who employ him in tenancy by destroying their property. "Barn Burning" is not only a story about white trash, but also about the pleasure of trashing other people's property.

The Snopes family travels from farm to farm with a ragtag collection of used-up things. The Snopes daughters sit "on and among the sorry residue of the dozen and more movings which even the boy could remember—the battered stove, the broken beds and chairs, the clock inlaid with mother-of-pearl, which would not run . . . which had been his mother's dowry."[9] Snopes's hat could have been a sculpture by Damien Hirst. It "had once been black but . . . had now that friction-glazed greenish cast of the bodies of old house flies" (11). In going to see Major de Spain, his newest landlord, Snopes smears fresh horse droppings on de Spain's property—dragging his stiff, manure-covered foot across de Spain's high-end carpet. The rug is, in its way, twice-destroyed. When Major de Spain delivers it to Snopes for cleaning, his tenant uses harsh, homemade lye to scour the rug's surfaces—laboriously changing bling into rubbish, high-end glitz into garbage.

Faulkner asks his readers to confront the ethical dilemma this trashing presents to Sarty, Abner's youngest son. Should he side with his barn-burning dad, or with the requirements of justice, of property rights? Named after "Colonel Sartoris," Sarty longs for his father to stop destroying other people's things. From a child's eye view Snopes's destructiveness looks random and chaotic. But thinking outside this box, we can also see that Snopes's laborious obliterations have a logic, as well as a resonance with postmodern destructivist artists who produced gorgeous, ruined

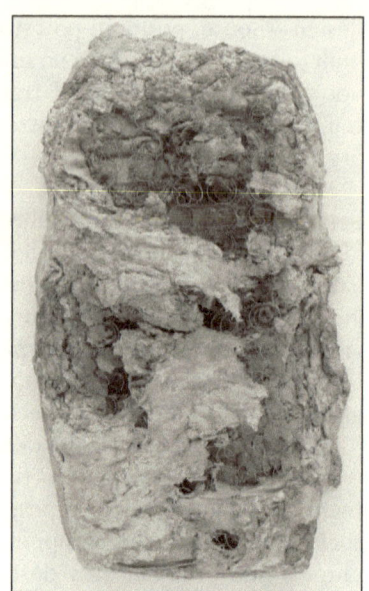

Fig. 2. Rafael Montanez Ortiz, *Archaeological Find, 3, Burnt Mattress*, 1961. *Burnt Mattress*, 6' 2⅞" × 41¼" × 9⅜". Courtesy of the artist and the Museum of Modern Art.

work in the 1960s and '70s. The manured, lye-washed rug reminds me of *Archaeological Find # 3* by Rafael Montanez Ortiz, a gorgeous *Burnt Mattress* that the Puerto Rican artist produced by marrying mattress and fire. The sensuous death of this sleepy synthetic produces plastic-charred mattress springs: a billowy marshmallow of formlessness and coiled metal. (Figure 2) The destroyed rug also calls to mind *Cut Piece*, a work Yoko Ono performed in Carnegie Hall in 1964. A member of the neo-Dadaist group Fluxus, Ono sat at the front of the stage and offered a pair of shears to her audience. She asked them to come up, one at a time, to cut pieces of clothing off her body—either until she was naked, or until the experience became too much to bear. As one critic says, this strategy was "designed to question the relationship between subject and object, victim and aggressor": a confusion Abner Snopes also aims for when he burns his employers' barns.[10] Refusing victim status, he also redoubles it, hoping de Spain's world will mirror his own collection of "sorry residue . . . the battered stove, the broken beds." But oddly it is also this life of remnants that allows the boy Sarty to elude de Spain later in the story. Sarty rats on his father; he warns de Spain that his barn is about to go up in flame. De Spain's slave grabs the child, but "it was too late this time too. The Negro grasped his shirt, but the entire sleeve, rotten with washing, carried away, and he was out that door too" (23). Sarty's raggedness saves him.

Fig. 3. Gordon Matta-Clark, *Day's End*
(Pier 52). Gansevoort Street and West
Street, New York, N.Y. Courtesy 2005
Estate of Gordon Matta-Clark / Artists
Rights Society (ARS), New York.

"Barn Burning" ends with the young boy's spring journey, just after
Sarty has warned de Spain and heard the gunfire aimed at his father. As
he runs away, young Colonel Sartoris Snopes is uncertain whether his
father is alive or dead; he aches to rationalize and memorialize his father's
past bravery. And Faulkner angles his images to make nature—and the
reader—approve of Sarty's "just" action. Day is dawning, the boy is at the
crest of a hill: "he went on down the hill, toward the dark woods within
which the liquid silver voices of the birds called unceasing—the rapid and
urgent beating of the urgent and quiring heart of the late spring night.
He did not look back" (25). Faulkner lavishes all the rhetorical stops he
can on awakening nature—and, by association, on the nonfamilial act that
preserves someone else's property. Awash in song and "liquid silver," we
find no celebration of the ashy sublime. There is no choir for the trashers
of culture.

As antidote, I propose a hypothetical alliance between Ab Snopes and
the twentieth-century visual artist Robert Matta-Clark. (Figure 3) As with
Ab Snopes's barns, Matta Clark's cut-into buildings no longer exist in the
world—except in photographic representations. His goal was to produce
"deliberately ruinous objects": art made from condemned or abandoned
buildings destined to be destroyed.[11] Most famous for a suburban "instal-
lation" called *Splitting on Humphrey Street in Englewood, New Jersey*,
Matta-Clark was intrigued with "unbuilding," with reapportioning others'
architecture by sawing through and unraveling it. His acts of disassem-
blage were more structured than those of Abner Snopes, but both men
based their destruction on a "luxurious squandering of energy."[12] Where
Ab Snopes used fire, Clark cut away the sides of houses, wharves, and
office buildings to let in transgressive, inappropriate light. (Figure 4) While
cutting a hole ("*Conical Intersection*") in a huge building within Les
Halles in Paris, next to the site of the proposed Centre Georges Pompidou,

Fig. 4. Gordon Matta-Clark, *Splitting: Interior*, 1974. 322 Humphrey Street, Englewood, New Jersey. Courtesy 2005 Estate of Gordon Matta-Clark / Artists Rights Society (ARS), New York.

Matta-Clark reported the delighted response of a seventy-year old concierge: "'Oh, I see the purpose of that hole . . . it is an experiment into bringing light and air into spaces that never had enough of either.' In this freeing up of a typical bourgeois interior, the hole was granted a liberating function, described by the artist as a 'son et lumiere' experiment."[13]

This allegiance to making detritus sublime (to dematerializing a culture that condemns its old buildings) takes another form in *Splitting*. (Figure 5) Matta-Clark begins by cutting a suburban residence into two halves with a chain saw. Using a jack, he then props the house open, tilting one half on its axis so that light and air (and wind and rain) could spill into old corners. The destruction the house was already destined for became willful, creative. By participating "in the collective imperative to waste," Matta-Clark veers away from capitalist manners.[14] He is deeply interested in nonproductivity (in not-progress), in shattering what exists to show the deep insecurities of the built environment. Making an art that makes the fragility of a suburban house beautiful (that celebrates an antiprogressive worklessness in the workaday heart of Paris), Matta-Clark makes each of these remnant buildings a torch song to not-progress, to uselessness. If Matta-Clark offers a critique of bourgeois enclosure (Figure 6), if he trashes homes and office buildings to challenge the hurry-up of new building and "growth," Ab Snopes shares with him the desire to dematerialize his culture. His burnt offerings, obsessive and vengeful though they be, also critique the place of his family in the material world—in the race and class inequities that allow the very rich to exploit the very poor.

Fig. 5. Gordon Matta-Clark, Untitled
(*Splitting* 2), 1974. 322 Humphrey Street,
Englewood, New Jersey. Courtesy 2005
Estate of Gordon Matta-Clark / Artists Rights
Society (ARS), New York.

Finally, like Matta-Clark, Snopes's actions approach the status of performance art. On the evening de Spain's barn burns, Sarty watches "his
father, still in the hat and coat, at once formal and burlesque as though
dressed carefully for some shabby and ceremonial violence," begin "emp-
tying the reservoir of the lamp back into the five-gallon kerosene can from
which it had been filled" (20–21). Snopes's hatred of others' material goods
has a bizarre theatrical quality. He sends a "strange negro" to announce
to his last employer-victim, Mr. Harris, that a performance is about to
begin. As Mr. Harris testifies, this "strange Negro" repeats a message from
Abner Snopes: "'He say to tell you wood and hay kin burn.' I said, 'What?'
'That whut he say to tell you,' the nigger said. 'Wood and hay kin burn.'
That night my barn burned. I got the stock out but I lost the barn" (4). If
there are pleasures to be had in Snopes's repeated destructions, they
are complex. These are working barns, not Matta-Clark's condemned buildings. But Snopes's lack of moral principles does not obliterate the fact that
each burning has an aesthetic and a polical—as well as a warped psychological—dimension. Snopes goes to de Spain to protest the fact that the
Major is about to own "me body and soul for the next eight months" (9).
At least until the late 1930s, and often beyond, tenant farmers' conditions
reflected "undeviating" powerlessness. It is this powerlessness that Ab
Snopes protests with his own brand of the trashy sublime. The story ends
not only with nature's silver, but with a sky "stained abruptly and violently
upward: a long swirling roar incredible and soundless, blotting the stars":
like a work of Abstract Expressionism, turning de Spain's barn to ash (24).

In this story, then, Faulkner is of both parties—celebrating a Blakean
destruction, as well as the child's love of commodified forms. But since
the celebration of the ashy sublime is buried in the midst of "Barn
Burning," since this hypothesis about a Snopes-based sublimity needs a
supplement, let me move to *The Hamlet* and compare its ending with

Fig. 6. Gordon Matta-Clark, *Splitting*, 1974. 322 Humphrey Street, Englewood, New Jersey. Courtesy 2005 Estate of Gordon Matta-Clark / Artists Rights Society (ARS), New York.

Claes Oldenberg's outlandish artwork *The Hole*. (Figure 7) Oldenburg was already well known as a major sculptor in the Pop Art idiom in 1967 when he made *The Hole*. In this public venue, he tries his hand at something resembling conceptual art. Oldenburg specialized in the satire of spatial enlargement. Common household objects were made immense, stuffed with kapok, and allowed to flop down. But this time, instead of making rigid things droopy, Oldenburg demonumentalizes the monument. He gets the city's permission (and its money) to dig a rectangular trench, six feet deep, six feet long, and three feet wide, sited behind the Metropolitan Museum. Dug from 10:30 a.m. to 12:30 p.m. on a summer's day, it gets filled in just after lunch. Having made an inverted sculpture or "imaginary recessed box" resembling the plain cubes that other sculptors "were producing in a style that would come to be called Minimal Art," Oldenburg in his journal calls *The Hole* a "nonvisible . . . monument."[15] (Figure 8) His "use of lowly soil" extended work that became fashionable in the 1950s of incorporating "dirt, sand, or urban detritus in painting and sculpture."[16] Why did art need expensive materials to create rich aesthetic value? Oldenburg focussed on matter out of place; his *Placid Civic Monument* was scoured with dirt that did not fit back into the hole.[17] Earth becomes the stuff of high art.

The first volume of the Snopes trilogy, *The Hamlet*, comes to its finale with a sense of equivalent anticlimax. Armstid, Bookwright, and Ratliff have bought useless property to make their fortunes; they are frantically digging a set of treasure-bent holes. Sure that they will find Confederate gold,

Fig. 7. Claes Oldenburg, *Placid Civic Monument* (also known as *The Hole*), 1967. Oldenburg with Doris C. Freedman and Sam Green. Photograph by Daniel McPartlin. Courtesy New York City Parks and Recreation Photo Archive.

conned by a Snopes (Abner's remaining, barn-burning son), Bookwright and Ratliff admit defeat; they begrudgingly admire the con, but Armstid, in his bitterness, refuses their knowledge. As an impoverished farmer, he feels that his hole has fit him too well; he is "waist-deep in the ground as if he had been cut in two at the hips, the dead torso, not even knowing it was dead, laboring on in measured stoop and recover like a metronome as Armstid dug himself back into that earth which had produced him."[18] Continuing to dig, refusing to recognize the absence of treasure ("spading himself into the waxing twilight with the regularity of a mechanical toy," Armstid sweats, and the whole county turns out to see him (405). And here is the consonance with Oldenburg's "sculpture." It becomes Mayor Lindsey's embarrassment, the talk of the town. No one can take it seriously, yet everyone has to see it. So in Faulkner, people come long distances to watch this spectacle of dirt, sometimes staying late to prolong the performance "even though it meant unharnessing and feeding and perhaps even milking in the dark" (404). This earthwork is absorbing; as Richard Godden argues, it makes Armstid an artist of his own life: "Part of Armstid may dig for the Frenchman's coin, but another part of him digs for his own sweat; to recover from the ground the lifetime's practice

Fig. 8. Claes Oldenburg, *Placid Civic Monument*. In the background, *Cleopatra's Needle*. Photograph by Daniel McPartlin. Courtesy New York City Parks and Recreation Photo Archive.

that he has put into it. . . . Having worked so hard, Armstid foolishly believes that there must be something [deep] in what he has done. For that treasure, different from Flem's or the Frenchman's, he digs."[19] What he produces for his countrymen is their own "civic monument" to injustice, ineptitude, poor soil, and capitalist cunning, but his hole still begs the question: do we read this earthwork as an instance of an earth-based sublime? Or does matter out of place represent, once again, Southern culture as devitalized remainder?

At the very least, we can say that Ab Snopes and Armstid create detritus as spectacle. There is something dramatic and overblown about each of their performances, as if the hyperbole of rich men's possessions creates a counterhyperbole in culture's destroyers: something that Armstid's audience recognize as a protoaesthetic that also recurs in *As I Lay Dying*.

In order to illuminate the detritus that flows through *As I Lay Dying*, we can contemplate *Fountain* by Sherrie Levine. Levine's *Fountain*, a gleaming brass urinal made in imitation of and homage to Marcel Duchamp, is another waste reservoir that gleams. (Figure 9) Duchamp's original urinal was among the first of his readymades: objects plucked (as early as 1913) from store shelf or wall and turned into art—by the mere act of declaiming them "art." As Duchamp explains, these objects were

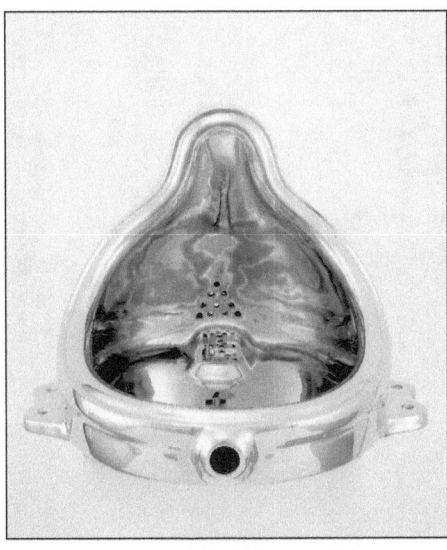

Fig. 9. Sherrie Levine, *Fountain (after Duchamp)*, 1996, cast bronze 17″ × 16″ × 12″. Edition of 6. Courtesy Paula Cooper Gallery, New York.

chosen with "a total absence of good or bad taste . . . in fact a complete anesthesia."[20] "Their startling originality emanates not from their physical form but from the unexpected act or gesture through which they were plucked from the everyday and designated as works of art."[21] Duchamp comments wryly on the omnipresence of the assembly line. In a world of identical products he individualizes this "one," giving it an arbitrary and comic aesthetic address, making it the hapless object of our helpless gaze. Eighty years later Levine remakes Duchamp's disappeared urinal in bronze, as if to pee is to gleam.

Like Duchamp, when Faulkner puts Addie Bundren's dead body at the axis of *As I Lay Dying* and gives it a smell, he enacts the unexpected. He connects with Duchamp's avant-garde in the savvy ridiculousness of the subject he chooses to put at the center of his novel. And, by choosing a corpse as his novel's centerpiece, he matches (or overmatches?) Duchamp's profundity by plucking Addie's body off the assembly line of death. Instead of joining the numbers of identical dead, Addie's body acquires a cortege and an odorous aura. But Faulkner's novel is also about the mass production of families, about the inexorability, the assembly-line features of hearth and home. Even as Addie's corpse escapes the fate of the copy, the reproduction, the same, her husband Anse is on his way to town to jumpstart the assembly line (to reproduce her selfsame, identical wife form): "'It's Cash and Jewel and Vardaman and Dewey Dell,' pa says, kind of hangdog and proud too, with his teeth and all, even if he wouldn't look at us. 'Meet Mrs. Bundren,' he says."[22]

Fig. 10. David
Hammons, *Toilet Trees*,
1990. Courtesy Jack
Tilton Gallery,
New York.

Fig. 11. Robert Gober, *Three Urinals*,
1998. Courtesy of the artist. Photo:
D. James Dee.

Others paying homage to Duchamp have played on the actual multiplicity of his urinal, its mimicry of every other urinal emerging from the
factory that day. The African American artist David Hammons installed
his *Toilet Trees* (1990) in a woodland at the Museum van Hedendaagse
Kunst in Belgium. (Figure 10) Hammons comments "on the social conventions that remove" natural bodily functions to "the confines of denat-
uralized, constructed space."[23] Robert Gober's *Three Urinals* is another
recontextualization of Duchamp's *Fountain*, this time as a way of evoking
and memorializing gay community in a time of AIDS.[24] (Figure 11) The
incongruous theatrics of each of these artists—featuring a receptacle for
human waste as high art—is a reminder of the insistent play of detritus
in modern/postmodern aesthetics. Similarly, the meditations of each of
Faulker's characters on Addie Bundren's body—or on the imagined boun-
ties the corpse's journey will bring—yield an equal and poignant play.
"My mother is a fish," says Vardaman, even as she splashes over him as
"pieces of not-fish now, not-blood, on my hands and overalls." When we
first meet this fish, "it slides out of [Vardaman's] hands, smearing wet dirt

onto him and flops down, dirtying itself again, gapmouthed, goggle-eyed, hiding into the dust like it was ashamed of being dead" (27). "My mother is a fish" takes all these loose, googly ends and gives to dead scale and dirt a sweet animistic life, as if, at least in Vardaman's mind, Addie Bundren still gleams.

What I've begun to establish is how closely Faulkner's characters are allied with detritus, ranging from the body in decay, to matter out of place (Armstid's holes), to Ab Snopes's world turned trash. If these recapitulations of Faulkner's fascination with all kinds of debris give us a world of both vitalized and devitalized remainders, making him of the party of both T. S. Eliot and Orson Welles, I want to look at one passage that seems to me unambiguous. This is the moment in "That Evening Sun" when Nancy starts to cry. Afraid to be alone, afraid for her life, Nancy (a black woman who cooks for the Compsons) gathers the Compson children around her. She lets them make popcorn, she tells them sad stories. But when they try to go and she hears someone coming, she breaks down: "Then Nancy began to make that sound again, not loud, sitting there above the fire, her long hands dangling between her knees; all of a sudden water began to come out on her face in big drops, running down her face, carrying in each one a little turning ball of firelight like a spark until it dropped off her chin. 'She's not crying,' I said. 'I ain't crying,' Nancy said. Her eyes were closed, 'I ain't crying. Who is it?' "[25] Nancy emanates tears, her own bodily wastes, as if they were jewels. Why?

The feminist artist Kiki Smith captures a similar set of bodily moments in her sculpture. (Figure 12) Where Oldenburg takes objects that are hard and makes them soft sculpture, Smith takes soft things and makes them hard, making them glitter, giving them gleams. In *Untitled (Train)* glass beads pour out of a woman's labia, as if the cosmos itself might flow from her uterus. Once again, human waste is on fire; it also shines in Smith's *Pee Body*, where the artist's tenderness toward a woman who squats vulnerably and crookedly near the floor to pee, gives the sculpture's protective rigidity a sweetness, a fragility belied by the tough little pearls that come out. (Figure 13) "There's a lot of life that's been left out of art," Smith says.[26] Here, the unspeakable liquids that come out of the body—urine and menstrual blood—become pearls of great price.

Next to these massive flows, Nancy's tears seem as nothing. But in the context of Faulkner's story, her brilliant tears mean a great deal. At first Nancy is associated with dirt or waste in her role as a laundress. The narrator notes that the city laundry now gathers "the soiled wearing of a whole week." But fifteen years ago, it was gathered by "Negro women with, balanced on their steady, turbaned heads, bundles of clothes tied up in sheets, almost as large as cotton bales" (289). What the children remark about Nancy as laundress is her steadiness: "Sometimes we would go a

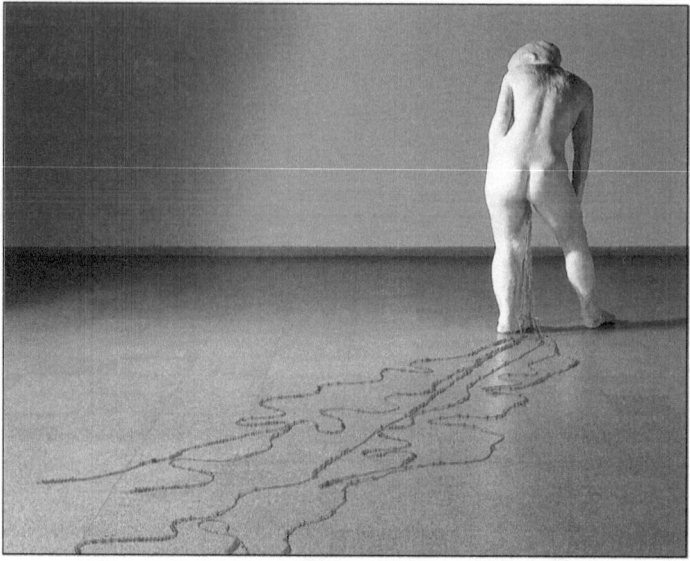

Fig. 12. Kiki Smith, *Untitled (Train)*, 1993. Courtesy of the artist.

part of the way down the lane and across the pasture with her, to watch the balanced bundle and the hat that never bobbed nor wavered, even when she walked down into the ditch and up the other side and stooped through the fence . . . her head rigid, uptilted, the bundle steady as a rock or a balloon," she would "rise to her feet again and go on" (290).

As we meet her in story time, Nancy is prostrate. She is terrified that she will be killed by Jesus, her black lover. This couple's lives are torn apart by injustice: "'I cant hang around white man's kitchen,' Jesus said. 'But white man can hang around mine. White man can come in my house, but I can't stop him. When white man want to come in my house, I aint got no house'" (292). Nancy's body, like her house, has become a disappearing act. A white man kicks her teeth in when she accosts him on the street and demands the money he owes her for sex. She goes to jail; he goes free; she tries to hang herself; the jailer cuts her down.

Living outside the protections of white society, Nancy cobbles together a living by doing laundry and cooking for the Compsons when Dilsey is sick. But when she sickens with fantasies about Jesus's wrath, she begins to disappear before the children's eyes: "Nancy whispered something. It was oh or no, I don't know which. Like nobody had made it, like it came from nowhere and went nowhere, until it was like Nancy was not there at all" (296). As a throwaway, Nancy tries to bed down with the children,

Fig. 13. Kiki Smith, *Pee Body*, 1992. Courtesy of the artist and Collection of Barbara Lee, Emily Pulitzer, and the Harvard Arts Museum.

but she is cast from their house, she can't find a place to thrive. As "water began to come out on her face in big drops, running down her face, carrying in each one a little turning ball of firelight like a spark" Faulkner gives us a glimpse of her interior. The sad thing about this story—and about Nancy's life—is that the spark lasts for only a sentence. Her life leaps out, it gleams, she could shine, but every circumstance is against her, her trauma made trash.

What do these images add up to? I've just scratched the surface of the enormous variety of detritus, waste, and bodily debris in Faulkner's fiction. As each of these stories suggests, Faulkner shares with other twentieth-century artists a preoccupation with detritus; it becomes a defining shelter for his characters' lives and rebellions. And this brings me to the most baroque space of detritus in Faulkner's canon, the apparition of Sutpen's Hundred at the end of *Absalom, Absalom!* As Quentin and Rosa approach this amazing, voracious, and beautiful ruin, it "loomed, bulked, square and enormous, with jagged half-toppled chimneys, its roofline sagging a little; for an instant as they moved, hurried, toward it Quentin saw completely through it a ragged segment of sky with three hot stars in it as if the house were of one dimension, painted on a canvas curtain in which there was a tear; now, almost beneath it, the dead furnace-breath of air in which they moved seemed to reek in slow and protracted violence with a smell of desolation and decay as if the wood of which it was built were flesh" (366).

In Chester Himes's *Cotton Comes to Harlem* a black junkman finds a $100,000 stash in a lost bale of cotton on the streets of New York and takes himself to Europe. In Welty's "The Burning" a black woman comes back to the plantation house that the Yankees who raped her have just burned down: she sees a charred mirror still blazing with baroque images of black men dressed in gold, and she leaves the scene with her son's bones and a jubilee cup. Here ashes (the throwaway) become sublime. But what Faulkner focuses on in the House of Detritus is its double melancholia.

First, he limns Sutpen Hundred's emptiness—its role as a stage set or a façade giving us a figure of hollowness, flatness. But this decayed house is also flesh (it has "a smell of desolation and decay as if the wood of which it was built were flesh"). When it disappears, it is not just Ellen's shopping or Sutpen's dream that goes up in ash, but the generational labors of Afro-Haitians, still covered in mud, and their children. These are the bodies Quentin Compson breathes in with the dust motes around him. "He could taste the dust. Even now . . . he could taste and feel the dust of that . . . (furnace-breathed) Mississippi September night" (362).

In *Song of Solomon* Toni Morrison creates a similar scene where an even more frightening trauma-detritus clogs the air:

> Every night now Guitar was seeing little scraps of Sunday dresses—white and purple, powder blue, pink and white lace and voile, velvet and silk, cotton and satin, eyelet and grosgrain. The scraps stayed with him all night and he remembered. . . . The bits of Sunday dresses that he saw did not fly; they hung in the air quietly, like the whole notes in the last measure on an Easter hymn.
>
> Four little colored girls had been blown out of a church, and his mission was to approximate as best he could a similar death of four little girls some Sunday, since he was the Sunday man. He couldn't do it with a piece of wire, or a switchblade. For this he needed explosives, or guns, or hand grenades. And that would take money. He knew that the assignments of the Days would more and more be the killing of white people in groups since more and more Negroes were being killed in groups.[27]

In a culture where not just commodities, but people are constantly dematerialized, we need to hang onto our detritus, to remember what used to be there. If we're lucky, it will shine and give us an archive of someone's lost life. But when it appears, like Sutpen's Hundred, as a devitalized remainder, we must still breathe it in. Only then will we feel the hot press of lost flesh as something beyond melancholy, as an actionable history.

NOTES

1. Norman Bryson, *Looking at the Overlooked: Four Essays on Still Life Painting* (London: Reaktion Books, 1990).

2. William Butler Yeats, "The Circus Animals' Desertion," in *The Collected Poems of W. B. Yeats* (New York: Macmillan, 1968), 336.

3. Elizabeth Bishop, *The Complete Poems, 1927–1979* (New York: Farrar, Straus & Giroux, 1983), 64.

4. *Citizen Kane* (Dir. Orson Welles, RKO Pictures, 1941).

5. T. S. Eliot, *"The Waste Land" and Other Poems* (1922; New York: Harcourt, Brace, Jovanovich, 1962), lines 176–82).

6. F. Scott. Fitzgerald, *The Great Gatsby* (1925; New York: Simon & Schuster, 1995), 27.

7. Mitchell Breitwieser, "Jazz Fractures: F. Scott Fitzgerald and Epochal Representation," *American Literary History* 12:3 (Fall 2000): 361–62.

8. William Faulkner, *Absalom, Absalom!* (New York: Vintage, 1936), 245.

9. "Barn Burning," in *Collected Stories of William Faulkner* (New York: Random House, 1950), 6.

10. Lisa Phillips, *The American Century: Art and Culture, 1950–2002* (New York: W. W. Norton and Company, Inc, 1999), 242.

11. Pamela M. Lee, *Object to Be Destroyed: The Work of Gordon Matta-Clark* (Cambridge: MIT Press, 2000), xiii.

12. Thierry de Duve, "Ex Situ," in *Les Cahiers du Musee national d'art moderne* 27 (Spring 1978), as quoted in Lee, *Object to Be Destroyed*, xv.

13. Lee, *Object to Be Destroyed*, 180.

14. Ibid., xv.

15. Suzaan Boettger, *Earthworks: Art and the Landscape of the Sixties* (Berkeley: University of California Press, 2002), 9.

16. Ibid., 8.

17. "This material is cheap, artistically lowly, and was used unprocessed and unrein-forced, thus producing a temporary form in contrast to the metals or stone of a work built for the ages. His adoption of non-fine art materials was something for which Oldenburg was . . . well known" (Boettger, *Earthworks*, 8).

18. William Faulkner, *The Hamlet* (New York: Vintage, 1990), 399.

19. Richard Godden, "Comparative Idiocy: A Phenomenological Reading of *The Hamlet* as a Rebuke to an American Century," in *Faulkner in America: Faulkner and Yoknapatawpha, 1998*, ed. Joseph R. Urgo and Ann J. Abadie (Jackson: University Press of Mississippi, 2001), 22–23.

20. Marcel Duchamp, "Apropos of 'Ready-mades'" (1961), reprinted in *The Writings of Marcel Duchamp*, ed. Michel Sanouillet and Elmer Peterson (New York: Da Capo Press, 1989), 141.

21. Martha Buskirk, *The Contingent Object of Contemporary Art* (Cambridge: MIT Press, 2003), 64.

22. William Faulkner, *As I Lay Dying* (New York: Vintage Books, 1987), 242.

23. Buskirk, *The Contingent Object of Contemporary Art*, 61.

24. Ibid., 62–63.

25. "That Evening Sun," in *Collected Stories of William Faulkner* (New York: Random House, 1950), 306.

26. Jo Anna Isaak, "Working in the Rag-and-Bone Shop of the Heart," in *Other Worlds: The Art of Nancy Spero and Kiki Smith*, ed. Jon Bird (London: Reaktion Books, 2003), 71.

27. Toni Morrison, *Song of Solomon* (New York: Signet, 1977), 174.

Flags in the Dust and the Material Culture of Class

KEVIN RAILEY

Based on Faulkner's own explanations, *Flags in the Dust* has been understood by many to be mainly concerned with the fading away of the Old South. Unlike the later Snopes trilogy, however, where the forces of Faulkner's New South are clearly identified, in *Flags* no new power overtly replaces the Sartoris family and all it represents. The novel seems more like a snapshot in time than an evolving narrative. Critics, including Faulkner's own literary agent, have noted this quality and lamented the book's lack of narrative unity. Surprisingly, when I turned to look at the novel through the lens of material culture, this structural feature became less of a deficit.[1] The text became what it perhaps was meant to be—a series of snapshots, a frieze on which figures stand next to one another, collectively representing a distinct moment in history but individually revealing no definite relationship to each other.

Pictures, though, do not tell their own story. Pictures are like objects in the world around us. Their meaning only emerges when the relationship to the world in which they exist comes into focus. An object's meaning only develops as it is utilized in a particular world and can only be fully understood when we come to understand its suprasensible qualities and symbolic significances. To analyze the relationship between material culture and *Flags in the Dust*, then, we must identify the signs and objects that signified the world of the past and unpack their meaning for that world. In turn, since the novel represents the hinge between two historical periods, we must ask how the new world redefines, refigures, or replaces those objects in its quest to reorder itself.[2] Here, I'll address these issues by looking through the multivaried lens of class.

The Past: High-Class Material

The pipe that Old Man Falls brings with him when he visits Old Bayard Sartoris is a significant object of material culture; it also symbolizes the particular past that is fading away in *Flags in the Dust*. Connected to that past, that world, and its leaders are all the lands owned by the Sartoris family for generations in both Virginia and Mississippi, the systems of planting, harvesting, and producing tobacco and cotton for consumption and profit, and the various preindustrial means of distribution. This pipe eventually winds up in the trunk of memorabilia that Bayard keeps in the attic, where he keeps many other artifacts from his high-class world—a brocade garment, a rapier, a cavalry sabre, dueling pistols, an army cap and Mexican machete, a locomotive oilcan, a Confederate grey coat (94–96). These objects serve as signs of the ways these men sought and gained power, how they held power over others, white and black alike, and the extent to which they would fight, die, and be killed in order to keep their place and power. As Bayard thinks to himself, somewhat ironically: "The proper equipment for raising tobacco [and cotton] in a virgin wilderness" (95).

That Old Man Falls had saved the pipe and now gives it to the son of the man who gave it to him reveals his respect for these men and their family. His actions reveal that, for him, these men were high-class material. That Old Bayard chooses to place it with his other memorabilia highlights its significance as a museum-like artifact representing the upper-class world of the Sartorises and the culture they created. All these objects, however, are saved not so much for the actions they represent as for the legend surrounding them—they need testimony to explain their significance. Like many upper-class families in the South, the Sartoris family had developed a legend surrounding its genealogy. This "blood precedent" (97), as Bayard's father labels it, develops the purported glorious context for all their actions. The objects and the legend mutually illuminate and interact with one another: the legend needing the objects to create a Sartoris identity, and the objects needing the legend, the stories, to become more than simply objects—to become, that is, material culture. Monarchies and royal families had been establishing dynasties and legacies by marking their identities with ritualized objects and putatively characteristic behavior for some time when the first Southern plantocrat perceived it might work for him too. In this world, Prince Albert coats take on associative resonance and anchovies take on mythic proportions because their value stems from their place within a story that indicates, supposedly, unique behavior denoting the superior characteristics of an entire clan. Old Man Falls and Bayard value the pipe because it represents a family history and a cultural order that both men feel is worthy of commemoration.

Though Bayard buries that pipe, he does not, of course, quit smoking. Rather, he replaces the pipe with the cigar. As Lori Merish discusses in the final chapter of *Sentimental Materialism*, the cigar came to have wide and deep symbolic power at the turn of the twentieth century in America.[3] It signaled America's growing dominance in the world as the country increasingly controlled the growth and distribution of many products, including tobacco, throughout the Americas. The cigar also became *the* symbol of masculinity for upper-class and middle-class men with cheap cigars extending the fraternity of male camaraderie to the lower classes. Merish claims that its particular masculine appeal was also connected to the growing feminization of American commodity culture and the fears of the overcivilization of American men—a feature symbolized for many by the leisure of the Southern upper class.[4] These discussions have various connections to the picture of Old Bayard and his symbolic role in the book.

The cigar symbolizes his financial power and social status. He is the only person who owns cigars, taking them from a humidor and smoking them at will. He is also the only person who has his discarded items— cigar butts and Prince Albert coats alike—collected and cherished by his servants. Both practices serve as signs of the hierarchical class structure to which Old Bayard still adheres. The cigar also signals the separation between Old Bayard and the next generation—whose significant representatives, the young Bayard and Harry Mitchell, both smoke cigarettes. Finally, when lit, the cigar also serves as a screen from Aunt Jenny's mothering. In these ways, the cigar stands as a symbol directly associated to Old Bayard's place within Yoknapatawpha.

At the same time, since only Old Bayard and his servant smoke cigars in this book, its symbolic potential to represent masculinity shared by men from all classes does not hold for Faulkner. Here, there are no social or business gatherings where men from all walks of life light up together, no celebrations where one man passes out cigars to all the men in town. The full cultural significance the cigar had for turn-of-the-century America does not carry over into Yoknapatawpha. Thus, the cigar seems to be the physical sign of the decision Bayard's father made late in his life—the refusal to avenge his own father's death in a way consistent with his heritage. This decision indicates a break in the behavior of the Sartorises, a break from the behavior expected from men as heirs to their family's culture. This break indicates that defending the family's honor through violence was a behavior that had strayed too far from a morality with which both Bayard's father and he could live. As E. Anthony Rotundo explains, in Western civilization in general masculinity was always associated with action in the world and with various types of physical prowess.[5] The Enlightenment increasingly characterized men as half-beast and half-angel and saw the rational mind as the power that would control the beast lurking within and lead men to civilization. The upper class, of course, was to epitomize civilized behavior. These dual demands placed contradictory pressure on men within the upper class. As Bertram Wyatt-Brown has detailed, these pressures were addressed in the upper class of the Old South by an elaborate system of controlled violence, controlled activity focused on the maintenance and continual challenge to one's honor where courage and character could be demonstrated.[6] In this culture, aggressive, even violent assertiveness and moral character were linked together. Old Bayard's father, however, cannot sustain this balance; he cannot find a way to act. In the moment that defines his life he cannot be true to both his upper-class status and himself, and he passes this legacy to Bayard. To redefine masculinity and honor seems necessary for these upper-class men, yet for them, morality comes to mean a type of passivity. Bayard's own inaction in the book verifies his connection to his father's legacy: whether in the bank, in the house, or in the front seat of his grandson's car, Bayard sits still and for the most part alone. Ultimately, the cigar serves as a sign of Faulkner's own affirmation of the moral stand Bayard's father took when he refused to kill as well as a sign of unrealized potential and fading power. Old Bayard, after all, never steps into the present.

Though associated with Old Bayard in many ways, Aunt Jenny highlights significant changes in roles in this new world. Clearly, Jenny's high-class identification is verified constantly in the book: she brings "leaded vari-colored panes" (13) of glass to the Sartoris home upon her arrival; she helps build the Sartoris legend; she demeans and patronizes all people she believes lower than she on the social/economic ladder; and she has a deep allegiance to Bayard. In keeping with this high-class identification, she exerts a strong power over behavior within the domestic sphere: she constantly corrects the behavior and language of both Sartoris men while they are in the house, and she consistently wants to serve milk rather than whiskey to young Bayard. As Ted Ownby has discussed at length, these types of roles had long been associated with women's power as moral agents within Southern culture. Women were to check the seeming natural inclinations of men to be rude sinners ready to upset the tranquility and nourishing power of the home.[7] At the same time, though, Aunt Jenny's sphere of influence has expanded during her lifetime. Shifting from old to new has not caused Jenny to become passive, like Bayard, just the opposite. Now, her power extends into the social arena. We witness this influence most pointedly in the way she cajoles Bayard to see Dr. Alford and the medical expert in Memphis. Her actions show further her affinity for the new middle class: her preference for Dr. Alford derives from the cleanliness of his office and the degrees he has—in contrast to the messiness of Loosh Peabody's office and the unscientific and dirty ways of Old Man Falls. Ultimately, Aunt Jenny links the past role of women to the new values of the middle class. Her relationship to the new world is best revealed by the comment she makes after she rides in young Bayard's car: "'I wished I smoked cigarettes'" (82). Implicitly rejecting the cigar and the horse, Jenny is moving, as we are, into a new world.

The Present (1): Objects and Men

The contexts that help explain the meaning of Bayard's failure to unite action with morality and the rise in social power for Aunt Jenny are numerous. The most relevant one is the rise of a dominant middle class in America, in the South, and in Yoknapatawpha. The new middle class sought to usurp social and economic power held by the class represented by Old Bayard. To accomplish its goal it had to restructure the ways people found personal identity and to redefine ideas about class. To this end, emerging powers sought to break the association between personal identity and family, lineage, and heritage and moved to create trans-class notions of identity. Gender was one of those arenas. Definitions of what it meant to be a man and a woman became more solely associated with gender than with class position. In this process, women came to be increasingly associated with morality and men more solely associated with action in the world. These definitions blended nicely with Southern evangelical Christianity, which had always defined men as being naturally more drawn to sin than were women.[8] New ideas about class, meanwhile, shifted value and worth away from the land one owned and the social power it assured toward more mobile forms of capital and psychological definitions of class. Historically, when young Bayard returns from the war, we are at the gates of this new world, the threshold of middle-class capitalism in the New South. We are also now in the land of cigarettes and automobiles.

Within the first minute he returns home and sits to talk with his grandfather, Young Bayard lights up a cigarette. Minutes later, he lights another. Like Popeye and Joe Christmas after him, Bayard's cigarettes appear moment after moment, a sign of both his incessant need and its eternal lack of fulfillment. For Faulkner and for the material culture of Yoknapatawpha the cigarette contrasts with the cigar in two significant ways. First, as Faulkner utilized the cultural and symbolic weight of the cigar to represent upper-class moral power and passivity, he utilizes the symbolic resonances of the cigarette to represent middle-class weaknesses and frenetic activity. Second, within the material culture of Yoknapatawpha the cigarette, not the cigar, possesses the full significance as a symbol for linking men in a fraternity of masculinity.

Faulkner's use of the cigarette as a sign of material culture within Yoknapatawpha relates to the ways in which it was figured in various political and advertising campaigns in the early twentieth century. One of these developments involved the way the cigarette played into the turn-of-the-century campaign for national reinvigoration. Addressing the fear that America was becoming overly feminized, national leaders like Teddy

Roosevelt exhorted America to exert a new manhood for the twentieth century. Inspired by Roosevelt, the leader of the Boy Scouts, Ernest Thompson Seton, phrased this point as follows: physical culture was necessary "to combat the system that has turned such a large proportion of our robust, manly, self-reliant boyhood into a lot of flat-chested cigarette smokers, with shaky nerves and doubtful vitality."[9] In this campaign the cigarette suggested the overfeminization of men and male impotence. *Flags in the Dust* reveals that Faulkner accepted these characterizations. Three men smoke cigarettes in the book—young Bayard, Hub, and Harry Mitchell. Bayard is a man victimized and destroyed by the demands of the modern world. Hub is a friend of the sewing machine agent Suratt; though married, he is described as a youth (144–45) and has no distinction at all except that he smokes and drinks with the boys and acts out a petulant rebelliousness. Harry Mitchell is Belle's "bullet-headed husband" (204) with bad teeth; he is a cotton speculator who supplies Belle with the material comforts and status symbols she craves but who cannot, it appears, satisfy her in other ways. None of these men represent positive figures for Faulkner: they are all weaklings with doubtful vitality.

It seems important, too, that no women smoke in the book. One might have suspected Joan Mitchell, Belle's sister, to be brazen enough to light up, but no. Though the cigarette became a symbol for the assertion of women's rights in the twenties—and Joan certainly epitomizes the assertion of a number of those rights—Faulkner does not make this association. In Yoknapatawpha's system of material culture smoking is for men only, and Faulkner uses this symbol to tell a story about the effects of the emerging New South on men. As action in the world in general came to be increasingly important, as the system of Southern honor faded, and as barriers between men from different classes eroded, men felt increasing pressure to reveal their manhood in all the public corners of their life and to defend their masculinity from challenges by all.[10] The full ramifications of this new reality are best revealed in the scene immediately following Bayard's fruitless attempt to ride the stallion.

In this long scene, the owner of a Ford car, Suratt, is asked to drive Bayard home. He and Hub agree to do so but proceed to get a jug of whiskey and to get drunk with Bayard. During the ride, both Bayard and Hub smoke cigarettes, and eventually Hub and Bayard both smoke from Bayard's pack. In conversation during this journey Suratt comments that he and Bayard have never shared a jug, revealing how their worlds have never intersected before this night because of a more rigid class structure. He also questions whether Bayard will lower himself to drink with them and if Bayard will be able to handle the moonshine. Bayard lives up to all expectations: he demonstrates his ability to drink, refrains from judging these men as lower class, and proves he is "all right" (149). Later in the night, all the boys switch from Suratt's car to Bayard's own and continue to drive around. Bayard does not return home—where his family nervously waits—even when he easily could have. He chooses instead to demonstrate his masculinity in the ways these other men and this new order have defined it for him: being a man means being a rabble-rouser; its proof of authenticity is the cigarette, the car, and the jug. All positive associations the car has for American masculinity in popular culture do not translate into the fictional world of Yoknapatawpha. For Faulkner, the cigarette, the car, and the jug represent and figure mobility and equality: all three men drink, all three drive, and two of them share cigarettes. They drive all over Yoknapatawpha County—all neighborhoods are explored, none are off limits. The new breakdown of barriers between people from all classes is thus epitomized by this nightly cruise. What the novel implies, however, is that by revealing they do not care about their class status, these men also reveal they have no class.

These scenes show how a society structured around notions of mobility works to tie subjective identities to gender—and to a shared material culture defining gender—rather than to family and class as the old order had. For Faulkner, as for much American and Mississippi history, common denominators unifying individuals in a shared definition of gender are often associated with *lowest* common denominators. Smoking, swearing, and drinking were always the signs of masculinity in Mississippi.[11] Despite the ways in which notions of Southern honor worked to link these behaviors, for some, to moral character, Mississippi's long history of evangelical Christianity had also characterized smoking, drinking, swearing, and fighting as characteristic behaviors of both men *and* immorality. These two parallel value systems created a paradox. On one hand, smoking, drinking, swearing, and fighting were the ways men could reveal their resistance to the over feminization of evangelical Christianity and prove their manhood; on the other hand, these activities were seen as corrupting the true nature of masculinity and as a sign of an allegiance to base pursuits. For Faulkner, Bayard's night out with the boys reveals one of the major effects of the changing class structure in the South. A man's main goal, now, is to prove to anyone and everyone that he is a man, and he can only do that by being base and immoral. To be a man means, it seems, to be an animal.

Present (2): Men as Objects

Clearly, the activities Bayard chooses are the material, cultural signs through which many signified a version of masculinity within American society in the twentieth century. In his attempt to reject his grandfather's response to the world, Bayard steps manically and desperately into the present to prove something. His most public attempt to prove himself during the book comes when he chooses to ride the stallion in front of virtually the whole town of Jefferson. That Faulkner has Bayard choose a horse, a symbol of the old order, and that he has Bayard fail open an important site of investigation into the differences between old and new. To fully understand this scene, we must understand how the move from a culture defined by class structure, family, and lineage to a society defined by mobility, autonomy, and individualism affects individuals, here young Bayard. Full understanding also requires us to consider how capitalism as a social and economic order based on production, distribution, and consumption of objects works in two ways: to project subjective identities into things in order to make them valuable and desirable, and to turn certain subjective identities into valuable objects to be consumed.[12]

Objects that have circulation and meaning within a given social order are part of the material culture of that society. Objects that become commodities have been given a commercial worth within the social order because of values and ideas projected into them. These values and ideas are suprasensible qualities—that is, they are properties people project into the object but they are not intrinsic to it. In this way, a type of subjectivity is given to objects. Behaviors, though, can also be seen as commodities, as objectifications of valued cultural understandings of identity. Material culture studies have opened our eyes to the fact that ideas exist in objects. But, we also cannot think about behaviors without recognizing how preexistent ideas often name, label, and thus commodify them. Behaviors can be said to be moving objects.

With these ideas in mind we can see that young Bayard does not just think that by moving, acting, driving, drinking, and smoking he will become a man. Rather, he acts as if doing these things makes him a man. Why else the constant action? Why the fear of rest? Young Bayard reveals he has accepted and internalized the various ways masculinity has become commodified and acts as if masculinity exists *in* these actions. His behaviors have everything to do with a sense that masculinity equals certain prescribed behaviors that can be consumed by those around him. As many attempts in the book reveal, there is no talking to Bayard—there is no subjectivity with which to engage. His behaviors are objectifications of masculinity having nothing to do with an individual man—his identity is the behavior. Bayard experiences the world, then, in a way similar to Harry Mitchell. Mitchell clearly represents the man who acts in order to gain wealth and to buy objects. Though, of course, he does smoke, drink, and drive, his identity is so completely connected to the objects he buys and to his ability to buy them that he even buys Belle a car after their divorce—not to buy would mean he is not a man. Though Bayard's and Harry's lives are not equivalent, they are parallel. For them and for many others, the worth of both exists in the ways they objectify and enact cultural understandings of masculinity, how they reveal their masculinity in and through objects.

Bayard's and Harry's situations in this new order reveal how the democratic form of society produces a concept of individualism but not individuals—how, that is, the assertion of worth and uniqueness fades in the face of conformity and uniformity.[13] In this light, Bayard *has* to be thrown from the stallion. Bayard seeks to establish his masculine identity through outward, external signs. These things will neither allow him to find peace nor help him ride a horse. Though in getting on the horse he demonstrates his desire to act in the world, this is not enough to ride the horse successfully. That ability—whether you are born with it or learn it—is something you either have or not. You cannot assert it; you cannot buy it; you cannot fake it. One's ability or skill in riding (or writing) has nothing to do with whether one is upper class or lower class, has nothing to do with whether one has money or not. This skill is something that exists inside a person, and though the opportunity to demonstrate it may be taken away, the skill itself cannot. Ultimately, what Bayard and other men seek—distinction, individuality, identity as a unique person of worth—cannot be found in objects or in objectified behaviors. For better or worse, the objects in the Old Bayard's trunk and the legend surrounding them gave the Sartoris family an identity, gave them distinction. When Old Bayard's father broke that chain of connection between past and present, he shattered that identity. The uncertainty that came with that move, along with the developments in this New South, leave young Bayard to seek endlessly for what was lost—something definite that can distinguish him from others. As Bill Brown states, "The triumph and trial of capitalism in America . . . amounts to the fact that in the midst of proliferating things, the *thing* is always missed" (48).

The Present (3): Objects and Women

In a good many places throughout the book, Narcissa associates Bayard with a beast, a savage, an animal. When Narcissa's cat leaps on a bird and kills it, she yells, "'You Sartoris!'" (76). She also claims that she hates watching Bayard do crazy, violent, and daring things, saying, "'You Beast, you beast . . . why must you always do these things where I've got to see them?'" (243). Bayard also frightens her at one point when he grabs her arm hard enough to leave a mark. Despite these reactions, Narcissa indicates that Bayard's actions have the power to move her: she feels butterflies in her stomach, runs from the room, and cries because of her emotions. This seeming paradox is explained, I think, by Narcissa's understanding of men. She has, in essence, internalized the objectifications of masculinity developed by her society—the New South. She has come to understand Bayard's behaviors as the real thing, and she has bought the package, so to speak. The text verifies the status of both characters as objects in the way it shapes their relationship. They do not interact much at all; there are no exchanges of intimacy. They watch each other, as consumers do in order to decide on a purchase. We also are never even told about the wedding or the pregnancy. Their marriage is the bonding of two objects for mutual future advantage. Benbow Sartoris, their baby, could not be named otherwise.[14]

Narcissa's status as an object is verified in other ways as well. Horace associates her with a vase, a particularly significant symbol. In terms of the material culture of this contemporary society, the vase can be seen to epitomize the processes of objectification and commodification in the way it signals both physical presence and emptiness.[15] Narcissa also takes pains throughout the book to repress her subjective feelings, seen mostly in her conversations with Aunt Jenny. This status makes her especially vulnerable to other people's projections onto her—a process epitomized by the character of Byron Snopes. Byron's desire to own and posses Narcissa is an intricate site of sexual politics at work. Narcissa is, of course, the ultimate commodity—beautiful and wealthy. Byron's desire to consume her can be read as a means to prove his own manhood by offering her what he thinks she secretly wants as well as a form of resistance to the oppression he experiences. She is the object of his lust but also an object the possession of which would symbolize his overthrow of the Sartoris legend, the assertion of his manhood and a victory for his class. Moreover, Byron has come to these fantasies precisely because of the ways the society is changing—mobility, moving up, as it were, is advertised and believed in, power is gained through accumulation and consumption. His fantasies reveal how he too has internalized the objectifications of men and women developed by his society.

The New Meaning of Class

Flags in the Dust implies that Byron's inability to affect Narcissa has more to do with a new meaning of class than it does with a misunderstanding of women.[16] Narcissa's entire personae in this novel serves to demonstrate new meanings associated with the term *class* and the ways the new middle class sought to establish its dominance. One way it achieved this dominance was in opposition to the working class through a discourse focused on issues of hygiene and cleanliness. Connected to this discourse was a new value on personal life and on the development of one's personal abilities. These distinctions work to separate Narcissa from Byron Snopes, whose physical hygiene is often implicitly questioned through descriptions of his drooling and sweating as if he continually needs to work at keeping himself clean. Narcissa's pure whiteness cannot be in the way Byron threatens to stain it. It would hurt her value and her status.

These distinctions also work to separate her from Belle Mitchell, whom Narcissa considers "dirty" (223), and this contrast emphasizes the shift in meaning of certain words. Belle Mitchell is not, of course, physically dirty as is implied about Byron Snopes. The feeling aroused in Narcissa stems more from what she considers to be the breaking of moral rules of proper and refined behavior. From Narcissa's perspective, Belle Mitchell has revealed she has no class because she has acted in improper ways and has shattered the feminine ideal by being motivated by sexual urges—and by admitting them. From this new perspective there is a qualitative difference between the two women; this difference forms through judgments that downplay economic and prioritize psychological and affective categories. The signs for this difference are pianos and houses.

In this new world, the piano is not a sign of one's ability to buy an expensive instrument or a verification of one's class status; it is a sign of a personal desire to develop one's abilities and a test of one's capacity for refinement—a similar quality to the ability to ride a horse. Belle Mitchell, in this regard, might have enough money to buy a piano, but she plays "with shallow skill" (211) and can only muster a "trite saccharine waltz" (219) during her daughter's recital. Narcissa's playing, meanwhile, opens the whole past for Aunt Jenny and is always associated with the high-class world of the Sartoris past. Similarly, houses are more than a manifestation of what an individual can afford; they are signs of character. Faulkner describes the Benbow house as one designed and built with good taste and judgment while the Mitchell home, as Aunt Jenny phrases it, is "the handsomest house in Frenchman's Bend on the most beautiful lot in Jefferson" (25)—otherwise described as "a majestic monstrosity" (195). In this new world constructed by the middle classes, both pianos and houses are signposts separating those with taste and class from those who are common, coarse, and somewhat less than human.[17] This new world pretended that a rigid economic class structure no longer existed and posited the ideals of equal opportunity and equality; Narcissa epitomizes the ways in which the new meaning of class sought to gloss over or ignore economic class relations and to focus on supposed differences of character. Here, good taste becomes the sign of social power and only those with class have it. Class still matters, now in more ways than one.

I want to end my discussion with Horace Benbow. Poor Horace Benbow. Has any Faulkner character been discussed as unsympathetically as he? I also want to confess—I now like Horace Benbow. After this project, I no longer see him as one of Faulkner's Prufrockian male failures. I no longer see him as a failed idealist. I no longer see him as a weak-willed reader of poetry.[18] I see him, rather, as an excellent tennis player with a natural ability at the game. I see him as sexually attractive. I see him as a man, unlike Byron Snopes, who can cope with his sexuality and not be obsessed, and who, unlike Bayard Sartoris, can act in the world and not be controlled by others. I see him as a man who resists the cultural objectifications that define other men and who resists the parochial moral pronouncements with which his sister attempts to control him. Mostly, I see him now as Horace the glassblower. Material culture is what rescues Horace.

The aspects of material culture associated with Horace are, I think, most indicative of the significance he has for the novel. Here is a description of Horace that many critics have overlooked: "He had five now, in different colors and all nearly perfect, and each of them had a name. And as he finished them . . . he must bring them across the lawn . . . in his stained dishevelled clothes and his sooty hands in which the vase lay demure and fragile as a bubble, and with his face blackened too with smoke and a little mad, passionate and fine and austere" (228). Here we have, I offer, someone who takes the raw materials of the earth and transmutes them into objects (into art?) through his own sweat and imagination and ability. He does so for the pure joy of creation—not, that is to profit or to prove something—and through the efforts of his own hands. That Horace engages in this task certainly can be seen to represent Faulkner's sense of the male creative drive versus the female procreative drive, but this description also contrasts Horace sharply with other male characters in the book. He is not passive like Old Bayard; he is not reckless or desperate like young Bayard. He does not maniacally work to own things as does Harry. Horace wants to make things and he wants to make things that accord with the images in his own head, not with those dictated by the values of commodity fetishism. And, he defies middle-class prissiness by getting dirty in the process. Horace represents, here, the creative man at work. The description of Horace as glassblower, I would suggest then, serves to exhibit the material culture of the art of being human, for lack of a better term—the material culture of real class.

The suspended moment represented in *Flags in the Dust* opens our eyes to the ways people became victimized by objectification or obsessed with objects. When they move, objectified, frozen figures move through the world like robots. Through this lens *Flags in the Dust* can be seen to participate in that post-World War I literary generation that explored the alienating and mechanizing effects of the new twentieth-century world on human beings. Faulkner is akin here to T. S. Eliot and others who testified to the wasteland effects on people in the emerging society. Faulkner also offers a picture of resistance—something he does not always do. Rather than doing things or owning things, people can make things. Both Eliot and Faulkner, of course, did just that, and they have taught us much. For them, as well as perhaps for us, a community of thinkers, makers, and teachers, real class exists in those significant personal, intimate exchanges and moments of creation where we resist the forces at work trying to define and control us. To be open to those and to enjoy them, we must be passionate, fine, and just a little austere.

NOTES

1. The study of material culture has been a growing interdisciplinary field since 1983. Two originators of its ideas and methods are Thomas J. Schlereth and Jules D. Prown. A good summary account of its significance for American studies is *American Material Culture: The Shape of the Field*, ed. Ann Smart Martin and J. Ritchie Garrison (Henry Francis du Pont Winterthur Museum, Distributed by University of Tennessee Press, 1997).

2. Behind my argument exists a long history of social and cultural criticism that includes, at least, Karl Marx's analysis of the role of the commodity in capitalism, Pierre Bourdieu's discussion of the category and importance of taste within the formation of middle class society, as well as ideas inspired by many discussions of the relationship between consumer culture, the American middle class, and personal identity. I utilize specific ideas from a couple of sources here, but my paper and thinking have certainly been influenced by a larger number of sources than the ones I directly cite. See Karl Marx, *Capital*, trans. Ben Fowkes (New York: Penguin, 1976), vol. 1; Pierre Bourdieu, *Distinction: A Social Critique of the Judgment of Taste*, trans. Richard Nice (Cambridge: Harvard University Press, 1984); Miles Orvell, *The Real Thing: Imitation and Authenticity in American Culture, 1880–1940* (Chapel Hill: University of North Carolina Press, 1989); Simon J. Bronner, ed., *Consuming Visions: Accumulation and Display of Goods in America, 1880–1920* (New York: Norton, 1989); Richard L. Bushman, *The Refinement of America: Persons, Houses, Cities* (New York: Knopf, 1992); William Leach, *Land of Desire: Merchants, Power, and the Rise of a New American Culture* (New York: Pantheon Books, 1993); Rachel Bowlby, *Just Looking: Consumer Culture in Dreiser, Gissing, and Zola* (New York: Methuen, 1985); Ted Ownby, *American Dreams in Mississippi: Consumers, Poverty, and Culture, 1830–1998* (Chapel Hill: University of North Carolina Press, 1999).

3. Lori Merish, "Not 'Just a Cigar': Commodity Culture and the Construction of Imperial Manhood," in *Sentimental Materialism: Gender, Commodity Culture, and Nineteenth-Century Literature* (Durham: Duke University Press, 2000), 270–303.

4. Merish cites these fears in the chapter cited above. This type of criticism of the Southern upper class is discussed in William Robert Taylor, *Cavalier and Yankee* (New York: G. Braziller, 1961).

5. E. Anthony Rotundo, *American Manhood: Transformations in Masculinity from the Revolution to the Modern Era* (New York: Basic Books, 1993).

6. Bertram Wyatt-Brown, *Southern Honor: Ethics and Behavior in the Old South* (New York: Oxford University Press, 1982).

7. Ted Ownby, *Subduing Satan: Religion, Recreation, and Manhood in the Rural South, 1865–1920* (Chapel Hill: University of North Carolina Press, 1990).

8. See Ownby.

9. Quoted in Merish, 284. Both Roosevelt and Seton are also discussed in Waller R. Newell, *The Code of Man: Love, Courage, Pride, Family, Country* (New York: Regan Books, 2003) but from a very different perspective than the one Merish applies.

10. This pattern began early for Bayard when he and his brother are pushed to defend their long hair by fighting in school. When their parents want to cut their hair to save them the pain of fighting, they protest, just as they protest whenever someone attempts to convince them to change their reckless ways—whether it be drinking or driving too fast. Within this new social order, these behaviors have meaning. The Sartoris boys have found ways to prove their masculinity and this status, not their status as upper-class gentlemen, matters to them. In an earlier time the choice of long hair would not have been questioned by anyone from a lower-class status, and an upper-class boy, man, gentleman would not have had to defend his masculinity by taking on all challengers. This pattern continues for both as they mature, and their constant and very public feats of daring can easily be seen as attempts to demonstrate their masculinity not just to other upper-class men but to all in society.

11. As explained by Ted Ownby in *Subduing Satan*.

12. My discussion of the significance of Bayard's attempt to ride the stallion has been inspired by reading Bill Brown, *A Sense of Things: The Object Matter of American Literature* (Chicago: University of Chicago Press, 2003). Brown's discussion of Twain's *The Prince and the Pauper* opened my eyes to a new way to understand Bayard.

13. See Bill Brown's similar discussion in chapter 1, especially p. 47.

14. It is also of interest to note that there are attempts by both Bayard and Narcissa to form what could be called a more intimate relationship: Narcissa's reading books to Bayard is her way to bring him into her (feminine) world and Bayard brings Narcissa hunting with him in order to share his (masculine) world. Both attempts have absolutely no effect; neither character is changed; both stay the objects they are socialized to be.

15. Faulkner is no stranger to citing the emptiness of particular characters and people. There are many statements throughout Faulkner's canon about hollow people—remember Mr. Compson's comments to Quentin about people filled with sawdust; Quentin's own fears of substanceless bodies; the imagery used to describe characters such as Popeye, Joe Christmas, and Flem Snopes in which they are described as all exterior, empty on the inside; and Faulkner's naming certain characters in such a way to make them a virtual commodity by definition—Montgomery Ward Snopes.

16. Narcissa, after all, keeps Byron's letters in her top drawer even though they have made her feel "filthy" (70). She also marries Bayard, who is associated with a long list of imagery very similar to that which characterizes Byron. Men are, in this world, animals, and women are to expect that. It is, then, not Byron's animal-like nature that disqualifies him as a potential suitor for Narcissa. It is his low-class status.

Bayard's status as upper class, on the other hand, allows him to be a potential suitor; then, he seems to make a deal with Narcissa that he will not behave in his crazy and violent way in front of her anymore—which he does not do after the marriage. Women, it seems, expect men will be animals but they do not wish to witness the overt public display of this type of behavior—which, after all, is low class.

17. In her introduction, Merish discusses how the formation of the middle class in America consistently and increasingly placed women in these roles of arbiters of taste. This was one step in the "refinement" of America.

18. For a discussion typical of many about Horace, see Philip Cohen, "William Faulkner, the Crisis of Masculinity, and Textual Instability," in *Textual Studies and the Common Reader: Essays on Editing Novels and Novelists* (Athens: University of Georgia Press, 2000), 64–80.

"Touch Me While You Look at Her": Stars, Fashion, and Authorship in *Today We Live*

D. MATTHEW RAMSEY

The benefits of a cultural studies/materialist investigation of William Faulkner are many—not the least being a demystification of the works and the man himself. In considering the material circumstances behind a text's conception, production, promotion, and reception, we can productively "unburden" the work and the author and get at seeming contradictions between the revered, canonical Faulkner and his less respected "hack" output. Richard Dyer has argued that works of a canonized author have often been treated "as illustrations of the author's biography . . . flying in the face of both the evident discrepancy between most authors' persons and their texts and also the vast range of public functions cultural production performs. In the interpretation of texts, the author was used as a means of fixing and giving weight to particular interpretations, rather than acknowledging the multiplicity of meanings and affects the readers generate from texts."[1] For a fuller understanding of an author and his/her works, we should consider authorship as multiple and performed within material and semiotic circumstances. Cultural materialism is insistent in its emphasis on the processes through which a text achieves its current estimation.[2] Film studies in particular has taken great pains to unburden the author figure and to emphasize the collaborative nature of filmic texts—which includes considering the function and reputations of the director, producer, actors, writers, the studio, even the costume designer—in order to understand how audiences might have reacted to the film and what their expectations may have been. Looking at Faulkner through the lens of recent materialist work on classic Hollywood film, particularly the notion of the "star" during the studio system, allows us to reassess his investment in popular culture, the value and aims of his screenwriting work, and to shift the emphasis from what Hollywood might have cost the writer to what he may have learned about his craft during his time working for the studios.

Biographies and criticism starting in the late 1940s necessarily and quite naturally have limited how subsequent readers and critics have made sense of "Faulkner," both as human being and body of work. The widespread disavowal of Faulkner's serious engagement with popular culture forms has led, essentially, to two ways of dealing with many of these less "literary" texts. On one pole of this binary, we excuse Faulkner from any responsibility, because he was, with these "hack" magazine stories and screenplays, simply trying to make some money so he could get on with his *real* writing. Or we claim that Faulkner was able to subvert these genres, to undermine the conventions in ways that *careful* readers and critics can pick up on. Both of these poles tend to oversimplify the matter and to suggest more clearly defined distinctions between high and low culture than actually existed during Faulkner's time in Hollywood. In each, Faulkner the *solitary* artist is stressed, and in each we see the suggestion that Faulkner did not willingly or enthusiastically engage or embrace popular culture—he participated out of necessity, he did the best with it he could.

The importance and complexity of the context within which Faulkner wrote has often been underestimated. Faulkner's reputation—shaped in part by Malcolm Cowley, Joseph Blotner, his friends and acquaintances, contemporary reviewers and critics, advertising—was in the early 1930s a particularly interesting point of contestation, of competing discourses and overlapping reputations. For "Turnabout," the 1931 short story from which MGM's *Today We Live* is adapted, these competing discourses included the reputations of Faulkner the serious writer, Faulkner the magazine writer, the *Saturday Evening Post*, the Algonquin Round Table, sailors, Faulkner's friends and acquaintances, American Modernism, and the constantly shifting representations of gender and homosexuality in American culture. There were also certainly limitations imposed on the writer, as well as other complicating factors, including the original story told by Robert Lovett, the requirements of the *Saturday Evening Post*, the WWI genre, and the short story form itself. But for "Turnabout," authorial control is understood to more or less remain with Faulkner. It is he who weaves, consciously or not, these parts together. By and large Faulkner as *ultimate* author figure remains relatively uncontested for "Turnabout."

The same cannot be said for the film MGM adapted from that story two short years later. What is interesting about *Today We Live* is that what little critical attention has been devoted to this film is largely characterized by the act of distancing Faulkner (and, for that matter, Howard Hawks, Joan Crawford, and Gary Cooper among others) from the material not so much because of its quality as because it resists easy placement within the narratives it might be seen to be a part of. There are so many competing reputations involved that critics cannot ascribe control over the text's meaning to anyone—not the director, the author(s), the stars, the studio, or the publicity department. Nor do they seem able to imagine what

audiences might have made of the film. It is generally agreed among contemporary critics that it is not a particularly good film, but the difficulty of
pinpointing precisely how and why this is so means that it gets overlooked.
Whether a critic is writing a narrative centered on Hawks or Faulkner or
Crawford or MGM, the blame is usually accorded in general terms to
some other participant in the process. The film seems to challenge the
cult of authorial control (be it in the realm of literature, or auteur theory,
or star power) and that, in combination with a failure to consider how the
film might have "worked" for the audience of its day, has consigned it to
virtual critical oblivion, despite the fact that it is readily available on video
and shown frequently on Turner Classic Movies.

The story of the "debacle" that doomed *Today We Live* is one of those
stories Faulkner (and Hawks) scholars love to tell. According to legend,
an unforeseen complication arose after Faulkner's first draft of the script.
Here is how Joseph Blotner recounts it: "As the pages of script accumulated, Hawks oversaw the other preparations for the actual shooting.
Gary Cooper would be available, along with Franchot Tone and Robert
Young. So, unexpectedly, would Joan Crawford. When Faulkner learned
from Hawks about Miss Crawford's availability, he remained silent for a
moment. Then he said thoughtfully, 'I don't seem to remember a girl in
the story.' 'That's the picture business, Bill,' Hawks told him. 'We get the
biggest stars we can, and Joan's a nice girl, too.'"[3] Some versions of this
story suggest the decision to include Crawford was Hawks's; others lay
the blame on a "venal" MGM and suggest that Hawks was exasperated
with the decision, but powerless to do anything about it. Blotner's version puts Hawks squarely in the driver's seat—the experienced director
leading his innocent, reluctant charge through the treacherous waters of
Hollywood.

Regardless of who ultimately made the decision to include Crawford
in the production, her presence obviously required major rewriting,
not only by Faulkner, but also by other screenwriters brought in later
to work on the project, including Dwight Taylor, Edith Fitzgerald, and
Anne Cunningham. Taylor and Fitzgerald, who both had experience pen-
ning "women's films," eventually ended up with screen-writing credit.[4]
Faulkner's listing in the credits is "Story and Dialogue by William
Faulkner." In order to accommodate Crawford, Faulkner came up with
the character Diana (called Ann throughout) Boyce Smith, Ronnie's sister, who has been "betrothed" since childhood to Claude, who has himself
been transformed into a ward of the family.

Criticism almost always suggests that Crawford's inclusion ruined the
film. Tom Dardis's *Some Time in the Sun*, an example of the "writer in
Hollywood" subgenre, suggests that: "The addition of a heroine entailed a

complete rewriting of the script, and the result was a lugubrious love trian-
gle. . . . The action sequences were the only good thing about the picture;
it failed with the critics and had a very modest financial success."[5] Hawks
scholar Gerald Mast writes, "The first, MGM half of *Today We Live* (the
stiff Joan Crawford part of the film) fails to fit its second Hawks-Faulkner
half (the vital 'men in war' part of the film, with Gary Cooper, Robert
Young, Franchot Tone, and a typical Hawks friend, Roscoe Karns)."[6] And
Thomas L. McHaney uses *Today We Live* as the most egregious example
of Faulkner's frustrations in Hollywood: "Faulkner's own movie adaptation of his all-male war story . . . was turned into a Joan Crawford vehicle
advertised in newspapers with a fashion spread on her movie wardrobe. . . .
Faulkner's concerns and strengths as a writer were different from those of
movie producers trying to appeal to a popular audience."[7] Peter Hogue
accurately sums up the film's rock and hard place: "Hawks aficionados
may find that the studio's emphasis on production values is distractingly
evident in the early parts of the film and Faulknerians may see the creation of a role for Joan Crawford as a typical Hollywood compromise with
the box office."[8]

What is interesting about this is the assumption made by so many critics that "Turnabout" would have made a good film and was perfect Hawks
material. "Turnabout" is not a typical men at war story, at least not in the
"ripping yarn" tradition. In fact, I would argue that it could be considered
more a slightly off-kilter male melodrama than the usual male-bonding
war story. Conflicted emotions, heated confrontations, misunderstand-
ings, desire from afar, stoic self-denial, ultimate sacrifice, sexual rivalry,
and the development of character through suffering and loss—these
themes characterize "Turnabout." This description does not, to my mind,
suggest solid Hawks material, despite Hogue's claim that it "has the fatal-
istic gallantry of *The Dawn Patrol* as well as the competitive camaraderie
of so many later Hawks films" (52). Hawks's best-known male-driven (or
male-bonding) films, such as *Scarface* (1932), *Only Angels Have Wings*
(1939), *Red River* (1948), and *Rio Bravo* (1959) certainly are not *all*-male
affairs, despite the emphasis placed on male relationships.

There are further reasons to challenge the idea of a perfect Hawks/
Faulkner collaboration that got ruined. How might the censors have
reacted? The climate in Hollywood was getting more and more repressive, particularly in terms of representations of "perversion" (partly due
to the optioning of *Sanctuary* a year earlier). As I have argued elsewhere,
"Turnabout" can (and I think should) be read not only as an entertaining,
adventurous war story about sacrifice and bravery but also as a narrative
about repressed homosexual/homoerotic desire.[9] Further, there is the
prospective audience to consider. An all-male cast would have seriously

limited box-office potential. MGM largely catered to the female audience (seven out of ten film-goers in the 1930s were women), and in that regard "Turnabout" would certainly have been a hard sell. Finally, it is questionable whether there is even enough *action* in Faulkner's story to sustain a full-length Hollywood film.

These are all issues Faulkner criticism does not tackle, questions it has not yet learned to ask. It is much easier to enlist a heartless studio and crass commercialism to explain why the author's original conception was altered. An attempt to sketch a fuller story is decidedly more complicated and thus less definite. A short summary of *Today We Live* will help us begin to explore how the competing reputations—of director, author, stars, studio, designer—were put into play in the production, publicity, and reception of the film, as well as reveal what sorts of changes had to be made in order to include Crawford's part. Ultimately, such an exploration allows us to go beyond the acknowledgment that Faulkner's story was changed and toward an understanding of how the changes offer an interesting interpretation of Faulkner's original text. Considering the intersections of various overlapping and competing reputations highlights the ways in which Faulkner may have gained insight as a writer, particularly in his treatment of class and the representation of female desire.

The final version of the film starts with a wealthy "neutral" American, Richard Bogard (Gary Cooper), who has come to England in 1916 in order to take over the Boyce Smith estate, which he has bought. The Boyce Smiths, an upper-class family, are down on their luck because of the war. The matriarch is apparently already dead, and Ann has gotten word of her father's death in battle just as Bogard appears at the estate for the first time. Her brother, Ronnie (Franchot Tone), and future fiancé, Claude (Robert Young), have joined the Royal Navy and are soon to ship out, leaving her with Bogard. Ann and her servants move to a small gardener's cottage on the estate and "make do." As an early drawing-room scene between Ann and Bogard makes clear, the Boyce Smiths have to ration everything. Ronnie and Claude appear for one last dinner before they head for France, and Claude and Ann make their engagement semiofficial as they exchange rings.

Ronnie and Claude ship out, and suddenly Bogard and Ann—seemingly after one bike ride—are declaring their love for each other, but she nobly realizes this is impossible because of her "pact" with Claude (and thus also Ronnie). She cannot let the boys down. So she leaves Bogard a quick note—"Richard. I love you. Sorry it had to be this way. Goodbye."—joins the Women's Auxiliary Ambulance Corps and leaves for London to avoid temptation (much to Bogard's chagrin and confusion). Ann is ultimately stationed in the same French town as Claude and Ronnie, who pilot a

Fig. 1. Lobby card. Bogard and Ann
reunite. Feel the heat.

small torpedo boat, their missions "very hush-hush." Alone with Ronnie,
Ann tells him about Bogard, but refuses to "let Claude down."

One day while Ann is working in the military hospital, Ronnie brings
her a list of those recently killed—Bogard has apparently died during
RAF cadet training. Ann now thinks her "true" love dead. Soon after,
Claude, drunk and angst-ridden, winds up on her front steps, and is set to
go, in a few short hours, on what seems a potentially fatal mission (a "special assignment"). So in order to do what's right by Claude, Ann decides
to sacrifice her ideals about romantic love and sleep with him (she simply
leads him into her room, but the implications are clear). Ann is clearly
not passionate with Claude, but he doesn't seem to notice. The next day
they tell Ronnie what they have done—"We didn't wait"—which curi-
ously seems to make Ronnie as happy as we have thus far seen him (he
beams at Ann and gives her a big kiss on the lips).

Of course, complications ensue. In a plot point that will be familiar to
anyone who has seen the recent *Pearl Harbor* (or any number of 1920s
and '30s romantic war films), it turns out Bogard is in fact alive and now
flying missions with the American Air Force (and just happens to be stationed in the same town). Visiting his mortally wounded front gunner, he
encounters Ann in the hospital corridor. At first Ann and Bogard embrace
and kiss (this somewhat chemistryless image, playing on the mix of war
and romance, dominates publicity materials for the film [Figure 1]), but
then Ann remembers her duty to Claude and reluctantly pulls away, and
Bogard is pushed out of the hospital by his friend and copilot Mac.

This is when the "Turnabout" section of the film begins, but it has taken
an interesting turn. Bogard and Mac encounter Claude, drunk and asleep
in the street. They take Claude "home"—which happens to be Ann's
room—and Bogard, filled with disgust and rage, finally understands what
is going on (or at least thinks he does). Later, Mac and Bogard encounter

Claude in a bar, and Bogard asks him to fly with them. Whereas in the short story it is Bogard's fascination with the "girlish" Claude and his need to protect the boy from Mac and others that leads to the invitation to join them on a mission as front gunner, here it is his hatred and his transparent desire to get Claude killed (since Bogard has already lost several front gunners).

Claude goes on the mission, performs bravely, and gains Bogard's grudging respect. At the same time, Ann learns from Ronnie what Bogard has done and understands how much he hates her now. Ronnie, trying to open Bogard's eyes and make him understand Ann's situation, asks him to come on a mission on their torpedo boat. Bogard goes on this typically dangerous mission (and does *not* act in a cowardly fashion, as he does in the short story), but Claude is blinded (although Bogard does not know it). Bogard leaves a note for Ann, telling her he understands everything now, everything presumably encompassing the tenuous nature of life and death and the constant risks Claude is under, as well as the deeply held bond between her and Ronnie and Claude. Ann, who was going to tell Claude about Bogard and pursue her true love, learns from Ronnie that Claude is now blind, and she refuses to let him down once again (despite Ronnie's urgings). But Claude now paradoxically (or Oedipally) "sees" things more clearly, and knows that she does not love him. He and Ronnie agree to undertake a suicide mission that Bogard has unnecessarily volunteered for, ostensibly to clear the way for true romance and Ann's ultimate happiness. The film crosscuts between Bogard and Mac in their plane and Ronnie and Claude in their boat as they approach the target, a large German cruiser (intercut with Ann pacing back and forth in her room—which of Ann's three loves will survive?). Ronnie and Claude arrive first, and nobly steer their boat, kamikaze-style, into the cruiser. Bogard and Mac witness their sacrifice and reluctantly fly off. The film ends with Ann and Bogard, arm in arm, silently looking at a memorial to the war dead, which includes the names of her father, Ronnie, and Claude. We then see the contented couple walking towards what is, we assume, *their* estate now.

The perception of popular culture as threatening Faulkner's reputation, combined with the difficulty of dealing with the complexities of audience response to film, in part explains why many critics find comfort in presenting Faulkner as subversive when it comes to classical Hollywood cinema.[10] Such supposed transgression of the conventions imposed on Faulkner allows these critics to often blame obtuse audiences (and other critics) for their perception of the relative failures of the film. But you have to see the film (and other 1930s women's films) to understand that, in fact, *Today We Live* is *not* particularly subversive, transgressive, or, on a narrative level, terribly interesting. It's hard to see how fifty other 1930s melodramas do not actually do relatively similar things in the course of their narratives, and often more satisfyingly. So let's see what happens when we break out of a "Faulkner versus" mode of thinking, as in Faulkner versus Hawks (for control), or Faulkner versus Hollywood. What if *Today We Live* does not fit well into the Faulkner (or Hawks) narratives because neither figure is ultimately *central* to the way the text worked—and what if we examine Crawford's insertion not as the irremediable problem of the text, but the key to understanding it? From this perspective, what can we learn not from Faulkner's control, but from his relative loss of control, and the potential benefits of this experience? Readings of *Today We Live* can and need to move beyond "Faulkner as Author" and begin to ask what other discourses, what other reputations, were in play as the film was being made, publicized, and received. One Hawks critic suggests that the first twenty minutes of the film are "so laboriously expositional that . . . the film was in a hole so deep it had no hope of climbing out. Hawks and his actors seem so ill at ease in the early drawing-room and church scenes that these emerge as among the worst scenes he ever directed. . . . The picture admittedly improves in its second half, which is where, not at all coincidentally, it converges most snugly with Faulkner's original."[11] In fact, for most 1930s audiences the first twenty minutes were likely the most satisfying and best represented what was expected. Joan Crawford's fans were most likely sorely disappointed by the emphasis on action, the stagnant nature of her character, as well as the lack of costume changes in the second half of the movie.

When one looks at the publicity and initial reception of *Today We Live*, what becomes immediately apparent is that neither Faulkner nor Hawks figures too prominently. A few reviews mention Faulkner's notorious reputation, but usually only to comment on how the film is so unlike the texts that purportedly secured this reputation. Richard Watts's review for the *New York Herald Tribune* is worth quoting at length in this regard:

> Although William Faulkner is billed as the author of *Today We Live*, the picture is no devastating survey of the degeneracy of the New South, filled with murderous neurotics and pathological passions. Instead, it is a lugubrious romance of the war, replete with clipped speeches, heroic sacrifices, self-effacing nobility and many cries of "stout fellow!" As a matter of fact, it is only when one of the characters begins to play quaintly with a cockroach that you see any particular traces of the Faulkner influence at all. For the rest of the time, the work seems more akin to *Journey's End* than to *Sanctuary* or *Light in August* and devotes most of its efforts to permitting Robert Young and Franchot Tone to destroy themselves gallantly so that Gary Cooper may henceforth live happily

with Miss Joan Crawford. It was my suspicion yesterday that their sacrifice was too great.[12]

Watts here seems already in 1933 to be ascribing to an auteurist vision of what is and is not "Faulknerian," and seems to denigrate the film for its melodramatic tendencies. Again, this echoes the notion of Hollywood as a business that could play a writer false, and predicts the Faulkner-as-subverter readings from more recent critics. Such reviews, however, are the exceptions, even as they point to interpretations to come. Most of the contemporary reviews, particularly those from newspapers in smaller, less cosmopolitan markets, do not even bother to mention Faulkner or Hawks at all. The real emphasis in most reviews is on Crawford, the love story, and fashion. Similarly, in newspaper advertisements Faulkner and Hawks are not featured prominently (if at all). In three of these ads neither the director nor the author is mentioned. In three others, Faulkner's name comes up, but not Hawks's. Hawks might have been famous (or infamous) for *Scarface* (1932) at this time, but he was not yet an advertising commodity.

When Faulkner is mentioned, it is usually in an attempt to cash in on the notoriety of *Sanctuary*. Two of the ads mention the novel, "William Faulkner (Author 'Sanctuary')," while another seems to conflate Faulkner's notorious novel with the little-read short story the film was based on: "From Wm. Faulkner's Celebrated Novel." (Figures 2, 3, and 4)

All of these ads, of course, feature Joan Crawford and Gary Cooper. And even the studio's reputation clearly was expected to signify more to potential viewers than either Faulkner or Hawks. Metro-Goldwyn-Mayer was, according to most film histories, the only studio in the early 1930s on solid financial ground, and it had a reputation for excess, "class," glossy productions, and big stars. The implication: MGM was the kind of place where straightforward, independent men such as Hawks and Faulkner would unproductively languish. And of course, the sheer size of the studio plays against Faulkner's reputation as a shy, naive foreigner overwhelmed by his surroundings.

But this reputation for ruthlessness, for the stifling of individual genius, certainly was not in place when *Today We Live* was being produced and promoted. Faulkner and Hawks critics seem to forget that audiences sought certain pleasures from an MGM film, were *seeking* the glossy production values and romantic twists and turns, and quite likely did not feel quite so betrayed by the end result. According to Howard Gutner, the "four most important participants on any MGM production were always the producer, the star, the set designer, and the costume designer. The last three were the primary selling tools of each film's marketing campaign."[13]

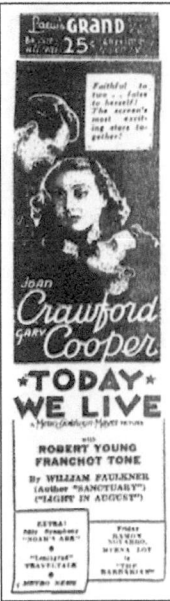

Fig. 3. Newspaper advertisement, *Atlanta Constitution* (26 May 1933).

Fig. 2. Newspaper advertisement, *Atlanta Constitution* (25 May 1933). "Faithful to two . . . false to herself!" Note the "William Faulkner (Author 'Sanctuary')" in this and the following figure.

The advertising for the film makes it very clear what kind of film audiences could expect.

In one magazine advertisement, a dapper, tuxedoed Leo the Lion (MGM's mascot), complete with monocle and crown, bows to a seated Joan Crawford, decked out in a fancy dress and hat (the glamorous outfit featured in the publicity does not actually appear in the film). (Figure 5) The dialogue is represented as follows: "Joan: I love my role in *Today We Live*. No part ever thrilled me so deeply, touched my heart so keenly. Do you think the public will like me in it, Leo? Leo: My child, the public always appreciates genius. It's a great emotional part. You are perfect in *Today We Live*." At the bottom of the ad the copy continues, "The finest picture Joan Crawford has yet made. . . . The scene at her home, where the sweetheart she believed dead returns and finds her the mistress of another—is as powerful an emotional scene as the screen has ever witnessed." The publicity for the film often makes it clear that thematically the film is guaranteed to deliver the emotional goods—Joan's is "a great emotional part." And audiences can expect one supposedly dazzling emotional scene—"as powerful an emotional scene as the screen has ever witnessed." The emphasis on the melodramatic aspects of the film suggests what kind of audience expectations were in place, and what kind of reputation MGM enjoyed at the time.

Fig. 4. Newspaper advertisement, *New York Times* (5 May 1933). "From William Faulkner's Celebrated Novel"?

Also telling is the evocation of fashion and elegance in the ad. Crawford might spend more than half of *Today We Live* in a military nurse's uniform, but that particular outfit figures in almost none of the advertising, and as I have noted, outfits that never appear in the film are presented in the ads. (Figures 6 and 7) It is worth pointing out that Cooper and Crawford never appear in tuxedo or evening dress, and this poster (Figure 8) is particularly misleading. (The magazine ads focus on the women's picture aspects, while many of the lobby cards and posters—publicity men might see as they stand outside the theater—feature the war elements.) (Figure 9) Contemporary reviews from the more sophisticated critics often focused on the seemingly outrageous outfits worn by Crawford in the film. Mordaunt Hall, for the *New York Times*, wrote, "It [the film] is also anachronistic, particularly as regards the costumes worn by Joan Crawford."[14] Pare Lorentz's review for *Vanity Fair* links Crawford's wardrobe with her reputation for overacting (or perhaps for acting in overly melodramatic films): "Joan Crawford, in an odd collection of clothes, stupidly displayed off-key and out of date with the story, gives the show away by acting her head off in . . . the best tradition of the 'Oh, the pain of it!' school."[15] These critics might take exception to the emphasis on fashion, but Crawford's fans could not get enough of it in her other films. Crawford and fashion became inseparable after the success of *Letty Lynton* (1932), a film that film historians identify as putting her on the same plane as the biggest female Hollywood stars: "The resounding success of *Letty Lynton* prompted MGM to put the publicity machine into high gear and publicize her as a glamorous star on a scale

Fig. 5. Magazine advertisement, *Vanity Fair* (April 1933). Joan Crawford in a glamorous dress not featured in the film.

with Greta Garbo and Norma Shearer."[16] One dress in particular solidified her position as "fashion plate" for future MGM films, and the reputation of costume designer Adrian. This dress came to be known simply as the "Letty Lynton dress." In their article on this dress and the phenomenon it sparked, Charlotte Cornelia Herzog and Jane Marie Gaines note how in the early 1930s fashion became *the* point of interest in a Joan Crawford film:

> Women went to Adrian-designed films just to see what the stars wore. It seemed to her that it hardly mattered at that time if the clothes were even appropriate for the scene. Both the sheer number of costumes and the look of expense were important to Crawford's promotion during the "clothes horse" phase of her career. The extensiveness of her personal wardrobe and the variety of costume changes in each new release were standard publicity topics, as was Adrian's financial extravagance. Crawford would recall that for these fashion plate films more was often spent on wardrobe than on the rights for the script. Critics at the time said that when there was little to remark about in the films, they could always write about the clothes.[17]

The preponderantly male critics at the time went out of their way to remark on the use (or rather misuse) of fashion in *Today We Live*, but incongruity was *not* the point. Many women (and presumably a lot of men as well) went to these lavish MGM films expecting to see gorgeous outfits. Ann Boyce Smith can barely afford to offer Bogard sugar for his tea, but that does not mean she can't wear a flamboyant dress complete

Fig. 6. Newspaper advertisement, *Washington Post* (5 May 1933). Crawford in another outfit not found in the film.

with totally impractical collar. But in addition to the mere spectacle of fashion, there were also often thematic reasons behind the creation of these gowns. Adrian himself noted: "Few people in an audience watching a great screen production realize the importance of any gown worn by the feminine star. They may notice that it is attractive, that they would like to have it copied, that it is becoming, but the fact that it was definitely planned to mirror some definite mood, to be as much a part of the play as the lines or the scenery, seldom occurs to them. But that most assuredly is true" (Gutner 9). Fashion played a vital part in Crawford's stardom, and she had become by 1933 a fashion arbiter for the entire nation. Part of the problem with *Today We Live*, it seems, is that the writers and director weren't quite sure how to incorporate the expected fashions into the usual Joan Crawford narrative.

Adrian's designs were, as Herzog and Gaines suggest and as we have seen in the publicity materials, a major part of the advertising and had a great impact on the reception of the film. In prerelease publicity for *Today We Live*, Crawford's connection to fashion is emphasized. A few examples from early 1933 should suffice. A January 7th issue of *Picturegoer* presented a fashion show of sorts under the title of "Joan Crawford—Mannequin." A March pictorial spread on Adrian, showcasing three costumes from *Today We Live*, was featured in *Silver Screen*.

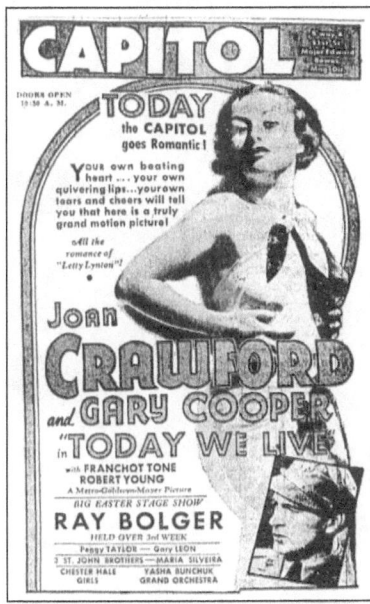

Fig. 7. Newspaper advertisement, *St. Louis Dispatch* (17 May 1933). "All the romance of 'Letty Lynton.'" Crawford in another Adrian design not seen in the film.

Photoplay, New Movie, and *Vogue* all between March and June featured pictorial articles on Crawford's wardrobe. Showcasing many (but not all) of these outfits, Crawford makes no fewer than four costume changes in the first twenty minutes of *Today We Live,* which isn't unusual for a Joan Crawford film. But by the 23rd minute, she is in her nurse's outfit, and even though she looks pretty smart in her military clothing, she is pictured only one more time in civilian clothes—in her final, silent scenes with Bogard at the end of the film. Although the dresses seen early in the film might appear anachronistic and unrealistic, Tapert suggests that seeming contradictions between the role the actress might be playing and her wardrobe were beside the point: "Crawford became an oracle for working-class girls, for she instilled in them the notion that a polished appearance was crucial to social advancement. So it didn't matter to them that her on-screen high-fashion clothes were completely incongruous with her 'shopgirl' parts. When reviewers criticized her for this, she was reminded by Joe Mankiewicz . . . that her female fans wanted to see her in a dreamy version of their own life: 'She doesn't want to see you in a housedress with armpit stains. She wants you dressed by Adrian, as she would like to be'"(54).

This suggests that the incongruity of Crawford's fashions in *Today We Live* does not fully explain audiences' and critics' dissatisfaction with the

Fig. 8. Window card. "Look, it's *Grand Hotel*. Oh, wait a minute. No it isn't." Gary Cooper and Crawford in evening wear they don't get a chance to wear in *Today We Live*.

film. Part of the problem, I think, is that the fashions in the film *only* act as spectacle. Other than her military uniforms, Ann's clothing doesn't signify. Crawford's Ann is not a shopgirl on her way up, but a privileged Englishwoman apparently on her way down (that is until she marries the rich American Bogard). Presumably Bogard is not won over by her outfits—social advancement is not really much of an issue in this particular film. And the film did nothing to enhance Crawford's new status as Hollywood clotheshorse. According to Gutner, *Today We Live* "was not the ideal vehicle either for promoting Hollywood fashion or for heralding Crawford's 'new look' . . . its message was too downbeat to inspire any real confidence in its fashion forecast. And while the costumes might have been interesting on a runway, they failed to embellish the narrative thrust of the film, as costumes in *Grand Hotel* and *Letty Lynton* had done so successfully" (125). Ann's choice of clothing in *Today We Live* has no impact on her status or on the overall trajectory of the narrative, and unlike other Crawford vehicles, changing fashion doesn't symbolize a change in the character she's playing. Ann never really demonstrates anything other than stoic acceptance of her fate and loyalty to the men in her life. The Joan Crawford character in the 1930s was understood to be a scrapper, a social climber who used the tools—most importantly, clothing—at her disposal to pull herself out of a bad situation.

This brings us to an interesting point made by Jeanine Basinger, who notes that Crawford, contrary to popular belief, did not really play a shopgirl often at all. She argues that this reputation is undeserved and brings to light the ways reputations shift during the course of an actor's career and

Fig. 9. 1–sheet poster. Street and lobby publicity often emphasized the war elements as well as the romance in order to pull in (or at least assuage the fears of) potential male audiences.

how the personal life of the actor impacts audience reactions to her: "Many people think that in the 1930s Crawford played the shop girl who rises to wealth, and that is her image for that decade. Yet in the twenty-six movies starring Joan Crawford released between 1930 and 1940, she played a shop girl exactly twice, in *Our Blushing Brides* and *The Women*. . . . This means that Crawford played an heiress or socialite eight times, or four times as often as she played a shop girl. . . . Here is another case of persona misfiring in the audience's memories. Joan Crawford in the 1930s was in movies to provide escape for audiences via stories of wealth that allowed her to wear the fabulous, angular clothes designed for her by the great Adrian."[18] Of course, such a reading doesn't fully work for *Today We Live* (a film, in fact, Basinger largely ignores), but her reading suggests something about how the personal lives of the stars (or at least the ways the lives of the stars were reported in fan magazines and studio publicity) factors into audiences' interpretations of what was going on up on the screen.

If Crawford's Ann is somehow striking a blow for women against patriarchy—as several Faulkner critics suggest[19]—part of that reading surely comes from Crawford's latter "shopgirl" persona and her reputation as a woman who had to scratch and claw her way to the top. As the character has been written, Ann transgresses certain social boundaries—such as sleeping with Claude out of wedlock—but her loyalty to a sense of moral duty doesn't seem particularly subversive. And her reward at the end of the film is, of course, patriarchal status quo as she walks arm-in-arm with her true love and reclaims her wealth and status (not to mention her estate). Crawford's presence as MGM star represents, for many critics who don't fully take into account the way fans may have responded to her as well as the integration of fashion, the crass commercialism of Hollywood itself: Joan Crawford = fashion = melodrama = appeals to women audiences. Such reductive readings cannot take into account how audiences might actually *resist* the roles as written and essentially create their own heroine or hero, based partly on their own desires and on their understanding of a star's reputation. Even though Crawford hardly ever played the social-climbing shopgirl, that is how audiences saw her, regardless of the role she was playing. And this might explain why many viewers found *Today We Live* unrewarding. Crawford's off-screen persona is distinctly *American*—the poor, fatherless girl who through her wits and incredible work ethic made good and became Hollywood royalty—and doesn't mesh well with Faulkner's script, with its English heroine who, while in danger of losing her social status, does nothing significant beyond remaining loyal to the men in her life and her own moral code. The awkwardness of the incorporation of Adrian's gowns in the narrative is, I think, symptomatic of this larger disconnect between Ann and the actress playing her. The extent to which this might be blamed on Faulkner's lack of knowledge of the expectations of the woman's film, or his misunderstanding of Crawford's persona, is impossible to gauge because of the collaborative nature of film. But it could certainly be argued that while Faulkner did go to the movies frequently, the 1930s woman's film might not have admittedly been his cup of tea. Later in his screenwriting career he appears to have been much more successful in helping with the creation of strong female characters in films such as *To Have and Have Not* (1944), *Mildred Pierce* (1945), and *The Big Sleep* (1946). It is likely that neither Faulkner nor Howard Hawks took into consideration how important the *plausible* integration of fashion was for a melodrama such as this. And Crawford didn't help matters any, as she reportedly demanded to have some of the dresses she had recently purchased in Paris put into the fashion rotation in the film (Gutner 122–24).

As I have been suggesting, a *strictly* formalist reading of *Today We Live* only gets us so far, since it ignores complicating factors such as competing reputations and audience expectations. But this still leaves us with a film difficult for most contemporary audiences to watch. It's almost impossible to identify with Crawford's character—upper-class English, able to stamp out her own emotional desires, stoic. She never really seems to love *any* of the men in her life and appears to do everything out of a sense of duty and not her own desires. If you add a woman to a war film, she has to be waiting desperately, and convincingly, for her man to return. That's the expected formula for emotional identification with a woman in a war film. I have to agree with most contemporary critics that *Today We Live* is not very satisfying on most levels. Cooper and Crawford do not have any

Fig. 10. Publicity still. Bogard and Ann meet for the first time. Gown (with amazing collar) by Adrian. This is the dress that most seemed to antagonize reviewers at the time.

real screen chemistry (this was the first, and last, film which cast them as lovers), the "clipped" dialogue, meant to approximate British speech, is often laughable, and Crawford's dresses (and multiple costume changes) are often disconcerting. Scenes end too abruptly, seemingly cutting off the actor's lines, or they drag on interminably. As Joanne Yeck has pointed out, visually the woman's film lacks innovation—the pace is slow, locales are generally confined to interior spaces, and actions limited largely to dialogue. The stylistic featurelessness of the woman's film functioned to focus attention on the star's face and costume.[20] Finally, the war scenes tend to mix uncomfortably with the romantic elements.

Having said all this, I still find enormous pleasures in the film, as I am sure many film goers did when it was first released. The "Gowns by Adrian" are fascinating (albeit absolutely impractical [Figure 10]), the romantic complications and shifting sources of sexual tension—and the plot machinations necessary to reveal them—are worthy of the better melodramas of the period. It is interesting to watch as the most convincing sexual chemistry develops between Ann and her brother Ronnie, not just because of the way this sublimated incest has clearly been written into the script, but also because Crawford and Franchot Tone were reportedly "falling in love" on the set during filming—Crawford would soon divorce husband Douglas Fairbanks Jr., and marry Tone. The war scenes are frequently exciting, even though the dogfights were reportedly recycled from Howard Hughes's *Hell's Angels* (1930). Also, there are great camp moments in the film (such as the over-the-top, homoerotically charged scene my title refers to, where the recently blinded Claude asks Ronnie to look at Ann and touch him one last time before they depart for their doomed mission).

But we do not get to discuss all this, as critics or teachers, unless we actually discuss the *film* and not something we can readily identify as *Faulkner's* text. This may require recognizing that *Today We Live* is interesting because what we perceive as failures in the film open up further questions that we might profitably explore. What I think is ultimately most interesting about *Today We Live* is the proposition that Faulkner might have actually *gained* something from the collaborative efforts—in particular, in being forced to imagine a different space for women than he might have been used to. Rather than think about Crawford's inclusion as another example of Faulkner being stifled/misunderstood/used, I find it more fruitful to use this particular moment in Faulkner's career to consider what he might have learned from the experience. Suddenly the author was presented with the task of imagining female desire, of finding not just a way to include an important female character but to represent the point of view of a woman sexually alluring, tragic, and noble all at once (in a very Joan Crawford way). And into an all-male, arguably homoerotic story at that. The love rectangle found here (Claude-Ronnie-Ann-Bogard) prefigures (with differences, of course) the relationships found in *Pylon*, another non-Yoknapatawpha work written less than two years after his work on *Today We Live*: Jack-Laverne-Roger-the Reporter. The difference, however, is that in *Pylon* we aren't privy to Laverne's thoughts or perspective—everything is seen through the men's eyes. As we watch *Today We Live* we realize, as Faulkner did, that this is Hollywood cinema, it is Crawford's film, and it is her perspective and fate that matter most.

A particularly telling mix—this seems to describe *Today We Live*, or at least what audiences were promised and presumably what some found there. Despite claims to the contrary, the film did solid box office business and was by no means a *commercial* failure. But the film has never fully entered the public consciousness and is not presumably part of the package Faulkner wanted to lay claim to given his reputation as American "man of letters."

What if we consider the possibility that Faulkner's time in Hollywood did not "cost" him books as many critics suggest but instead gained him perspective that contributed to his major works still to come? How might we further trace the dilemma of female desire in later works? Perhaps the "forced" inclusion of female desire in this all-male scenario led Faulkner to recognize the ways in which "Turnabout" represents on some levels "the easiest of loves" and had some sort of impact on his subsequent works. How might Faulkner have been influenced not only by Symbolist poetry and T. S. Eliot, but by imagining a role for Joan Crawford in a melodramatic "woman's picture" early in his career?

If we examine the many layers behind the production and reception, *Today We Live* becomes more interesting and we have a great potential to see what Faulkner might have learned about both literary and cinematic writing from the experience. The author undoubtedly knew that he wasn't being asked to include "a girl" into the film—he was adding Crawford, who came with her own reputation and audience expectations. And regardless of the outcome, Faulkner need not "subvert" the Hollywood conventions of the woman's film—the fans do it themselves, something he no doubt understood. Rather than threatening Faulkner's reputation, his "sojourn" should be seen to enhance it.

My investigation of *Today We Live* has also led inevitably to a more complex understanding of how Joan Crawford's multiple, ever-changing reputations may have affected the production and reception of the film. And this led to my thinking about how considering Faulkner as a "star" in the cinematic sense might be a productive endeavor. Stars are quite often made up of contradictory discourses, created by personal biography, publicity, self-presentation, the works themselves, and the criticism of those works. At times stars are seen to be supporting the status quo, at others exhibiting transgressive qualities. Coming to terms with how historical spectators/readers group texts and then read them (or vice versa) is necessary in developing a materialist history of interpretation.

The suggestion that Hollywood distorted Faulkner's works relies on the supposed unity of the literary object and a priori assumptions about coherence, intention, imagination, and effect. It's worth thinking about Faulkner as a star, complete with seemingly contradictory messages, an ever-shifting image, and as the product of promotion, publicity, his works, and criticism: "The social film historian derives the image of a star from the texts that collectively embody that image, not for the purpose of determining the 'correct' meaning of that star, but rather to determine how the image has been structured, the range of possible meanings at any given time, and the changes that might have occurred to that image over time. . . . It enables us to better understand what meanings were available to *be used* by individuals and groups within society at a point in history. It is clear that stars form an aesthetic intertext that audiences use to derive meaning and pleasure."[21] Sometimes we need to rethink the academic rules for making texts coherent and to consider what readings have been available for different audiences. Some reading strategies available for 1930s audiences—Crawford, Adrian, Cedric Gibbons, MGM—have largely been lost on the contemporary viewer. Faulkner's role in *Today We Live* becomes oversimplified—or overemphasized—and bears an unfair burden when we neglect to pay closer attention to the material realities of the film's production and reception.

NOTES

1. Richard Dyer, "Believing in Fairies: The Author and the Homosexual," in *Inside/Out: Lesbian Theories, Gay Theories*, ed. Diana Fuss (New York: Routledge, 1991), 186.

2. Alan Sinfield, *Cultural Politics—Queer Reading* (Philadelphia: University of Pennsylvania Press, 1994), 28.

3. Joseph Blotner, *A Biography*, 2 vols. (New York: Random House, 1974), 781. Blotner clearly believed that Faulkner's time spent in Hollywood was detrimental, albeit not ultimately fatal, to the author's career. In his 1966 article "Faulkner in Hollywood" this attitude is clear: "The creator of Yoknapatawpha County, from the early 1930s the most famous of Mississippi's sons, was to spend a total of nearly four years in California working for various studios. This time was accumulated during a period of twenty-two years in often painful sojourns of varying lengths. . . . The work itself, as compared with the anguishing that went into most of his novels, was slight; it was the expense of spirit that was costly for Faulkner, who wanted above all to be a serious artist" (*Man and Movies*, ed. W. R. Robinson [Baton Rouge: Louisiana State University Press, 1967], 262).

4. Edith Fitzgerald worked on many early 1930s "women's films," including *Many a Slip* (1931), *Compromised* (1931), *Susan Lenox (Her Fall and Rise)* (1931), *Laughing Sinners* (1931) (another Joan Crawford vehicle), *Ex-Lady* (1933), and *The Painted Veil* (1934). Dwight Taylor had worked on only a few films prior to *Today We Live*, including *Secrets of a Secretary* (1931) and *Are You Listening?* (1932). He went on to work at RKO on several Fred Astaire/Ginger Rogers romantic musicals such as *The Gay Divorcee* (1934), *Top Hat* (1935), and *Follow the Fleet* (1936).

5. Tom Dardis, *Some Time in the Sun* (New York: Scribner's, 1976), 94.

6. Gerald Mast, *Howard Hawks, Storyteller* (New York: Oxford University Press, 1982), 354.

7. Thomas L. McHaney, *Literary Masters: William Faulkner* (New York: Gale Group, 2000), 134.

8. Peter Hogue, "Hawks and Faulkner: *Today We Live*," *Literature/Film Quarterly* 9 (1981): 51.

9. D. Matthew Ramsey, "'Turnabout' Is Fair(y) Play: Faulkner's Queer War Story," *Faulkner Journal* 15.1, 2 (1999/2000): 61–81.

10. The best example of this is John Matthews's intriguing argument that Ann represents Faulkner's transgressive transformation of classical Hollywood cinema expectations. "Faulkner and the Culture Industry," in *The Cambridge Companion to William Faulkner*, ed. Philip M. Weinstein (New York: Cambridge University Press, 1995), 51–74. While I find Matthews's reading compelling in many respects, I think he tends at times to reify the high/low culture divide as he suggests that Faulkner *always* attempted to subvert the popular culture forms within which he was working: "Although one can see Hollywood conventions reshaping Faulkner's story, one can also see his imagination resisting too slick a repackaging" (66).

11. Todd McCarthy, *Howard Hawks: The Grey Fox of Hollywood* (New York: Grove Press, 1997), 184–85.

12. Quoted in Lawrence J. Quirk, *The Films of Joan Crawford* (New York: Citadel Press, 1968), 104.

13. Howard Gutner, *Gowns by Adrian: The MGM Years, 1928–1941* (New York: Harry N. Abrams, 2001), 105.

14. Mourdant Hall, "The Screen," *New York Times* (6 May, 1933): 11.

15. Pare Lorentz, "The Screen," *Vanity Fair* (June 1933): 37–38.

16. Annette Tapert, *The Power of Glamour* (New York: Crown Publishers, 1998), 53.

17. Charlotte Cornelia Herzog and Jane Marie Gaines, "'Puffed Sleeves before Tea-Time': Joan Crawford, Adrian, and Women Audiences," in *Stardom: Industry of Desire*, ed. Christine Gledhill (New York: Routledge, 1991), 77–78.

18. Jeanine Basinger, *A Woman's View: How Hollywood Spoke to Women, 1930–1960* (New York: Knopf, 1993), 172–73.

19. In addition to Matthews, see Dallas Hulsey, "'I don't seem to remember a girl in the story': Hollywood's Disruption of Faulkner's All-Male Narrative in *Today We Live*," *Faulkner Journal* 16.1, 2 (2000/2001): 65–77.

20. Joanne L. Yeck, "The Woman's Film at Warner Brothers, 1935–1950" (PhD dissertation, University of Southern California, 1982), 48.

21. Robert C. Allen, "The Role of the Star in Film History," in *Film History: Theory and Practice*. Reprinted in *Film Theory and Criticism*, ed. Leo Braudy and Marshall Cohen, 5th ed. (New York: Oxford University Press, 1999), 548.

Order and Rebellion: Faulkner's Small Town and the Place of Memory

MILES ORVELL

We are not always fortunate enough to be present at the primal scene in an artist's work, but we are, in a sense, when Faulkner gives birth fictionally to the town that he'd already been writing about for twenty years or more before he came to imagine its "founding." Here is that moment, in "The Courthouse" section of *Requiem for a Nun*, where its first construction, in the 1830s, is described: one of the townsmen utters the name that is the town, after initially thinking that "the thought was solitarily his":

'By God. Jefferson.'
'Jefferson, Mississippi,' a second added.
'Jefferson, Yoknapatawpha County, Mississippi,' a third corrected.

Faulkner dwells on the moment, describing it as "one conjoined breathing, one compound dream-state, mused and static, well capable of lasting on past sunrise too," when suddenly Compson (the "gnat, the thorn, the catalyst") interrupts the premature celebration of the town's founding, and brings the enthusiasts back to earth:

'It aint until we finish the goddamned thing. . . . Come on. Let's get at it.'[1]

By the time Faulkner was writing "The Courthouse" in 1950, he was looking back on a mythology that had been two decades in the making, and one that he'd previously amplified in such summary narratives as "Appendix: The Compsons," which he wrote for Malcolm Cowley's 1946 *The Portable Faulkner*. Given how firmly Jefferson had become fixed in Faulkner's imagination by this time, it's not surprising that he would encompass not only the stories of families past and present, but stories of the place itself, the logs and bricks that made up the buildings that made up the town that was the imaginative matrix for his creations. The governing principle here connecting story and material object is the one enunciated by Gavin Stevens in the third section of *Requiem*, "The Jail": "If you would peruse in unbroken—ay, overlapping—continuity the history of a community, look not in the church registers and the courthouse records, but beneath the successive layers of calcimine and creosote and whitewash on the walls of the jail, since only in that forcible carceration does man find the idleness in which to compose, in the gross and simple terms of his gross and simple lusts and yearnings, the gross and simple recapitulations of his gross and simple heart" (184).

1

What did it mean for Faulkner to found the town of Jefferson as the setting for his fiction? And how did his thinking about the town change over the period from *Sartoris*—where it is first used, in 1929—to *Requiem for a Nun* in 1950? I am not concerned here with the relationship between the fictive Jefferson and the actual Oxford, Mississippi, a subject that has been treated before me by scholars who have examined the congruencies and the dissonances in great detail and with great authority.[2] Nor have I the space to offer an exhaustive survey of Faulkner's use of the town as a fictional place. Rather, I want to examine a few representative works, not only to better understand the meaning of place in Faulkner but to frame that problem within the larger issue of how the small town generally has figured in the American cultural imagination.

In these days of global empire, of America writ large across the earth, for better or worse (and mostly for worse), it might seem quaint to consider the small town, in regard to Faulkner or in any other context. The leading paradigms in American studies have been global imperialism and border crossing, reflecting the social and economic dynamics of American society in the last twenty-five years, as we have grown into a society of increasingly multicultural dimensions and a nation that has exerted its power across the world. Yet the business of discovering the antecedents of our contemporary world, of tracing the roots and lineage of our cultural identity, has largely neglected the small town, overlooking its significance in the formation of contemporary American culture. What Thorstein Veblen said many years ago is still, in many ways, true today: "The country town is one of the great American institutions; perhaps the greatest, in the sense that it has had and continues to have a greater part than any other in shaping public sentiment and giving character to American culture."[3]

The small town continues to maintain its hold on the American imagination, not only in film and fiction, but in the ongoing construction of our built environment; the town is the leading spatial archetype of the postwar period, the model for the vast majority of developments being built in this country now, whether in the guise of the new urbanism, the new suburbanism, or the ubiquitous gated communities that make willing prisoners of their inhabitants. Simultaneously, we have been worrying as a society about the fate of community and how to revive it, whether in the streets, on the Internet, or in the bowling alley, neglecting to examine the model of community, such as it is, in the small town. Faulkner, whose creation and exploration over many years of Jefferson and Yoknapatawpha County is at the core of his fiction, may thus serve as a rich model for understanding the literary representation of place and the meaning of community.

In the face of our contemporary neglect, there is, of course, a long tradition in American literature that explores the life of the small town, from both positive and negative perspectives. As early as 1772, the young Philip Freneau was imagining "The American Village" as a middle ground, a pastoral retreat somewhere between the "howling forest" (those were Indians howling in that forest, of course) and the distractions of urban life. ("Sweet haunt of peace whose mud'wall'd sides delight, / The rural mind beyond the city bright.")[4] And this idealized vision of the village or town remained a strong current through the nineteenth century, centering on the New England towns that would be more closely and critically examined by New England writers such as Harriet Beecher Stowe, Mary Wilkins Freeman, and Sarah Orne Jewett, and continuing into the twentieth century with middlebrow writers like William Allen White, Booth Tarkington, and Zona Gale, who shifted the scene to the Middle West.

A somewhat more complex vision of the small town is initiated by Hawthorne, who established the archetype of the town that conceals within its seemingly placid surface the torments of suspicion, dread, and evil spite. It is this distortion of character in the crucible of small-town life that began to occupy the satirists of the early twentieth century who emerged from the Midwest, writers like Edgar Lee Masters (*Spoon River Anthology*, 1916), Sinclair Lewis (*Main Street*, 1920), and Sherwood Anderson (*Winesburg, Ohio*, 1919). In their hands, the pastoral simplicity and democratic egalitarian ideals of small-town life mutated into a cauldron of gossip, backbiting, malevolence, and thwarted sexual desire, a vision of America that can be taken as part of the general reaction against Puritanism and its repressive heritage on the part of a younger generation of writers. In this environment, the only healthy response to the repressive order of the town, we find again and again, is the path of rebellion—to leave the local village for Greenwich Village, to head out for the big city, where tolerance of sexual difference and aesthetic ambition is presumably to be found, and such is the pattern in Lewis, in Anderson, and in Willa Cather, among others. (Henry Seidel Canby, in "The Two Americas" [1921] argued that the opposing visions of the small town—center of everything good in American values versus the drab and ugly—were not only a reflection of authorial perspective but of the actual complexity and contradiction within the American social landscape.)[5]

Faulkner, coming of age as a writer at the height of the antivillage sentiment, seems to have experienced the ambivalence of small-town life first hand. (In the biographical sketch he wrote for the publication of *The Marble Faun*, he wrote—after detailing his occupations and peregrinations: "Present temporary address, Oxford, Miss." It's the word "temporary" that is so striking, in retrospect.)[6] The dullness of the small town is captured in the character of Margaret, when she asserts, in *Soldiers' Pay*, "You see, I lived in a small town and I had got kind of sick lazing around home all morning and dressing up just to walk downtown in the afternoon and spending the evenings messing around with men, so after we got in the war I persuaded some friends of my mother's to get me a position in New York."[7] Faulkner too ventured away from Oxford several times during the early 1920s—to Connecticut at Phil Stone's invitation; to New York, at Stark Young's invitation; and of course most notably to Toronto, to join the Royal Canadian Air Force, at his own invitation. But he kept coming back, finally settling into the respectable job of University of Mississippi Postmaster.

Faulkner as postmaster? The report we get of him during the few years that he served in that position suggests that if he had settled into Oxford, he had also settled into the role of village malcontent, of alienated artist, superior to his small-town surroundings. In the letter of charges from the Postoffice Inspector in Corinth, Mississippi, to Postmaster Faulkner (2 September 1924), the following items are noted:

> 1. That you are neglectful of your duties, in that you are a habitual reader of books and magazines, and seem reluctant to cease reading long enough to wait on the patrons; that you have a book being printed at the present time, the greater part of which was written while on duty at the postoffice; that some of the patrons will not trust you to forward their mail, because of your past carelessness and these patrons have their neighbors forward same for them while away on their vacations. . . .
> 2. . . . that on another occasion a contractor working at the University was compelled to get your father to help him get a package out of the office, which you had held for two or three days. . . .
> 3. That you are indifferent to interest of patrons, unsocial, and rarely ever speak to patrons of the office unless absolutely necessary. . . .
> 4 . . . that you have thrown mail with return postage guaranteed and all other classes in the garbage can by the side entrance. . . . that this has gotten to be such a common occurrence that some patrons have gone to this garbage can to get their magazines, should they not be in their boxes whey they looked for them.[8]

We know Faulkner's own opinion of the post office customer, from *Soldiers' Pay*, where he remarks, authorially, "The mail was in and the window had opened and even those who expected no mail, who had received no mail in months must needs answer one of the most enduring compulsions of the American nation" (111). If the mail was somewhat unreliable under Postmaster Faulkner, we might say that the cause of letters was nevertheless somehow being served, with the government of the United States giving Faulkner a kind of postal fellowship, or at least he interpreted it as such, the opportunity to get the kind of education he had missed in more formal terms.

Following his dismissal from the post office, from the mid-twenties to 1930, Faulkner is on and off the road at regular intervals, as if unable or unwilling to settle in a place that might best serve his purposes: he visited New Orleans, took a tour of Europe for several months; then moved back to New Orleans, then back to Mississippi again, then back again to New Orleans, and so on, finally settling down in 1929 in Oxford when he married Estelle Oldham and the next year purchased Rowan Oak. But the pattern of departure and return continued as a constant, if moderated, habit in the following years and even decades, with Faulkner based in Oxford, but working for shorter or longer stints in Hollywood, traveling to New York, Europe, and so on. Yet despite the bodily peregrinations, mentally Faulkner was, beginning in 1929, dwelling more and more in Oxford, or rather the fictive Jefferson, which had become by 1929, in *Sartoris*, his steadily explored imaginative base. What is interesting is that Faulkner seems to have settled on a modus vivendi that was the perfect compromise and the expression of his unavoidable ambivalence: he was there and not there. He was in the place, but not of the place. Clearly he had come to realize that, however much he might feel the urge to leave Oxford, it was the nursery and constant feeding source of his literary imagination.

We might date the sea change in Faulkner, when he would decisively turn to the small town as his fictive world, somewhere around 1925. In that year, during a visit to New Orleans, Faulkner met Sherwood Anderson, who was a catalyst for the writer's movement from the European aestheticism that had earlier attracted him to the homegrown materials of the American Modernist.[9] Fascinated by Faulkner's tales of his family and background, Anderson certified the legitimacy of the South as Faulkner's subject, urging him to root his work in the local (the aesthetic program that William Carlos Williams was likewise championing for American poetry), to use his native materials, "Because one place to start from is just as important as any other." The South, Anderson said, "is America too . . . as little and unknown as it is."[10] Faulkner was reading Joyce's *Ulysses* in the early twenties, and the Irish writer provided yet another model for the combination of the intensely experimental and the intensely local in his extravagant anatomy of Dublin. It was just this amalgam in Faulkner of the powerfully imaginative with the embodied realism of place that Eudora Welty celebrated, in her famous essay on *Place in Fiction*

(1957): "Yoknapatawpha County, so supremely and exclusively and majestically and totally itself, is an everywhere, but only because Faulkner's first concern is for what comes first, Yoknapatawpha, his own created world. I am not sure, as a Mississippian myself, how widely it is realized and appreciated that these works of such marvelous imaginative power can also stand as works of the carefullest and purest representation."[11]

Standing at our own moment in time, in the midst of the exuberant rootlessness of postmodernism, we can see this rootedness in place as a characteristic aspect of American Modernist practice, perhaps even a defining one, yet one that seems on the surface to derive from the regionalism of late nineteenth-century realism. There is, however, a major difference between Modernist localism and Realist regionalism: Realism was interested in the representation of place and the revelation of character in a specific context; place in the nineteenth century was self-contained, the local was generally sealed against the larger national influences; place had the power to define character in high relief, whether we are talking about Twain's Hannibal or Jewett's Dunnet Landing. The distinction of Modernist localism is that it placed the local within the larger currents of national change and the pressures of modernization. Modernist place is, as geographer Stephen Oakes puts it, "the very terrain of modernity's paradoxes and contradictions."[12]

The Faulknerian small town is not simply a site of nostalgia (though there are certainly elements of the remembered past) but rather of modernity's ambiguities; it is the place where local events intersect with larger historic forces; it is the matrix of identity that places the individual subject at the juncture of two currents moving in opposite directions: backward into the past, which is visible as the physical and material embodiment of cultural memory; and forward into the future, as the larger world of mass culture impinges upon the small town life. Entering the discourse of the small town in the late 1920s, Faulkner offered a vision of far greater complexity than either the satirists or the middlebrow idealists. He offered the town of Jefferson as a study in paradox, a place of memory that embodied, in its history and in its shaping power, the contradictions of order and rebellion.

2

The complexity of this vision was not something that came immediately to Faulkner, if we can judge from the early *Soldiers' Pay* (1926), where the author pauses in the narrative to describe the town square of Charlestown, Georgia (not Jefferson, but from the same litter), which, "like numberless

other towns throughout the south, had been built around a circle of teth-
ered horses and mules."

> In the middle of the square was the courthouse—a simple utilitarian edifice
> of brick and sixteen beautiful Ionic columns stained with generations of casual
> tobacco. Elms surrounded the courthouse and beneath these trees, on scarred
> and carved wood benches and chairs the city fathers, progenitors of solid laws
> and solid citizens who believed in Tom Watson and feared only God and drouth,
> in black string ties or the faded brushed gray and bronze meaningless medals
> of the Confederate States of America, no longer having to make any pretense
> toward labor, slept or whittled away the long drowsy days while their juniors of
> all ages, not yet old enough to frankly slumber in public, played checkers, or
> chewed tobacco and talked. (112)

What's interesting about this description is that it seems written in a self-
conscious way that would soon disappear, and for a non-Southern audience. Faulkner writes with an insider's knowledge of the mores and
manners of the townsfolk and with an intimate familiarity with the material
structure of the courthouse square, but he is also writing from the outside, slightly ashamed perhaps, but equally amused at the way the human
presence has stained and carved itself into the material objects (tobacco-
stained columns, scarred wood benches). He is ironic in his observation
of the political culture of this place—the city fathers, "solid citizens who
believed in Tom Watson," who embody the complacency of the privileged,
white townsfolk, supporting the racist, anti-Socialist, anti-Semitic fulmi-
nations of the former Populist leader. Most significantly for an author
who would in the future dwell so richly on the South's past, there is the
dismissive reference to the faded dress and "bronze meaningless medals
of the Confederate States of America." Not that a Southerner might not,
for the amusement of other Southerners, poke fun at the courthouse old-
timers, fixed in the glories of the past, but the passage taken as a whole
is self-consciously distant from the local color, as if written by and for the
outsider.

In his next novel, *Sartoris* (completed in 1927, published in early
1929)—also about the fate of the soldier returning from World War I—
Faulkner moves closer toward acceptance of his materials, beginning to
treat it with some of the complexity it will henceforth always possess. As
he said famously in an interview: "Beginning with *Sartoris*, I discovered
that my own little postage stamp of native soil was worth writing about
and that I would never live long enough to exhaust it, and that by subli-
mating the actual into the apocryphal I would have complete liberty to
use whatever talent I might have to its absolute top. It opened up a gold
mine of other people, so I created a cosmos of my own."[13]

Some of the features of the newly created Jefferson are identical to the town as depicted in *Soldiers' Pay*—there is the courthouse with the monument of the Confederate soldier, "his musket at order arms, shading his carven eyes with his stone hand"—but now Faulkner places the town square within the broader context of the changing and already changed world of mass culture. Approaching the square, Faulkner expands the temporal context, reminding us that "the town proper had been built these hundred years and more ago," but the scene confronting the contemporary eye is of the modern world of commerce and popular culture: "the street became definitely urban presently with garages and small shops with merchants in shirt sleeves, and customers; the picture show with its lobby plastered with life, episodic in colored lithographed mutations" (142–43). The automobile and the airplane are also factors in these changes. Young Bayard, back from the war in Europe having lost his twin brother in an air battle, has "a racing automobile and he spends all his time tearing around the country in it" (143). It is the "snake" in the putative garden of Eden that is Jefferson, and Bayard will, by the end of the book, complete his self-destructive goals by dying while test-flying an airplane.

Against the chaos of modern life that these events represent, Faulkner poses the relative order and sanctity of the town. Class and race are represented in terms of the fixed hierarchies of place (where identity determines where it is permissible to sit, to stand, to walk) as well as the signifying colors of dress. While the "drifting Negroes" and "country people" are wearing the casual colors of World War I dress (khaki and olive drab), the memory of the War between the States is visible as well. "Beneath the porticoes of the courthouse and on benches about the green, the city fathers sat and talked and drowsed, in uniform too, here and there. But it was the gray of Old Jack and Beauregard and Joe Johnston [Stonewall Jackson, General Pierre Gustave Toutant Beauregard, Civil War generals], and they sat in a grave sedateness of minor political sinecures, smoking and spitting, about checkerboards. When the weather was bad they moved inside to the circuit clerk's office" (143).

Faulkner is being satiric, true, but it is a more tolerant satire, written more from an insider's point of view, than was the case in *Soldiers' Pay*. There has been a significant shift in tone, from the sharper cartoon of the earlier book to the more genial realism of the later one. And most importantly, the town has taken on a broader meaning as a symbol of order, stability, and peace, in the context of the recent world war, which Horace Benbow (who had stayed at home) describes to his sister as "an experience that pretty well shook the verities and the humanities" (144). As Horace and Narcissa continue their walk through the town, they leave behind the "shabby small shops" and traverse an older, more spacious neighborhood of shady lawns.

Faulkner writes: "These homes were quite old, in appearance at least, and set well back from the street and its dust, they emanated a gracious and benign peace, steadfast as a windless afternoon in a world without motion or sound. Horace looked about him and drew a long breath. 'Perhaps this is the reason for wars,' he said. 'The meaning of peace'" (144–45). Horace's theory of war—we fight to defend our privileges, to defend our gracious way of life, to defend the order of the world—is one that is spoken out of the chaos of the postwar moment; but in a way it is a theory consistent with the South's rebellion as well—a war fought to "defend our gracious way of life," to protect the status quo of privilege.

The richest, most complex portrayal of the courthouse is in *Requiem for a Nun* (1951). Faulkner had begun *Requiem* in the thirties, but put it aside until around 1950, when he completed it in the form of a play, each of whose three acts was prefaced by a historical prose narrative relating to the founding of Jefferson—"The Courthouse" and "The Jail"—and with a middle narrative ("The Golden Dome") on the statehouse in Jackson, Mississippi. (Faulkner called these introductory prose sections "interludes . . . prefaces, preambles," and he may have had more invested in them than in the relatively tedious drama of Temple, Gavin Stevens, and Nancy, to which they are tangentially related and which I will largely ignore.)[14] Faulkner begins the story by placing the courthouse immediately within a layered temporal context. It is, he tells us, "less old than the town," which had begun as a settlement by virtue of the documents and papers associated with the land, property, slaves, taxes, and so forth. It came into existence by chance events that resulted in the dismantling of the jail by a band of robbers being held there overnight (they literally take down the log wall, piece by piece, and make their escape). Needing a structure to replace that previous building, the settlers construct a courthouse. Before undertaking the telling of that tale, Faulkner briefly catapults us into the present tense—mid-twentieth century, that is—observing parenthetically and with sublime authorial omniscience, "(overnight it would become a town without having been a village; one day in about a hundred years it would wake frantically from its communal slumber into a rash of Rotary and Lions Clubs and Chambers of Commerce and City Beautifuls: a furious beating of hollow drums toward nowhere, but merely to sound louder than the next little human clotting to its north or south or east or west, dubbing itself city as Napoleon dubbed himself emperor and defending the expedient by padding its census rolls)" (4). The effect of these dislocations, the equivalent in temporal perspective of the multiple spatial perspectives of cubism, is to create an irony of comic dissonances, which is how Faulkner writes history.

Besides the historical theme, the other major theme in "The Courthouse" is the relationship of Jefferson, the town, to the larger federal structure, the nation. The connection between town and nation inheres in the mail pouch, which is saddled with a fifteen-pound lock (later used more functionally, though otiosely, to lock the jail), and it is the locking of the mail pouch, Faulkner writes, that is a "gesture of salutation," the linking of the settlement to Washington, and a symbol of "respect without servility, allegiance without abasement to the government which they had helped to found and had accepted with pride but still as free men, still free to withdraw from it at any moment when the two of them found themselves no longer compatible" (Requiem, 11). By the end of that sentence we have unexpectedly but inevitably approached the Civil War.

Though Faulkner gives us that look forward, it is the moment of the building itself that is, for now, even more important, for the act of reconstructing the jail, which is prelude to the building of the courthouse two years later, is an act of bonding, an act of social transformation that changes these individuals responding to a crisis—their jail has been dismantled—and turns them into a community with a name. (Incidentally, Faulkner is not following actual Oxford history here—the jail was built after the courthouse—but this is his story, his Jefferson.) Between the first day and the second, Faulkner tells us, the "same men met on the project before sunrise on the next day, which was already promising to be hot and endless too, but with the rage and the fury absent now, quiet, not grave so much as sobered, a little amazed, diffident, blinking a little perhaps, looking a little aside from one another" as they realize collectively their new identity: "'By God. Jefferson'" (28).

The courthouse itself is built with the aid of a "tame Parisian architect," whose contempt for the townsfolk is complemented by his arrogant regard for his own plans. He teaches them how to mold and lay the brick and he lays out the design of the courthouse and the town, and here again Faulkner makes a leap forward: "'In fifty years you will be trying to change it in the name of what you will call progress. But you will fail'" (34). What the architect gives them is the order of civilization, each building and institution around the square "in its ordered place," and the progression of the town's growth, along the chartered streets, each year pushing back "the wilderness and its denizens" (34). The "order" brought by the courthouse is not simply architectural; it is also moral and political: "protector of the weak, judiciate and curb of the passions and lusts, repository and guardian of the aspirations and the hopes." Faulkner's panegyric to the courthouse, which encompasses the law is, to say the least, an idealistic one; and it grows even more panglossian when he describes the Negro worker's enthusiasm for the construction effort, thrilled that he was "helping to build not only the biggest edifice in the country, but probably the biggest he had ever seen. . . . it must raise all of their hopes and aspirations level with its own aspirant and soaring cupola," allowing them to believe, with humility, that "all men, including themselves, were a little better, purer maybe even, than they had thought, expected, or even needed to be" (37). All of this may be related to the story that is to follow, which centers on Nancy, the African American who worked for Temple, and her seemingly perverse act of killing one of Temple's children in order to prevent the mother from destroying even more of her family than she already has, and of Nancy's willingness to accept the mortal consequences at the hands of the justice system. But it seems also a reflection of the historical moment itself: In 1946 President Truman had created the President's Committee on Civil Rights, whose recommendations the following year would set the agenda for the civil rights challenges of the early fifties: to eliminate segregation in housing, health facilities, interstate transportation, employment, and public accommodations; to make lynching a federal crime; to abolish the poll tax, protect voting rights, and prohibit discrimination in the armed forces and federal government.

If there is indeed an idealism in this encomium to the courthouse, it is balanced by the realism of the conclusion, where Faulkner moves from a description of the emplacement of the eight marble columns, brought by steamboat up the Mississippi River, to the incident in 1861 on the eve of the War between the States. On one of the balconies, Sartoris "would stand in the first Confederate uniform the town had ever seen, while in the Square below the Richmond mustering officer enrolled and swore in the regiment which Sartoris as its colonel would take to Virginia as a part of Bee" (i.e., Confederate General Bee's force at Manassas) (39). The further history of the courthouse is even more embroiled in the war: it is burned in 1863 and although it survives, according to Faulkner, it takes twenty-five years to rebuild. (For the record, the actual Oxford courthouse was more thoroughly destroyed than Faulkner's Jefferson one.) Faulkner needs to have his own courthouse survive because it serves, in its survival, as a symbolic construction, an emblem of heroism and doom: "Because its fate is to stand in the hinterland of America: its doom is its longevity; like a man, its simple age is its own reproach, and after the hundred years, will become unbearable" (41).

But the image Faulkner uses to conclude the courthouse narrative is not one of endurance; it is, instead, a startling image of birth. Pigeons have developed the habit of nesting in the courthouse, Faulkner tells us, and when the bells ring in the belfry, they are jolted into flight, "bursting in one swirling explosion . . . as though, the hour, instead of merely adding one puny infinitesimal more to the long weary increment since Genesis, had shattered the virgin pristine air with the first loud ding-dong of time and doom" (42). It is a brilliant image, offering us two "readings" of the bell's sounding that are simultaneously present: the tolling of the bell adds yet one more hour to the procession of history, and yet it is, contrarily, the *beginning* of time and history. The courthouse, by the end of the first narrative, has become not only the ordering principle of civilization, but the symbol of cosmic order.

3

We can't explore the courthouse in Faulkner without acknowledging the Confederate soldier monument standing before it, not only in Jefferson, but in so many other Southern towns as well. If the courthouse represents the principle of order in Faulkner's universe, the instauration of law in the otherwise barbarous frontier community, the Confederate soldier monument, its complementary asset, might seem to represent the principle of rebellion. But Faulkner's soldier, however literally monolithic it may be as an obelisk, is not of monolithic significance.

Before discussing the Faulkner version of the Confederate soldier, I must provide some background on Civil War monuments generally, which were erected in cemeteries and in towns throughout the South from the late 1860s through the early twentieth century. Two types of monuments were generally constructed: one is the funereal type, featuring grieving figures and texts lamenting the dead; and the other is the monument to the common soldier, where the figure stands high on a pedestal, which is usually decorated with text or flags in relief. There are two monuments of the latter type in Oxford (statues of the common soldier on a pedestal), both of which were erected during the height of the construction of Civil War memorials in the South, from 1900 to 1912, when approximately 190 soldier memorials were put up in towns, according to Gaines M. Foster's tabulations in *Ghosts of the Confederacy*.[15] In the preceding years, from 1865 to 1900, only 41 were erected in town centers. Moreover, when the Oxford monuments were constructed, the soldier type was greatly surpassing in popularity the earlier funereal monuments; given the growing distance from the war, memory of the loss was being transmogrified from grief into something else—perhaps "determination." (From 1900 to 1912 only 37 funereal monuments were built, in comparison to the 190 soldier statues.) It's worth noting as well that the location of the monument had gradually shifted from the late nineteenth-century preference for the cemetery to the town center, especially after the turn of the century, when more than 85 percent were placed in courthouse squares.

What's implicit in this shift is a cultural movement from grieving the loss of the dead and lamenting the lost Rebel cause, to a celebration of the soldier's duty. As opposed to the monument to the individual leader, which was tailored to the hero's story, these so-called common soldier monuments were more conventional, portraying simply the readiness of the soldier to serve: the soldier is posed standing at ease, alert but relaxed, resting his hands on his upstanding rifle. The influential Reverend Moses Drury Hoge, in appealing to donors for funds to construct a Richmond statue, affirmed the inspirational value of the monuments: "Books are occasionally opened," he said, "monuments are seen every day, and the lesson of that lofty figure which is to tower over Libby Hill . . . will be. . .: 'Live nobly; there is a reward for patriotic duty; republics are not ungrateful.'"[16] By the first decade of the twentieth century, "the real war," as Whitman put it, had not only failed to get into the books, it had failed to get into the public sculpture as well; instead, the call to noble sacrifice, a readiness to die for one's country, was the lesson put before the townsfolk of the nation, North and South. Moreover, according to Foster, a good many of these monuments were reproduced en masse and sold by monument companies, hence their not coincidental similarity. Whatever the individual life was valued at during the war, in the aftermath, the rule of the memorial was ultimately "one size fits all." And at least some Southerners saw the common soldier statues as lacking in all passion. Calm and passive, they failed to make "anybody's heart beat faster," a North Carolina editor complained in 1915; they gave no "child a vision of the spirit, heroism and pathos of our Civil War period."[17] "Pathetic" is how William Alexander Percy described them.[18]

Whether or not Faulkner saw the typical common soldier monument as "pathetic," I don't know, but significantly he did order one of a different type for Jefferson, making use of the nearby model on the campus of the University of Mississippi. Refusing the soldier "at ease," Faulkner gives us instead the soldier on watch, shading his eyes, looking out (one presumes) for the enemy. That image of the common soldier statue appears in the early novel, *Soldiers' Pay*, in a section I discussed earlier. After satirizing the townsfolk in the vicinity of the courthouse, Faulkner takes his two characters, the rector and Mr. Saunders, on a stroll through the square: "They passed beneath a stone shaft bearing a Confederate soldier shading his marble eyes forever in eternal rigid vigilance" (112). The conversation between the two continues to flow around this reference to the statue, which reminds us in passing of the price the soldier in the novel has paid for his own vigilance on behalf of his country. But what is noteworthy is the momentary elevation of tone, now dignified and grave, that Faulkner employs to describe the soldier—"shading his marble eyes forever in eternal rigid vigilance"—so different from the satiric tone used to describe the square. It's as if Faulkner is himself paying his respects to the memorial.

But why did he change the pose of the statue? Faulkner of course took other liberties with "fact," in transmuting the Oxford he knew into the Jefferson that he imagined, but this change is especially striking, in moving the pose from the passive to the more active. As he describes the image, it takes on an almost heroic quality—"shading his marble eyes forever in eternal rigid vigilance"—as if to measure the heroism of the World War I pilot against the Civil War prototype of heroic vigilance. And yet a far different description of the statue occurs at the end of *The Sound and the Fury*, published a few years later, in 1929. In this most famous of Faulkner's scenes, the one that concludes the novel, Luster is entertaining Ben by taking him on a surrey ride, behind Queenie: "They approached the square, where the Confederate soldier gazed with empty eyes beneath his marble hand in wind and weather."[19] Seeking to show off his rig and his skills, Luster cuts Queenie with the switch and swings her to the left at the monument. This deviation from the expected order of things is of course completely disruptive to Ben: "For an instant Ben sat in an utter hiatus. Then he bellowed. Bellow on bellow, his voice mounted, with scarce interval for breath. There was more than astonishment in it, it was horror; shock; agony eyeless, tongueless, just sound." Jason is attracted by the uproar in the square, comes running out, bashes Luster, takes Queenie in hand, and corrects the course of the surrey so that it swings to the right of the monument, at which point Ben quiets down. The book concludes: "The broken flower drooped over Ben's fist and his eyes were empty and blue and serene again as cornice and façade flowed smoothly once more from left to right, post and tree, window and doorway and signboard each in its ordered place" (336).

Faulkner is setting up a tension here between the immobility of the Confederate soldier—impassive, unmoving stone, regardless of "wind and weather"—and the fragility of Ben, lacking in equilibrium, exploding into rage and grief, subject to the externalities that control his responses. Nothing could be more different, it would seem, than the revered soldier and the despised idiot. So much is obvious. But the fact that Faulkner has given both the soldier and Ben the same eyes adds another dimension to the scene: the soldier gazes with "empty eyes," while Ben's eyes are "empty and blue and serene." There is, Faulkner implies, an unsuspected kinship here between the soldier and this ruined Compson, innocent victims both, it would seem, of the tragic history of the South.

The last use of the soldier monument that I want to consider is in *Requiem for a Nun* where, in "The Jail" section, Faulkner brings us to the dedication ceremony. In *Requiem*, the Confederate soldier is, above all, an anachronism, tied to the past in the midst of the onrushing modern world, a talisman for the "unvanquished women" who are "irreconcilable" and who "instigated and bought the monument" (206). Faulkner focuses on the unveiling of the monument on Confederate Decoration Day, in 1900. (Again, Faulkner here departs from the actual unveiling dates of the Oxford monuments, half a dozen years later.) At the unveiling, however, there is a surprise: no one involved in the construction of the monument, from sponsors to architect to builders, "had noticed that the marble eyes under the shading marble palm stared not toward the north and the enemy, but toward the south, toward (if anything) his own rear—looking perhaps, the wits said . . . for reinforcements" (206–7). Although the ladies take the statue very seriously, Faulkner allows us to take a more ironic attitude, suggesting that "with the old war thirty-five years past . . . you could even joke about it." In any case, by the time he composed *Requiem for a Nun*, in 1950, the Confederate monument had come to seem emblematic of a misguided nostalgia, celebrating and perpetuating the myth of a heroic past. What begins as tragedy and mourning, we might say, ends as farce.

4

But *Requiem*'s final word on Jefferson is a more complex statement, occupying the final half of "The Jail." Here, Faulkner places his town in the rushing events of the twentieth century, offering an image of the sweeping changes passing through Jefferson, transforming the fabric of its life: the town witnesses such things as macadam roads, gasoline buggies, and screen doors; it sees the advent of neon signs and Pittsburgh plate glass and "the corpse-glare of fluorescent light" (210); it endures the loss of the forest trees that had shaded the courthouse and the coming of "formal synthetic shrubs" (209). Jefferson witnesses the coming of the WPA (in the 1930s), as it endures the displacement of the mule by the machine and the disappearance of "an entire generation of farmers" (211). Absorbing these changes, Jefferson is at peril of losing its identity. Radio airwaves carry the same comedians and vocalists from Los Angeles to New York and everything in-between: "one air, one nation" (210). The erasure of identity in the town even extends to the deathless Lost Cause, which itself devolves into the mock observances of "tiny Confederate battle flags among the thronged Saturday afternoon ramps of football stadia." The passage of time here and its erosion of memory is, of course, Faulkner's preeminent theme. Here, it takes an explicitly historical cast, and a cosmic dimension, as Faulkner places the fate of America within the larger cosmos, with the individual standing amidst the "radar waves from the constellations" bouncing back at him (213). Anticipating the arguments that would lead cultural geographers to lament the growing "geography of nowhere,"

Faulkner sums it up in a phrase: "One nation: no longer anywhere, not even in Yoknapatawpha County."

But Faulkner doesn't rest in this sense of contemporary anomie and rootlessness. There is a remnant of the past that has survived and endured in Jefferson: it's the old jail, "indisputable in authenticity" (214). And he imagines the "old irreconcilables" actually increasing in numbers as the twentieth century progresses, people moving back to Jefferson, treasuring the stories of the jail, and possibly removing the entire wall and window (with its old legend of the girl's name engraved on it and the young man who comes back to marry her) to place it "embalmed and intact into a museum," the image and trace of her individual life preserved in glass like a daguerreotype (219). Jefferson, suffering the onslaught and erosions of modernity, the transformations of our national culture that turns everyplace into a simulacrum of everyplace else, somehow manages to hold onto itself, in Faulkner's quasi-historical discourse, becoming itself a shrine for visitors from outside to come and marvel at this representation of a past long gone but still surviving.

The town itself, which had represented in its founding the establishment of order in the wilderness, comes round, in the twentieth century to represent a kind of stubborn rebellion, to the extent that is possible, against the strong currents of modernity. What we are left with, in Faulkner's evolving representation of Jefferson, is a modernist paean to rootedness, to endurance, a not unfamiliar Faulkner message, one might say, but brought presciently into the postmodern era of flux and impermanence. What is most prescient about this vision is the way Faulkner subjects it to the ironies of post-World War II history as it has emerged, a history of memory, of looking back, of preserving the traces of a more authentic past, in the treasures of the relic, the daguerreotype, the museum artifact, the reenactment. Faulkner's place, the Jefferson of his fiction, is conflated with the idea of community, but a community of difference, of contained opposing forces: courthouse and monument, black and white, male and female, soldier and idiot, order and rebellion. It is the place where individual fate is achieved amidst the larger forces of history and war, the place that is at once a microcosm of the larger nation and also a place away from it, the place of the local as well as the place of the cosmic. Containing these paradoxes, Faulkner's Jefferson is the place of memory in a culture of change.

NOTES

1. William Faulkner, *Requiem for a Nun* (1951; New York: Vintage, 1975), 28–29.
2. See, for example: Dale J. Breaden, "William Faulkner and the Land," *American Quarterly* 10 (Autumn, 1958): 344–57; G. T. Buckley, "Is Oxford the Original of Jefferson

in Faulkner's Novels?" *PMLA* 76 (September 1961): 447–54; Calvin S. Brown, "Faulkner's Geography and Topography," *PMLA* 77 (December 1962): 652–59; Charles S. Aiken, "Faulkner's Yoknapatawpha County: Geographical Fact into Fiction," *Geographical Review* 67 (January 1977): 1–21; Charles S. Aiken, "Faulkner's Yoknapatawpha County: A Place in the American South," *Geographical Review* 69 (July 1979): 331–48;

3. Thorstein Veblen, "The Country Town," from *Absentee Ownership and Business Enterprise in Recent Times*, chapter 7 (1923; *The Portable Veblen* [New York: Viking, 1948]), 407.

4. Philip Freneau, "The American Village," *Poems of Freneau*, ed. Harry Hayden Clark (1929; New York: Hafner, 1960), 214.

5. Henry Seidel Canby, *Saturday Papers: Essays on Literature from the Literary Review* (New York: MacMillan, 1921), 15–22.

6. *Selected Letters of William Faulkner*, ed. Joseph Blotner (New York: Vintage, 1978), 7.

7. William Faulkner, *Soldiers' Pay* (1926; New York: Liveright, 1970), 162.

8. "The Postmaster," *New Yorker* (21 November 1970), 50.

9. See Daniel J. Singal, *William Faulkner: The Making of a Modernist* (Chapel Hill: University of North Carolina Press, 1997), 57–58.

10. William Faulkner, "A Note on Sherwood Anderson, 1953," *Essays, Speeches, and Public Letters*, ed. James B. Meriwether (New York: Random House, 1965), 8.

11. Eudora Welty, *Place in Fiction* (New York: House of Books, 1957), n.p.

12. Stephen Oakes, "Place and the Paradox of Modernity," *Annals of the Association of American Geographers* 87 (1997): 510.

13. *Lion in the Garden: Interviews with William Faulkner, 1926–1962*, ed. James B. Meriwether and Michael Millgate (New York: Random House, 1968), 255.

14. On the question of why he chose to tell the story with this structure, Faulkner said "that the story of those people fell into the hard simple give-and-take of dialogue. The longer—I don't know what you would call those interludes, the prefaces, preambles, whatever they are—was necessary to give it the contrapuntal effect which comes in orchestration, that the hard give-and-take of the dialogue was played against something that was a little mystical, made it sharper, more effective, in my opinion" (6 May 1957). *Faulkner in the University: Class Conferences at the University of Virginia, 1957–1958* (New York: Vintage, 1965), 122.

15. See Gaines M. Foster, *Ghosts of the Confederacy: Defeat, the Lost Cause, and the Emergence of the New South, 1865–1913* (New York: Oxford, 1987), Appendix 1.

16. Hoge, Peyton H. *Moses Drury Hoge: Life and Letters* (Richmond, Va.: Presbyterian Committee of Publication, 1899), 460–61. Quoted in Foster, 129.

17. Clarence Poe to Benjamin Sledd, 21 September 1915, Clarence Poe Papers. Quoted in Foster, 129.

18. William A. Percy, *Lanterns on the Levee: Recollections of a Planter's Son* (New York: Alfred A. Knopf, 1941), 11–12. Quoted in Foster, 129.

19. William Faulkner, *The Sound and the Fury* (1929; New York: Modern Library, 1946), 335.

Faulkner, Photography, and a Regional Ethics of Form

Katherine R. Henninger

It (the talking, the telling) seemed (to him, to Quentin) to partake of that logic- and reason-flouting quality of a dream which the sleeper knows must have occurred, stillborn and complete, in a second, yet the very quality upon which it must depend to move the dreamer (verisimilitude) to credulity—horror or pleasure or amazement—depends as completely upon a formal recognition and acceptance of elapsed and yet-elapsing time as music or a printed tale.

—William Faulkner, Absalom, Absalom!

There is no link that could move from the visible to the statement, or from the statement to the visible. But there is a continual relinking which takes place over the irrational break or crack.

—Gilles Deleuze, Foucault

Picture the South. There's a good chance the image that comes to mind, especially, perhaps, if you're not from the South, is an image based on a photograph. No one, Southern or not, will deny the ubiquity of photographs in American culture or their power in shaping our notions of the subjects they depict. What exactly is the source of this power? Is it the material photograph, a piece of paper with light waves recorded upon it, a potentially permanent record of "reality," not only of a place but of a specific moment in time? Or is it our cultural ideas about what photographs are, what we believe they tell us about ourselves and the world, our desires and our fears about truth and time? And what, if anything, does region have to do with it? It makes very little material difference if a photograph is made in Oxford, Mississippi, or Fargo, North Dakota: generally, the same papers, chemicals, and cameras have been used all over the country. Beyond obvious issues of content—Fargo's photographs will be a lot snowier—does the culture wherein a photograph is made make a difference in its meaning?

I will argue in this essay that it does, using an unlikely source—William Faulkner's fiction—to show some of the ways how. As Kenneth Haltman reminds us, "Material culture begins with a world of objects, but takes place in a world of words."[1] For material culture critics like Jules Prown, who believe that objects have their own language, it is a long-troubling fact that "it is necessary to convert vision into words, to say what you see, even if only to yourself, in order to actually see it."[2] For Faulkner, that fact is not troubling at all—as a novelist, it is his stock in trade. There are no actual, material photographs in Faulkner's works, but there are plenty of fictional photographs: that is, photographs represented in writing.[3] As distinguished from actual photographs, fictional photographs separate the physical object we know as a photograph from its cultural photographic effects, and reembody these effects in a new object, the printed word. Oddly, eliminating the primary material aspect of the photographic image may make the cultural dynamics of material and visual representation more visible. These dynamics, as portrayed in literature by William Faulkner, are the subject of my analysis.

In part, what I'll be discussing is an abstract debate about form: What does it mean to change a photograph into words? What does it mean to change spoken words into print? Formal debates are never "just" abstract questions of essence or knowledge (matters of epistemology), but central questions about how human beings can and do encounter each other (matters of ethics). In short, they are questions about the ethics of form. What forms best represent a people or a culture like the South, and who decides this and why? How does the choice of one form over another reflect wider cultural beliefs, or battles, about what or who should be represented as a legitimate part of that culture? As we shall see, for Faulkner, issues of representational form—especially the choice between visual or oral expression—are integrally tied to these issues of representational politics. Formal ethics are always created in and through larger cultural trajectories of desire and power.

The notion that visual and oral forms are in strict dichotomy is a false one. As W. J. T. Mitchell has succinctly put it: "all media are mixed media, and all representations are heterogeneous; there are no 'purely' visual or verbal arts."[4] Far from a natural or inevitable division, the formal split between the oral and aural on one hand, and the visual on the other, is ideological, ethical, and political. Distinguishing one form from others, drawing and policing the borders between them, is a cultural matter. Formal division often stands in for greater cultural tensions and the cultural desire for borders: between space and time, object and action, artifact and history, for example—or between groups of people.

This is clear in the South. Faulkner was a writer of visualized, printed words in a Southern culture that was deeply ambivalent about literature and, to some extent, about visual representation in general. History and circumstance (and, I will argue, politics) had prompted the South to proclaim itself "truly an oral society."[5] For Southerners and Southernists, the "great oral tradition" of the South regularly holds the status of a historical given, noted in activities ranging from sermonizing to mule trading, quilting-bee gossip to oration, gospel singing to lynch-mob baiting, dialect writing to singing the blues. The South's oral traditions are, a vast critical and historical corpus would have it, a cornerstone of Southernness itself. Even in light of such a rich and varied oral heritage, however, why make the critical leap of labeling the South "truly an oral culture"? Would it not be equally appropriate to proclaim the South "truly a visual culture"? In a culture where visual signs—the shape of a lip, a skin's shade, external sex characteristics, the carriage of one's body, the condition of one's clothing—determine "place" (and may literally mean the difference between life and death), surely the visual may be said to reign supreme. Are there particular interests at stake in maintaining a certain distance between representational forms, and privileging one over the other?

In the South, formal divisions are intimately intertwined in the constructions of gender, race, and class distinction so crucial to, and contested within, Southern identities. I believe that the tensions between oral and visual representation embodied in Faulkner's work originated in the competing desires of white and black Southerners, and their Northern counterparts, to construct and preserve "Southern identity" and "the South" in the form of strategic, nationalist narratives. Benedict Anderson has famously defined "nations" as imagined political communities that are imagined in terms not only of what or whom the community includes, but also what or whom it does not.[6] In the South, visual signs—often maddeningly ambiguous ones—were meant to signify the material "reality" of the racial, class, and gender differences that determined one's place in the community. For different reasons, both black and white Southerners stood in uneasy relation to this visual ambiguity. In part to counter this unease, oral traditions came to figure prominently in emerging concepts of Southern communal identity, though they performed different strategic functions for white and black Southerners.[7]

The briefest of examples will have to suffice here. Constructing and defending their difference from Northern cultures, and especially against attacks like H. L. Mencken's castigation of the South in 1917 as "The Sahara of the Bozart," white Southerners fell back, as it were, on their strengths: an organic, agrarian culture and an oral tradition that could be traced to ancient English roots and that culminated in the high art form of political oration.[8] Agrarians John Crowe Ransom and Donald Davidson defended Southern artistic traditions against Northern standards, highlighting oral folk expressions and political oratory as examples of organic, antimaterial art practice.[9] The strategic significance of African American oral traditions is also understandable in terms of resistance to competing white Southern narratives, which visualized "Negroes" into an ironically invisible and silent social "place." Frederick Douglass's account of slave song is an early revelation of the subversive, unifying power of African American oral expression: the singing is misidentified by whites as evidence of contentment, but to Douglass's ear it conveys a "testimony against slavery, and a prayer to God for deliverance from chains."[10] Tracing these soundings from ancestral African roots adds a powerful, nationalist cast to black Southern orality, defining an incipient black Southern national identity not only as a response to white oppression, but as the call to origins and claim to continuity that Anderson posits as essential to national imagining.

In the contexts of this Southern privileging of the oral, and of Faulkner's avowed interests in matters of form and cultural politics, it is not surprising that Faulkner's literary works manifest tensions between orality and printed/literary text, between the oral and the visual, between image and word. In interviews, Faulkner expresses his desire to capture oral cultures in a visual-literary form as a strategy to perpetuate life itself: by embodying the ebb and flow of life in a still object—the printed word on a page—there was the possibility that a reader would come along and put those words back into motion, back into life. Faulkner's representational techniques—his use of imagery, metaphor, language, and tone—engage a formal tension between powerful Southern oral traditions and his own writerly project: a tension that constructs and challenges notions of Southernness itself. Embodying an image/text/oral nexus, fictional photographs figure these tensions in Faulkner's work, in ways that query not only material "representations of reality," but also the Southern cultural "realities"—dynamics, tensions, anxieties, and rewards—of representation, including the ethics of formal division and formal choice. At times in conjunction with and at others in opposition to (represented) orality and aurality, fictional photographs appear as complex figures of what I call "cultured vision"—gendered, racialized, strategic viewing. Performing so, they enact an ethical encounter of claim and acknowledgment that models the productive encounter of reader and text.

I propose briefly now to examine photography in Faulkner's literary texts to show not only how Southern contexts shape Faulkner's treatment of image/text/oral tensions, but also how notions of Southernness are in turn constructed and challenged through literary debates over representational form. My purpose is to demonstrate how Faulkner's use of fictional photographs to highlight and negotiate these tensions is informed by a specifically Southern version of formal ethics, a version at the heart of the construction of the South itself.

Faulkner's fascination with photography is well documented. Beginning at least as early as 1918, Faulkner staged or commissioned photographs of himself in various poses: sometimes, as in the 1918 photographs of himself as a wounded "war hero" in the Royal Canadian Air Force, with an obvious intent to stretch the truth; other times, as in the numerous personal and publicity portraits taken by his hometown photographer, Colonel J. R. Cofield, with an apparent, but entirely conventional, desire to control his own public image.[11] As his fame grew, numerous "outside" photographers sought Faulkner's image: he posed for some, including, famously, Henri Cartier-Bresson, yet in time Faulkner seems to have become increasingly reticent about having his photograph made (Rankin 294, 309–12, 315). The desire to obtain photographs of famous people (some would say the desire to photograph at all) and the interest scholars have shown in Faulkner's images point to epistemological matters: The photograph is a document, a piece of evidence, a way to knowledge about its subject. Once we know from other, more reliable sources that Faulkner never even flew in the Royal Air Force, the epistemological quandaries deepen; we are reminded (again) of the power of the camera to lie, and the photograph then becomes a metaphor for the ambivalent status of knowledge in the modern (and postmodern) world. But Faulkner's use of real photography and his use of fictional photographs tend to lead us away from epistemology and toward ethics. What is evidenced in the multiple images of "Count No 'Count" seems less the manipulation of truth or knowledge (though there is that), than the important role of the visual in constructing identity, in the ability to take on or assign different roles, and in comic yet serious, potentially subversive play. Crucially, vision and the visual are constructed in and by their social, political, cultural context, in an encounter between two (and what can feel like three) performing subjects—an author/shower and a reader/viewer and a mediating photograph—where recognition and acknowledgment are key to the creation, perpetuation, and revision of the cultural codes, or scripts, that constitute the subjects themselves. In other words, here we glimpse the role of vision in (re)creating identity, in perpetuating life.

Significantly, when Faulkner formulated his own artistic struggle with the forces of time and space, mortality and immortality, he chose a visual metaphor: "The aim of every artist is to arrest motion, which is life, by artificial means and hold it fixed so that 100 years later when a stranger looks at it, it moves again since it is life. Since man is mortal, the only immortality possible for him is to leave something behind him that is important, since it will always move."[12] This famous statement is usually noted for its compelling first clause, useful for explicating the multiple strategies Faulkner uses for arresting motion, the numerous moments in his text where time seems frozen, fixed, suspended, "like something moving forever and without progress across an urn."[13] These crystalline moments—the view of Caddy's muddy drawers in the tree in *The Sound and the Fury*, Popeye and Horace Benbow's prolonged staring across the stream in *Sanctuary*, the "yellow slashes of mote-palpitant sunlight" that refuse to move higher on the wall as Rosa tells her story in *Absalom, Absalom!*—might be described as photographic, especially in the modernist sense: carefully composed, static surfaces, snatched from time, from a singular perspective, emphasizing relations between angle, light, and surface.[14] Some seem intentionally to echo the photographic images of the South made by Farm Security Administration documentarians in the thirties, like this passage from "Old Man": "the convicts sat in a line along the edge of the platform like buzzards on a fence, their shackled feet dangling above the brown motionless flood out of which the railroad embankment rose, pristine and intact, in a kind of paradoxical denial and repudiation of change and portent, not talking, just looking quietly across the track to where the other half of the amputated town seemed to float, house shrub and tree, ordered and pageant-like and without motion, upon the limitless liquid plain beneath the thick gray sky."[15]

Indeed, there are ample instances in Faulkner's works of fictional pictures, especially portraits, as metaphors for stasis. As she attempts to convert Joe Christmas in *Light in August*, Joanna Burden's "calm profile in the peaceful firelight was as grave and tranquil as a portrait in a frame" (268–69), and only twenty pages later, the townspeople look down at Joanna's murdered body, "with that static and childlike amaze with which adults contemplate their own inescapable portraits" (288). The Reverend Gail Hightower is so ensconced in past images he has become "disassociated from mechanical time" (366); after losing his church, he becomes an art teacher and photo processor, developing other people's frozen moments. This imagery suggests that stopping motion, or time, is a mode of description, a way of representing, and perhaps containing, the temporal world. It suggests a dynamic that lends itself to epistemological configurations of subject/object relations. As Gary Stonum has asserted, "The question of arrest turns in part on the relation of subject to object. Arresting is the means by which the subject represents the object, that is, the world in motion, to himself."[16] It is a dynamic often ascribed to vision itself, often in ethical terms of mastery or domination, as in the case of the objectifying male gaze or the colonizing racist gaze, and also to the photograph, in equally ambivalent terms. Susan Sontag, for instance, is famously critical of the "perennial successes of photography . . . [in] its strategy of turning living beings into things" (98) and fragmenting history and narrative.[17]

But Faulkner's statement has an equally compelling second clause, the crucial turn in the sentence: "when a stranger looks at it, it moves again since it is life." This clause emphasizes the interactive role of the stranger/viewer in bringing the arrested motion—which itself seems to have an agency that "is life"—back into time and motion. In this context it is especially interesting that photographic metaphors in Faulkner's work more often figure becomings, process, and irresolution, than stasis and resolution. Joe Christmas watches his own naked body in the light from an approaching car, "grow white out of the darkness like a kodak print emerging from the liquid" (*LIA* 108).[18] Little Belle's photographed face seems "to swoon in a voluptuous languor, blurring still more, fading, leaving upon [Horace Benbow's] eye a soft and fading aftermath of invitation and voluptuous promise" (*Sanctuary* 234). And Quentin's early attempt to envision and contain Rosa's narrative of the Sutpen family as a conventional photograph, "with formal and lifeless decorum . . . [seen] as the fading and ancient photograph itself would have been seen enlarged and hung on the wall" founders because of its "quality strange, contradictory and bizarre; not quite comprehensible, not (even to twenty) quite right" (*AA* 9). Quentin's mental gesture epitomizes a narrative, thematic precept in *Absalom, Absalom!*, operative as well in *Light in August* and *Sanctuary*: attempts to know, or figure, the truth are frustrated, utterly contingent, and ultimately not the point. Our best technologies for, as Sutpen describes it, "fixing things right," such as photography—or the "technologies" of race, gender, and class[19]—explode upon us, proliferating, rather than containing, meaning, knowledge, and desire. In Faulkner's work, we are led away from what Judith Sensibar has called "the epistemologically dazzling vista" of the fictional photograph (295), to its equally complex role in the ethical play of recognition and acknowledgment.

The most compact illustration of Faulkner's use of fictional photographs to model the move from epistemology to ethics is the creased and dog-eared magazine photo, perhaps of Caddy Compson, in the appendix Faulkner added to *The Sound and the Fury* in 1946. In an interview at the University of Virginia, Faulkner portrayed the origin of *The Sound and the Fury* as "the picture of the little girl's muddy drawers, climbing that tree to look in the parlor window with her brothers that didn't have the courage to climb the tree waiting to see what she saw."[20] Nearly twenty years after its original publication, after spending some time in Hollywood, Faulkner returned to *The Sound and the Fury* and reenvisioned Caddy, this time in a fictional photograph discovered by Jefferson's librarian, Melissa Meek, in a "slick magazine" (*SF* 415). This photograph, described in greater detail than any other in Faulkner's published work, is "a picture filled with luxury and money and sunlight—a Cannebiere backdrop of mountains and palms and cypresses and the sea, an open powerful chromiumtrimmed sports car, the woman's face hatless between a rich scarf and a seal coat, ageless and beautiful, cold serene and damned; beside her a handsome lean man of middle-age in the ribbons and tabs of a German staffgeneral" (415).

"Aghast at her own temerity," Melissa Meek takes the photograph first to Caddy's brother, Jason, and then to the Compson's nearly blind former mammy, Dilsey, seeking recognition: first of the image as Caddy's and, second, of the need and responsibility to "save" Caddy from her pictured fate. Jason capitulates, first claiming the photo is of Caddy, then denying it derisively; Dilsey declines even to look, saying her eyes are no longer "good," that she "can't see it" (418). Critical discussions of this photograph have centered, as does Melissa Meek, on the question of whether the photograph actually is of Caddy, and the implications of the determination either way. For Thadious Davis, accepting Melissa Meek's conclusion that it *is* Caddy and that Dilsey *"didn't want to see it know whether it was Caddy or not because she knows Caddy doesn't want to be saved hasn't anything anymore worth being saved for nothing worth being lost that she can lose"* (*SF* 419–20, emphasis original), means recognizing Caddy as the "central, othered presence" inscribed under a male gaze, a symbol of Faulkner's "latent sense of the moral corruption of Southern white women."[21] Patricia Angley finds in Dilsey's refusal to look a refusal to "fix Caddy in her gaze."[22] She argues that, by leaving open the possibility that it is *not* Caddy in the photograph, Faulkner undercuts the authority of his own apparent judgment, enabling Caddy to "[dance] past him" and resist closure in the text (184). Like Susan Donaldson and Minrose Gwin, Angley sees in the elisions and gaps of Caddy's silence (and invisibility) a kind of space-between, a "form of speaking against the language of southern culture" (179).[23]

But of course, as readers we can never know the true subject of the photograph: we cannot see the photograph beyond its textual description (and even if we could, who among us could "recognize" Caddy in the traditional sense?). Faulkner brings us a fictional photo, which Melissa Meek is desperate to have serve as "evidence," and even "shows" it to us through ekphrasic description, only to shift the terms of engagement. Finally, it matters less that Caddy is in the photo than that we consider the conditions where Caddy could actually be seen (acknowledged, accommodated) and what such acknowledgment would mean, for her, for Jason, the librarian, Dilsey, the South—and for us. These conditions and their implications are clearly ideological and political. In the last lines of the "Candace (Caddy)" section of the appendix, Faulkner startlingly links the metaphoric looking at the photograph with the metaphoric reading of a book: Melissa Meek is on a train returning to Jefferson, where "life lived too with all its incomprehensible passion and turmoil and grief and fury and despair, but here at six oclock you could close the covers on it and even the weightless hand of a child could put it back among its unfea-tured kindred on the quiet eternal shelves and turn the key upon it for the whole and dreamless night" (419). "Too," like the photograph, the written story of *The Sound and the Fury* "is life," "but here," contained in the cir-cle of cultural (un)acknowledgment, and perhaps *unlike* the still radically uncontained photograph, it can be set aside. By suggesting that the photo-graph (and by association, Caddy) may continue to exist outside Jefferson's acknowledgment, and by simultaneously invoking the power of even the lightest of reader's hands, Faulkner rhetorically inscribes both the threat of unacknowledgment (death) and the hope for defiance of that death that is in the hands of his own present reader. Readings such as Angley's open up interesting possibilities for Caddy's freedom outside the acknowledg-ment by her own Southern culture; these possibilities are contingent on the reader's acknowledgment of Caddy's claim as a character outside the frame of the novel, but inside the reader's frame of experience. The power of the metaphoric photograph in this passage is to evoke the old rhetorics of true evidence and knowledge, in order to frustrate them by revealing their ideological, political bases. Seen this way, "Caddy's" photograph does not refuse its representative function; rather, what it comes to represent is the ethical frame around the contingency and process of representation.

Faulkner's epic novel, *Absalom, Absalom!*, takes the contingency and process of representation as its central subject. Once again, criticism of this novel has classically focused on epistemological questions of true knowl-edge and/or the impossibility of such, of the slippery and elusive nature of representing the real.[24] I want to argue instead that *Absalom, Absalom!* prefigures the move from epistemology to ethics that Faulkner illustrates in his 1946 appendix to *The Sound and the Fury*. In formulating my argu-ment, I agree with Warwick Wadlington, who asserts that "the question of knowledge is a subset, an included issue" of the novel's central con-cerns with catharsis, spoken voice, immortality, and accommodation (173), and with Philip Weinstein, whose reading of the novel ultimately makes sense within "the frame of a giving and taking whose mutual name is acknowledgment."[25] *Absalom, Absalom!* relays its central concern—the crucial human need for acknowledgment across and beyond cultural divi-sions of race, class, and gender: the "no" to death—in a narrative structured around formal tensions between oral representation, with its associations with temporality and life flow, and visual representation, associated with spatiality and the artifacts of history. In a novel all about "strategies of composition,"[26] formal ethics take center stage. In portraying a powerful Southern voice (so powerful that even the Canadian Shreve is drawn to speak it) in a written, spatial form, Faulkner confronts a formal division constitutive of Southern identity, a division that threatens his own writerly project of "arresting motion" to perpetuate life itself. The tensions surrounding this division are figured in *Absalom, Absalom!* in a series of fictional photographs that reveal the interconnections of representational form and representational politics in the South. These photographs come to embody Faulkner's own strategy of composition, a strategy that attempts simultaneously to challenge the essentializing tendencies of Southern identity narratives, and to make room for Faulkner's artistic project.

Much has been written on the tensions between orality, the written text, and visuality in *Absalom, Absalom!* Most notably, Stephen Ross has focused on Faulkner's use of the Southern oratorical voice as a strategy for "overcoming the silence that threatens all writing."[27] The ornate, voluble style of narrative voices in *Absalom* is derived from a specifically Southern tradition of oratory concerned to overpower any doubt of the speaker's authority with "sheer prolixity" (Ross 197) and to erect a monument to its own endeavor (to evoke community or the past), safe from the passing exigencies of speech. This oratorical voice, according to Ross, is the mode by which "written fiction comes to be invested simultaneously with the vigor of performance and the structured permanence of monument, as the time bound process of storytelling is paradoxically brought to the service of eliminating temporality and process" (236). Taking a different tack, Wadlington finds in Sutpen's monumental oratorical style the epitome of his tragic error: reducing dialogue to monologue. Seeking in monologue an invulnerable, autonomous Voice, Sutpen devastatingly silences the reciprocal vocal performance that constitutes human subjects: the novel thus "dramatizes not so much the failure to know others as the failure to acknowledge and accommodate others adequately" (218). To Wadlington, *Absalom*'s tensions are not those of an inscribed, print medium's inadequacy in conflict with a culture's oral base. Rather, the novel invokes the conventions of *trans*cription that can accommodate Southern voice and thus "can offer itself to the reader as an occasion for consummating performance" (210). Tensions arise from the possibility that the text (or, potentially, the reader) will not fulfill the expectation, implicit in the South's honor-shame culture, to fill in or embellish the silences left by what the culture cannot say.

Both discussions are useful for understanding the nation-building function of the constructed tension between orality, textuality, and visuality in the South, and in Faulkner's novel. Thomas Sutpen's overly wrought, "bookish" speech (the very "set of his shoulders forensic, oratorical" [221]) reflects the determination with which white Southern nationalists attempted to cement the authority of their version of Southern identity, in relation to their white Southern audiences. Quentin and Shreve's "happy marriage of speaking and hearing" (253), Rosa Coldfield's furious insistence on telling her story to Quentin, Mr. Compson's variation on that same tale—all partake in conventions of embellishment and amplification central to Southern oral traditions. These traditions, *Absalom* seems to posit, are essential to Southern identity itself. Yet as the novel so persistently demonstrates, this Southern orality, or voice, is integrally connected to Southern visions, especially the tragic visualizations of race, gender, and class inherent in white Southern identity. In conjunction with, and sometimes in opposition to, Southern orality, Faulkner's novel presents an equally cultured vision: a gendered, racialized, strategic mode of viewing that in *Absalom, Absalom!* erupts from its place as the silent other in the white South's constructions of itself. In a novel full of photographic "instants," "flashes," and "exposures," this eruption ironically takes place in the form of an encounter, a repeated scene of potential recognition and acknowledgment that mirrors the thematic struggles of the tragic subjects in Faulkner's novel. Taking advantage of their culturally endowed ability to configure space and time, visual and verbal, seer and seen, Faulkner configures fictional photographs as the site where the Southern oral and visual traditions meet and recognize, or misrecognize, each other.

Parsing this encounter thoroughly would take more space than available here. My readings, of necessity, will be comparatively brief and incomplete. It will be "probably true enough" (as *Absalom*'s narrator concedes on page 268) to begin, as does the novel, with Rosa Coldfield who, in relation to the Compsons and to Shreve, embodies gendered seeing in the South. Having summoned twenty-year-old Quentin Compson to hear her story of Thomas Sutpen and to assist her in investigating the old Sutpen mansion, sixty-three-year-old Rosa is introduced as sitting on a too-tall chair, resembling, as seen through Quentin's eyes, a "crucified child," whose feet dangle above the floor "with that air of impotent and static rage like children's feet" (4, 3). Rosa is further infantilized, and stilled, by her male observers throughout the book: she is a "little girl of the dead time" (14), whose "lonely thwarted old female flesh" (9) has coalesced in the form of a "mechanical doll" with a "fixed sleep-walking face" (297). Quentin's father's voice briefly interrupts Quentin's listening to Rosa's story, to explain Rosa's position within Southern society: "Years ago we in the South made our women into ladies. Then the War came and made the ladies into ghosts. So what else can we do, being gentlemen, but listen to them being ghosts?" (7–8). Like his father, Quentin misreads Rosa—as is foreshadowed by his inability to recognize Rosa's handwriting as "cold, implacable, and even ruthless" (6), and as he himself realizes in the final pages of the novel—mistaking her trembling eagerness to reach the mansion for terror or alarm (291). Rosa, as Judith Sensibar and others have argued, is an artist figure, engaged in telling her own story and, through Quentin, "publishing" it to a broader audience. She may be a town joke, the subject of jumprope rhymes, but, as Shreve finally reminds Quentin, "she refused at the last to be a ghost" (289). Yet, however hard (or ambivalently) she works to subvert her own image,[28] Rosa's status as Southern female ensures that her voice will be positioned within traditional (patriarchal) visualizations of Southern white women.

The most telling encounter between Rosa's (positioned) voice and her own (embodied) cultured vision takes place as she narrates her adolescent love for Charles Bon, the intended (by Judith's mother) fiancé of Rosa's niece, Judith Sutpen. To support her repeated denials that she loved Bon, Rosa uses terms that could equally inscribe Faulkner's relation to the narrated past of the story: "I never saw him. I never even saw him dead. I heard a name, I saw a photograph, I helped make a grave: and that was all" (117). The photograph Rosa sees of Bon, which is mentioned only by Rosa and apparently does not survive elsewhere, is framed in the tensions between envisioned cultural desire and the self-consciousness of a speaking artist: "I dont know even now if I was ever aware that I had seen nothing of his face but that photograph, that shadow, that picture in a young girl's bedroom: a picture casual and framed upon a littered dressing table yet bowered and dressed (or so I thought) with all the maiden and invisible lily-roses, because even before I saw the photograph I could have recognised, nay described, the very face. . . . so who will dispute me when I say, Why did I not invent, create it?—And I know this: if I were God I would invent out of this seething turmoil we call progress something (a machine perhaps) which would adorn the barren mirror altars of every plain girl who breathes with such as this—which is so little since we want so little—this pictured face" (118). Here Rosa, in a more obvious way than Quentin's initial attempt to "photograph" the Sutpens, introduces the rhetoric of cultural desire that surrounds and is embodied in the fictional photographs throughout *Absalom, Absalom!* The camera has provided the only literal trace of Charles Bon except his gravestone, yet Rosa raises the possibility that this trace, the photograph, is immaterial: what matters is her vision and, most importantly, the vision of her culture. The machine Rosa would invent is not the camera; it is something that would encode and embody even more perfectly the abstract image of cultural desire. Judith Sensibar has compellingly argued that Rosa is an "expert at reading photographs of desire," because her gaze, unlike the objectifying gaze of Horace Benbow in *Sanctuary*, is self-conscious; Sensibar attributes to Rosa a desire to abstract and analyze her own motivated gaze that "questions all the premises upon which such objectification is based" (309).

Nonetheless, Rosa as a character is limited in what she can see, or analyze, by the constraints of that same cultural desire. As Rosa admits, she loved Bon before she saw him, loved the imaged idea of him such that it was hardly necessary for his actual body to exist.[29] If the "maiden and invisible lily-roses" have disappeared from Rosa's vision in the wake of her actual, brutal experience with Thomas Sutpen (who proposes to Rosa that she have a child and, if it is a boy, *then* he will marry her), Rosa's mature vision, evidenced in her final interactions with Quentin and Clytie, seems finally to leave abstracted images of gender and, especially racial, Southern identities in place.

The character that most fully embodies the inherent ambiguities of these desired raced and gendered identities is of course Charles Bon, who is represented both as the abstract image of Southern masculinity and as slightly feminine, "even catlike" (76); who may or not be Charles Sutpen's son; and who may or may not have part "black blood." But the site where these structures and ambiguities meet most forcefully is in a fictional photograph that Faulkner leaves even more radically undeterminable than Rosa's image of Bon. This photograph is narrated in different forms by Rosa, Mr. Compson, Quentin, and Shreve: in Rosa's version, it is unproblematically a photograph of Judith, enclosed in a metal case, which Judith has given Charles Bon and which Judith retrieves from Bon's newly dead body. For the three male narrators, the photograph is actually two: the one given by Judith, and the other of Bon's octoroon wife and their child. With the exception of Rosa, who claims to have seen Judith holding the photograph (in its metal case) "casual and forgotten against her flank as any interrupted pastime book" (114), the photograph is unseen by any of the narrators. Yet in "telling" the photograph(s), each male narrator embodies his own cultured vision in the image the metal case contains. For Mr. Compson, the photograph of the octoroon and child is the crucial evidence of bigamy and miscegenation which, upon finding it on Bon's dead body, prompts Judith to destroy his letters, save the one she passes on to Quentin's grandmother. For Quentin and Shreve, the two photographs, inexorably making their way to Charles Bon, are pawns, strategic distractions from the greater drama of patriarchal unacknowledgment, potential incest, and miscegenist defilement they envision enacted between Sutpen, Henry, Bon, and, almost incidentally, Judith. In this story, the photograph of Bon's octoroon wife and their son stands in for, or replaces, Bon's own racial impurity: Bon, as Shreve channels his voice, places the photograph in Judith's metal case to communicate his own unworthiness to her, to say "*I was no good; do not grieve for me*" (287).

Significantly, this most potent image of envisioned race is never "seen." Faulkner's choice here is in stark contrast to one of the original versions of *Absalom, Absalom!*, the unpublished 1931 short story "Evangeline." In that story, the photograph in its metal case plays a more straightforward role as the final, all-revealing piece of evidence. Judith and Bon exchange tokens before marriage: Bon gives Judith an engagement ring and takes with him to New Orleans "Judith's picture in a metal case that closed like a book and locked with a key."[30] Judith and Bon successfully marry in "Evangeline"—after Bon and Henry meet to overcome Henry's mysterious objections, one hour before both men leave for the Civil War. The reason for Henry's objection to the marriage is revealed by an ancient Negro woman (a storytelling prototype of Clytie) not to be Bon's first, still-living wife, but something worse, that can't be spoken. This unspeakable sin is revealed, definitively, by the locket photograph, to which, following Bon's death, Judith takes a poker to beat permanently shut. After the Sutpen mansion burns down, the story's narrator/protagonist (an obnoxious prototype of Shreve) uses an axe to pry open the lock, revealing the intact picture: "the smooth, oval, unblemished face, the mouth rich, full, a little loose, the hot, slumberous, secretive eyes, the inklike hair with its faint but unmistakable wiriness—all the ineradicable and tragic stamp of negro blood" (608). To the narrator, this "doomed and passionate face" is definitive evidence of "what to a Henry Sutpen born, created by long time, with what he was and what he believed and thought, would be worse than the marriage and which compounded the bigamy to where the pistol was not only justified, but inescapable" (609).

While "Evangeline" turns on a simple mystery, solved by an unproblematic photographic "truth," *Absalom*'s use of fictional photographs marks a shift from epistemology to ethics that may model a productive encounter between visual and oral forms, and between reader and text. The photograph's frustrating status in *Absalom* as evidence/not-evidence seems designed to mirror the frustrations of the various narrators as they create their versions of the Sutpen saga, a process Faulkner ties (through Mr. Compson) to the alchemic process of reading: "There [the Sutpens] are, yet something is missing; they are like a chemical formula exhumed along with the letters from that forgotten chest, carefully, the paper old and faded and falling to pieces, the writing faded, almost indecipherable, yet meaningful, familiar in shape and sense, the name and presence of volatile and sentient forces: you bring them together in the proportions called for, but nothing happens; you re-read, tedious and intent, poring, making sure that you have forgotten nothing, made no miscalculation; you bring them together again and again nothing happens; just the words, the symbols, the shapes themselves, shadowy inscrutable and serene, against that turgid background of a horrible and bloody mischancing of human affairs" (80). The image of the Sutpen family, the graphic and spatial word on a page, both shaped and static, are in Mr. Compson's narrative a barrier to the viewer/reader's will to know, or re-create, the real. But in Quentin and Shreve's cocreated narrative, these frustrations cede to the more urgent (and even more frustrated) need to effect cultural acknowledgment across static race, gender, and class lines in the South. The tale that Quentin and Shreve weave around the unknowable fictional photograph in the metal case points to Faulkner's greater concern for the integrated narrative and visual basis of that cultural accommodation (or its denial). For if it is clear that Bon is not black until he is "called" black, it is equally clear that being called black affects how Bon can be seen. In the relation of these contingent "truths," Southern notions of racial "essence" are unhinged.

Yet *Absalom, Absalom!* makes painfully clear that this unhinging is a utopian gesture, incomplete and perhaps unachievable in the South of the novel. In Shreve's narrative, the fictional photograph found on Bon's body takes its place in the series of "long tension-building delays, which result in explosions of insight or action which turn out to be, in fact, not culminating but which leave something more to be resolved" that Wadlington has described as part of the reader's "schooling in unfinality and inexhaustibility" (215). Shreve, glaring and encroaching upon Quentin, refutes Mr. Compson's telling of the photo: "And your old man wouldn't know about that too: why the black son of a bitch should have taken her picture out and put the octoroon's picture in, so he invented a reason for it. But I know. And you know too. Dont you? Dont you, huh?" (286). But Shreve's "truth," although it is "probably true enough" within the story that Quentin and Shreve have up until this point built together, and although Quentin does accede to it, is anticlimactic. In a narrative built around "playing" with Bon's racial and patrilineal identity, Shreve's parodically vicious stamping of Bon as a "black son of a bitch" potentially reinscribes as much as it unhinges Southern race ideology. This scene mirrors Thomas Sutpen's epiphanic initiation into class consciousness, where he recognizes that racial division is a "balloon-faced" red herring, that "they (the niggers) were not it, not what you wanted to hit" (186), only to have what arises "like a monument" in the "explosion" and "bright glare" of his analysis be "the severe shape of his intact innocence," rather than new awareness (192). Shreve parodies as well Quentin's own monumental "innocence" and cultural intransigence as he tries to interpret the metaphoric portrait he himself has created. Through this narrative repetition and parodic revision (which may or may not be intentional parody on Shreve's part) the reader is further schooled in pressing borders, and surviving frustrated desire. Whether these survival skills will be enough to unhinge the divisive Southern notions of "essence" that hamper cultural acknowledgment across racial, class, and gender lines is as open a question as Bon's inscrutable metal-encased photograph.

Faulkner's use of fictional photography in *Absalom, Absalom!* illustrates not only that the meaning of a photograph lies in its use, in its narration,[31] but that there is also something important about what is represented, or not represented, by the photograph's inscrutability. The ability of the fictional photograph to represent the seen *and* the unseen may figure, or model, the written text's desire simultaneously to exist in the spatial and temporal realm: to be the "is life" of Faulkner's arrested/reanimated motion equation. Or it may represent the power of what the printed text cannot represent: actual, vocalized speech and actual, unvocalized vision. Both possibilities point to the crucial role of the reader, who is also outside the text—"a stranger [who] looks at it"—who will not only recognize the graphic marks on the page as "arrested motion," but who will acknowledge and assimilate them, perpetuating them in time and life. As Charles Bon discovers, recognition (the ethical basis of "separate but equal" in the South) is not enough; only human acknowledgment effects cultural accommodation.[32] The "politics of inscription" is thus integrally tied to a politics of reception, intimately involved in identity formation and nation-building.[33] Faulkner's artistic desire to "arrest" Southern orality in written form in *Absalom* is an effort to affect cultural memory, both of and within the South, and for outside readers. Claiming, and winning acknowledgment of, the utter contingency of visual and verbal representations alters the formal as well as the political identity of the South, and opens space for Faulkner's literary project. As cultural memory is by definition a collective remembering—a field where individuals interact in complex, highly political negotiations to create cultural meaning—Faulkner must depend on a radically unforeseeable stranger, a reader, to interact with and enact his text. The radically unseen and unseeable fictional photographs in *Absalom, Absalom!* stand in for this encounter and model the hoped-for interaction between reader and text.

NOTES

1. Kenneth Haltman and Jules David Prown, eds., *American Artifacts: Essays in Material Culture* (Michigan State University Press, 2000), 4.

2. Jules David Prown, "Material/Culture: Can the Farmer and the Cowman Still Be Friends?," in *Learning from Things: Method and Theory in Material Culture Studies*, ed. W. David Kingery (Washington, D.C.: Smithsonian Books, 1996), 23.

3. I use the term "fictional photographs," following Judith Sensibar's lead, because it most accurately describes the metaphoric aspect of the figurative photograph in a specifically literary form. By the modern logic, perhaps best articulated by Roland Barthes, that "language is, by nature, fictional," all photographs described in linguistic form, including text, are "fictional," but I intend that the popular association of "fiction" with written literature will help anchor the more general "figurative photograph" in a textual, literary context. Judith Sensibar, "Faulkner's Fictional Photographs: Playing with Difference," in *Out of*

Bounds: Male Writers and Gender(ed) Criticism (Amhearst: University of Massachusetts Press, 1990), 290–315. Roland Barthes, *Camera Lucida* (New York: Farrar, Straus and Giroux, 1981), 87.

4. W. J. T. Mitchell, *Picture Theory* (Chicago: University of Chicago Press, 1994), 5.

5. Waldo Braden, *The Oral Tradition in the South* (Baton Rouge: Louisiana State University Press, 1983), ix.

6. Benedict Anderson, *Imagined Communities*, rev. ed. (London: Verso, 1991).

7. I explore the differing relations of black and white Southerners to this visual legacy of the South in much greater detail in my forthcoming book, *Ordering the Façade: Photography in Contemporary Southern Women's Writing*.

8. H. L. Mencken, reprinted in *Prejudices: Second Series* (New York: Knopf, 1920).

9. *I'll Take My Stand* (1930; Baton Rouge: Louisiana State University Press, 1977), 12, 52–60.

10. Frederick Douglass, "Narrative of the Life of Frederick Douglass, an American Slave, Written by Himself (1845)," reprinted in *The Oxford Frederick Douglass Reader*, ed. William L. Andrews (New York: Oxford University Press, 1996).

11. Faulkner's interactions with and attitudes toward photographs and the many photographers who wished to photograph him are most extensively discussed by Thomas Rankin in "The Ephemeral Instant: William Faulkner and the Photographic Image," in *Faulkner and the Artist: Faulkner and Yoknapatawpha, 1993*, ed. Donald M. Kartiganer and Ann J. Abadie (Jackson: University Press of Mississippi, 1996). Further references will be cited in the text. See also Sensibar, "Faulkner's Fictional Photographs," 300–2, and Joseph Blotner, *Faulkner: A Biography* (New York: Random House, 1974), 1: 232.

12. James B. Meriwether and Michael Millgate, eds., *The Lion in the Garden: Interviews with William Faulkner, 1926–1962* (New York: Random House, 1968), 253.

13. Faulkner, *Light in August* (1932; New York: Vintage International, 1990), 7. Further references will be cited in the text.

14. Faulkner, *The Sound and the Fury* (1929; New York: Vintage, 1946); *Sanctuary* (1930; New York: Vintage, 1993); *Absalom, Absalom!* (1936; New York: Vintage International, 1990), 15. Further references will be cited in the text.

15. Faulkner, *If I Forget Thee, Jerusalem (The Wild Palms)* (1939; New York: Vintage, 1990), 61–62.

16. Gary Lee Stonum, "The Fate of Design," in *William Faulkner's Absalom, Absalom!*, ed. Harold Bloom (New York: Chelsea House Publishers, 1987), 35–55.

17. Susan Sontag, *On Photography* (New York: Farrar, Straus and Giroux, 1977), 98.

18. This metaphor takes on special significance as it comes after the description of Hightower's sign on page 58: "carpentered neatly by himself and by himself lettered, with bits of broken glass contrived cunningly in the paint, so that at night, when the corner street lamp shone upon it, the letters glittered with an effect of Christmas:

REV. GAIL HIGHTOWER, D.D.

Art Lessons

Handpainted Xmas & Anniversary Cards

Photographs Developed

19. I adapt the notion of a "technology of gender" from Theresa de Lauretis, who in turn adapted it from Michel Foucault's "technology of sex," in *Technologies of Gender: Essays on Theory, Film, and Fiction* (Bloomington: Indiana University Press, 1987).

20. Frederick L. Gwynn and Joseph L. Blotner, eds., *Faulkner in the University* (Charlottesville: University Press of Virginia, 1959), 1.

21. Thadious Davis, "Reading Faulkner's Compson Appendix: Writing History from the Margins," in *Faulkner and Ideology: Faulkner and Yoknapatawpha, 1992*, ed. Donald M. Kartiganer and Ann J. Abadie (Jackson: University Press of Mississippi, 1995) 245–46.

22. Patricia B. Angley, *"Just Words": Reading Faulkner Writing Women* (Ann Arbor Mich.: University Microfilms, 1998), 179. Further references will be cited in the text.

23. See Susan Donaldson, "Reading Faulkner Reading Cowley Reading Faulkner: Authority and Gender in the Compson Appendix," *Faulkner Journal* 7 (Fall 1991–Spring

1992): 28, and Minrose Gwin, *The Feminine and Faulkner* (Knoxville: University of Tennessee Press, 1990), 60–62.

24. See Warwick Wadlington's brief outline of this criticism in *Reading Faulknerian Tragedy* (Ithaca: Cornell University Press, 1987), 173–74. Further references will be cited in the text. What Wadlington calls the "cognitive frame" within which such criticism houses the novel is sometimes applied directly, as in Cleanth Brooks's influential declaration that *Absalom, Absalom!* concerns the "nature of historical truth and . . . the problem of how we can 'know' the past" and is "a persuasive commentary upon the thesis that much of 'history' is really a kind of imaginative construction" (309, 311–12), and sometimes less obviously, as in Donald Kartiganer's rhetorical conclusion to his discussion of the novel's symbolic form and strategies of composition: "But where does self-serving strategy end and 'truth' begin? . . . At what point does fiction intersect with reality even as it preserves a discontinuity we have come to insist on?" *The Fragile Thread: The Meaning of Form in Faulkner's Novels* (Amherst: University of Massachusetts Press, 1979), 72.

25. Philip M. Weinstein, *What Else But Love?: The Ordeal of Race in Faulkner and Morrison* (New York: Columbia University Press, 1996), 193. Jay Watson makes a related argument that "*Absalom*'s greatest mystery is not so much epistemological as practical, ethical: not who did it or why he did it but how to live with the terrible knowledge you have gleaned, how to put that knowledge to best use," in "And Now What's to Do: Faulkner, Reading, Praxis," *Faulkner Journal*, 16 (Fall 1998): 70.

26. Kartiganer, 72.

27. Stephen M. Ross, *Fiction's Inexhaustible Voice* (Athens: University of Georgia Press, 1989), 234. Further references will be cited in the text.

28. Rosa's efforts are sometimes maddeningly ambivalent, though familiar, to feminist readers. Rosa understands her power as contingent on the very image her artist's position as "all polymath love's androgynous advocate" might work to subvert: her ability to summon Quentin as audience, her justification of her response to the happenings at Sutpen's Hundred, and indeed her ability to survive as a (nominally) respected citizen depend on the patriarchal codes surrounding Southern womanhood being maintained and closely followed.

29. Rosa's statement, and the persistence of her cultured desire, is echoed in Josephine Humphreys's *Dreams of Sleep* (New York: Penguin, 1984), when Will Reese's mistress, Claire, tells him, "I loved you before I loved you" (119).

30. Faulkner, "Evangeline," in *Uncollected Stories of William Faulkner*, ed. Joseph Blotner (New York: Vintage Books, 1981), 588. Further references will be cited in the text.

31. For a theorization of the relation between photographs, descriptive language, use, and meaning, see Mary Price, *The Photograph: A Strange, Confined Space* (Stanford: Stanford University Press, 1994), especially 1–21.

32. I use "acknowledgment" in a broad sense here. The specific acknowledgment Bon seeks is from his father, Thomas Sutpen, who has, according to Quentin and Shreve's narrative, abandoned Charles and his mother because of the mother's black ancestry. Thus, racial acknowledgment is portrayed within the frame of the family, which, as Weinstein shrewdly notes, mirrors what at the time of *Absalom*'s writing was a primary strategy of white Southern apologists: mythologizing the South into a culture by seeking to "anneal racial difference into family understanding." Faulkner's "narrative lens" is focused on Southern constructions of family, which prevents him from "reading his black portraits outside the themes of damage, disinheritance, and nonacknowledgment" (77). In his comparative reading of *Absalom, Absalom!* and *Jazz*, Weinstein suggests that Morrison hears in Bon's (and by extension, Faulkner's) "syndrome of outraged innocence," "a certain note, finally, of adolescent complaint" (149).

33. See Mitchell's discussion of the "politics of inscription" in *Picture Theory*, especially 109–50.

True and False Things: Faulkner and the World of Goods

T. J. Jackson Lears

The burden of Southern history comes in many forms. Mine was a burden of *faux* Southern history, some might say, though such distinctions are not always easily made. My father was a professional Southerner, even though (or maybe especially because) he was from the border state of Maryland. My brother was named for Robert E. Lee, and I was named for Stonewall Jackson; we also had a dog named Jefferson Davis—which pretty well captures the Southern view of how those gentlemen stacked up. This obsessive Southernism played itself out in my father's publicity stunts (designed to promote his furniture business); it also promoted—in me—a certain ambivalence toward things Southern.

When I was growing up in the 1960s, Faulkner was, of course, the quintessentially canonical Southern writer. So to my father he was our guy, even if we lived in Maryland not Mississippi, and even if my father had never read any Faulkner beyond his stories in the *Saturday Evening Post*. It was a complex fate, being the son of a professional Southerner, and one of its consequences was a tendency to guard against a superstitious overvaluation of Faulkner. I remained cautious regarding his work, teaching and admiring *The Sound and the Fury*, trying to penetrate *Absalom, Absalom!*, but not much else.

Now, thanks to the University of Mississippi's kind invitation, I've read much more of Faulkner, and I find it hard to avoid superlatives, superstitious or otherwise. A big part of the reason for that is the extraordinarily sensitive way he illuminates a territory that has fascinated historians (including myself) for the last twenty years or so: the social and personal meanings of things, and how those meanings changed with the coming of a mass consumer culture in the early twentieth-century United States.

Faulkner is prominent among an extraordinary group of writers and thinkers I like to call antimodern modernists: Henry Adams, T. S. Eliot, Willa Cather, Sherwood Anderson, Ralph Ellison, Walter Benjamin, Gabriel García Márquez—to mention a few of the most prominent. They used modernist forms to promote a critique of bourgeois modernity; they took sympathetically and seriously the people left behind by the Twentieth-Century Limited. Some focused on the meretriciousness, the inauthenticity, of mass consumable goods, and exalted preindustrial craft as an authentic alternative; they distinguished between true and false things. Antimodern modernism shaded over into the "producerist" critique of consumer culture, which has animated thinkers from William Morris to Wendell Berry. This remains a powerful and important, though unfashionable, critical tradition.[1] Faulkner participates in this tradition, but his world view contains and transcends the producerist perspective. My title thus embodies a characteristic academic bait and switch—I want to show that, while Faulkner *does* distinguish between true and false things, he also complicates that distinction in creative ways.

Faulkner illuminates the complexity of things largely through his sensitivity to aesthetic form. Like Oscar Wilde, he recognized that appearances, surfaces, mattered. Also he recognized with Wilde that the self, like the work of art, was a made thing and not an unchanging given. And yet if the form was fine enough, the art itself might come to resemble Keats's Grecian Urn, a timeless realm where Quentin and Caddy Compson could play in the stream forever, where forever would he love and she be fair.

Faulkner's outlook on things, in short, took three major forms. He was a producerist critic of mass consumer culture; he was also an anthropologist of that culture and a successful confidence man who recognized the social and personal meanings of things—their susceptibility to being used in the construction of a self. And finally he was a vernacular aesthete who sympathized with the longings embodied in things, from cheap trinkets to certified *objets d'art*—their capacity to convey a numinous, fetishlike power.

Faulkner's criticism of mass culture was rooted in his own experience as a professional writer—his desperate attempts to make money by producing pulp fiction and his hatred of himself for doing so. He was, he complained in a letter to his agent in the 1930s, "out of touch with the Kotex Age."[2] Here as elsewhere he revealed the misogyny characteristic of male modernists. Like them he linked mass culture with femininity and filth, but also, more broadly, with mindlessly destructive inanity. Joe Christmas reads a pulp magazine cover to cover before killing Joanna Burden. The tall convict in *The Wild Palms* is inspired to his stupid crime by a story in a mass-market detective magazine. Critics and scholars have noted the neon wasteland in Faulkner's fiction, the blighted wilderness of commercial signs and their frequent association with human degradation. In *The Sound and the Fury*, billboard boosterism ("Keep Your Eye on Mottson") reflects the character of Jason Compson, who is mean, petty, vindictive, calculating—a pathetic caricature of economic rationality. Whenever the

subject of mass culture comes up in one of Faulkner's loquacious character's monologues, one has to be prepared for a rant against inauthenticity.
In *The Wild Palms*, Wilbourne engages in regular tirades like this one:

> . . . we have got rid of love just as we have got rid of Christmas. We have radio
> in the place of God's voice and instead of having to save emotional currency
> for months and years to deserve one chance to spend it all for love we can now
> spread it thin into coppers, and titillate ourselves at any newsstand, two to the
> block like sticks of chewing gum or chocolate from the automatic machines. If
> Jesus returned today we would have to crucify him quick in our own defense,
> to justify and preserve the civilization we have worked and suffered and died
> shrieking and cursing in rage and impotence and terror for two thousand years
> to create and perfect in man's own image; if Venus returned she would be a
> soiled man in a subway lavatory with a palm full of French post-cards.[3]

Gavin Stevens passes equally harsh judgments in *Intruder in the Dust*
(1949). An embodiment of displaced patrician honor, he disdains "all the
spurious uproar produced by men deliberately fostering and then getting
rich on our national passion for the mediocre." Americans, he says, are
"the only people on earth who brag publicly of being second-rate, i.e. low-
brows." A once-great nation has become "a mass of people who no longer
have anything in common save a frantic greed for money and a basic fear
of a failure of national character which they hide from one another behind
a loud lip-service to the flag." Old ideals of duty and sacrifice have given
way to "a national religion of the entrails in which man owes no duty to
his soul because he has been absolved of soul to owe duty to and instead is
static heir at birth to an inevictable quit-claim on a wife a car a radio and
an old-age pension."[4] Despite flashes of insight, Stevens's tirades eventually descend to a parody of mid-century mass culture criticism. Recoiling
from the noise and crowds on the Jefferson town square, the yards and
flowerbeds cluttered with ornaments, he identifies the automobile as a
substitute phallus for the castrated American male.

Yet Faulkner's evocation of the destructive power of modernity involves
insights more subtle than Stevens's armchair sociology. Like William
James, Max Weber, and the Nashville Agrarians, Faulkner was involved in
a critique of rationalization. Like them he questioned the consequences
of the effort to exert systematic control over all aspects of natural and
human life. Consider the picture of Doane's Mill in the opening pages
of *Light in August*.

> All the men in the village worked in the mill or for it. It was cutting pine. It
> had been there seven years and in seven years more it would destroy all the
> timber within its reach. Then some of the machinery and most of the men
> who ran it and existed because of and for it would be loaded onto freight cars
> and moved away. But some of the machinery would be left, since new pieces

could be bought on the installment plan—gaunt, staring, motionless wheels rising from mounds of brick rubble and ragged weeds with a quality profoundly astonishing, and gutted boilers lifting their rusting and unsmoking stacks with an air stubborn, baffled and bemused upon a stumppocked scene of profound peaceful desolation.[5]

The passage distills volumes of social theory. The mill owners deploy apparently rational and certainly up-to-date managerial strategies—buying new machinery on the installment plan—with the single purpose of quick profits. Transforming trees into lumber, nature into commodity, they lay waste to the land and move on. Their men are as mobile and expendable as their machines. The mill, embodying the merger of industrial technology and money worship, reveals the vapidity of phrases like "economic development" and "creative destruction."

In the same novel, Faulkner also takes on the less tangible aspects of rationalization, the disenchantment of culture, the harnessing of even religion to managerial standards of efficiency. So the defrocked preacher Hightower laments that "what is killing the Church . . . [are] the professionals who control it and who have removed the bells from its steeples."[6] The loss of music suggests the disappearance of soaring aspirations amid the professionals' quest for control and predictability. As an alternative to this lifeless new world, Faulkner sometimes invoked the producerist vision of the simple life—as Gavin Stevens does in Intruder in the Dust when he pays tribute to Lucas Beauchamp. Lucas, says Stevens, possessed

> not even just the will but the desire to endure because he loved the old few simple things which no one wanted to take from him: not an automobile nor flash clothes nor his picture in the paper but a little of music (his own), a hearth, not his child but any child, a God a heaven which a man may avail himself a little of at any time without having to wait to die, a little earth for his own sweat to fall on among his own green shoots and plants.[7]

Faulkner was looking for the solidity he found in Holston House, with its "original log walls and puncheon floors and hand-mortised joints of which are still buried somewhere beneath the modern pressed glass and brick veneer and neon tubes." We are in the familiar producerist trope of decline from authenticity to artifice. Just as the copper light in August— "an older light than ours"—contrasts with the inauthentic glare of commercial neon, the old ways are somehow more "real" than the new.[8]

However simpleminded or easily parodied, this antimodern conviction has shown remarkable staying power. For decades, ordinary folk as well as high modernists have continued to believe that the price of modernity— especially capitalist modernity—has been to a severing of ties to older, more authentic ways of doing things. Hence the centrality of craftsmanship to the producerist critique. In Cash Bundren of *As I Lay Dying*, Faulkner created a clear-cut example of the craftsman as hero. The Bundrens' neighbor Tull comments: "I have seen him spend an hour trimming out a wedge like it was glass he was working, when he could have reached around and picked up a dozen sticks and drove them into the joint and made it do."[9] Cash himself muses, after his brother Darl has just been packed off to the state insane asylum in Jackson for setting a barn on fire:

> ... it's a shame in a way. Folks seem to get away from the older right teaching that says to drive the nails down and turn trim the edges well always like it was for your own use and comfort you were making it. It's like some folks has the smooth, pretty boards to build a courthouse with and others dont have no more than rough lumber fitten to build a chicken coop. But it's better to build a tight chicken coop than a shoddy courthouse.[10]

Cash's skill and care with things stands out against the ineptitude of the rest of his family, especially his pathetic and ludicrous father, Anse, who conceives the lame idea of putting a cement cast on Cash's broken leg. This botched piece of craftsmanship leaves his son crippled for life, while Anse, at the close, is a rejuvenated man with a new wife, new teeth, and a new graphophone. The Bundren kids, meanwhile, get bananas and not the shiny toy train that Vardaman craves but that only town boys can afford. So these uprooted producers are left adrift in a tawdry consumer paradise, one where the most desirable goods are unaffordable except on the installment plan. The graphophone is one example. Yet despite its associations with the cheap and meretricious, the graphophone is not a totally false thing. It makes music, which (even the Bundrens seem to agree) can put one in touch with the ineffable.

Here, at the close of *As I Lay Dying*, we see a hint of something more than producerist moralism—an aesthetic intervention in everyday life. This was Faulkner's way. To be sure, he was a producerist with respect to his craft. He believed in the solidity of words as things and treated them with respect accordingly. But he was no plain speaker, no icon of authenticity; in fact he was a poseur throughout his life. Faulkner epitomized the artist as confidence man, who realized how much art (and life) could be constituted through the creation of convincing narratives—stories of obscure war injuries, or of bastard children tucked away. After his largely successful imposture of an ace aviator, Faulkner adopted a series of roles throughout his life: the bohemian genius, the humanist sage, the gentleman riding to hounds. So it should come as no surprise that in his writing as in his life, Faulkner was a producerist critic of mass consumerism but also a shrewd observer of the meanings of things.

As an anthropologist of American material life, Faulkner rivaled Henry James and Edith Wharton. Deploying various props in his own performances, he understood the power of appearances, of surface display, as a source of social, personal, and even spiritual significance. He recognized that artificial materials could be used to fashion an authentic self.

Faulkner became a bourgeois realist at large, dissecting status amid stuff with the zeal of a Dickens or a Balzac. He recognized the profound social gulf between Thomas Sutpen, whose mansion was to be his crown of conquest, and Will Varner, who stood before another mansion "trying to find out what it must have felt like to be the fool that would need all this . . . just to eat and sleep in." He knew how even a small proportion of power could make a difference, as he described "the rich and white lawyers and judges and marshals talking to one another around their proud cigars, the haughty and powerful of the earth" (from Lucas Beauchamp's point of view) or contrariwise, how important a small proportion of submission could be too as Lucas acknowledged when he made his wife, Molly, take off her headkerchief for the portrait that hung in their cabin. "I didn't want no field nigger picture in the house," Lucas said. Clothes could signify social stasis, a caste and class system as solid as iron or wood, as in the "trucks filled with wooden-faced country people in garments like a colored wood meticulously carved," driving into town to contemplate the prospect of Lucas's lynching.[11]

But Faulkner also realized that clothes and other goods could signify social fluidity and possibility—longings for status ascent, or for an escape from status markers altogether. Consider Virgil Snopes and Fonzo (of *Sanctuary*) in Memphis for the first time: "carrying their new, imitation leather suitcases, their new hats slanted above their shaven necks." Or Popeye's "tight suit and stiff hat all angles, like a modernistic lampshade." Or the bohemian's progress of Harry Wilbourne, from arriving hopelessly overdressed in a dark suit at Charlotte Rittenmeyer's party to the appearance he and Charlotte present to the suspicious doctor on the desolate beach where the wild palms clatter: "the man . . . in a pair of disreputable khaki slacks and a sleeveless jersey undershirt and no hat in a region where even young people believed the summer sun to be fatal." The woman in "them pants that was just exactly too little for her in exactly the right places." Harry and Charlotte have tried to escape the world of ascribed status and rigid convention, to become unclassifiable. It's worked for them, for a while, as it did for Joe Christmas, who when he first showed up at the mill looked to Byron Bunch "like a tramp, yet not like a tramp either."[12]

Apart from clothes, other kinds of things could embody meanings more complex than status ascent or self-assertion—longings for human connection, as in the "stale and flyspecked box of candy" Joe Christmas gives to Bobbie in a clumsy attempt at courtship; desires for an aura of domestic comfort, despite all odds, as in the Grand Rapids mission furniture the bachelor Gavin Stevens rents for his digs, or in the San Antonio brothel Wilbourne visits in *The Wild Palms*, with its "bone veneered dining room table bearing an imitation cut-glass punch bowl and scarred by the white rings from damp glass bottles, a pranola slotted for coins and twelve chairs ranged along the four walls in orderly sequence like tombstones in a military graveyard, where the maid left him to sit and look at a lithograph of the St Bernard dog saving the child from the snow and another of President Roosevelt."[13]

There is a vein of vitality running beneath the tawdriest assemblies of stuff, Faulkner implies. Not even the "paintless Negro cabins" can resist the imprint of their inhabitants' things. Those cabins were "where on Monday morning in the dust of the grassless treeless yards half naked children should have been crawling and scrabbling after broken cultivator wheels and worn out automobile tires and empty snuff-bottles and tin cans and in the backyards smoke-blackened iron pots should have been bubbling over wood fires beside the sagging fences of vegetable patches and chicken runs which by nightfall would be gaudy with drying overalls and aprons and towels and unionsuits."[14] This is the anarchy but also the dignity of poverty, of poor people trying to create a humane way of life amid the detritus of the transition to modernity.

So Faulkner sympathized and identified with the longings embodied in things, even shoddy and mass-produced things. He also understood how things could be freighted with strange and revelatory powers. Faulkner's recognition of the fetishistic power of things placed him alongside Walter Benjamin, Joseph Cornell, and other modernist alchemists of the quotidian. He had a rare capacity for capturing the way objects could acquire a magical aura, at least in the eyes of their perceiver. He brilliantly caught Vardaman's child perspective on the sustainable, repeatable magic of the toy train, contrasted with the disposable ordinariness of the bananas. "Bananas are gone, eaten. Gone. When it runs on the track shines again." For Lucas Beauchamp the magic is harnessed in the divining machine he acquires to search for buried treasure. He held the machine "before him as if it were some object symbolical and sanctified for a ceremony, a ritual." But for young Gail Hightower the thing magic asserts itself in more troubling ways when he finds his father's old frock coat, "almost unrecognizable with patches." When Gail sees a blue patch, he feels "a kind of hushed and triumphant terror which made him a little sick." He is convinced that the blue patch came from the coat of a Yankee his father had killed; he stares at his father with awe and fear. The boy will be haunted by dreams of lost heroism for the rest of his life.[15]

For Harry Wilbourne in *The Wild Palms*, the fetishlike thing that brings magical self-transformation is the wallet full of money that he finds in a trash can. He drops a pair of bricks in the trash can, part of his elaborate scheme for making his rendezvous with Charlotte seem respectable. What happens next is a clever foreshadowing of the consumer culture that, for a while in Chicago, will sustain and frame their fate: "the edges of the papers merely tilted and produced from among them, with the magical abruptness which the little torpedo containing charge from a sale emerges from its tube in a store, a leather wallet."[16]

Certain things can promise a more sinister sort of transformation, can bring the observer to the brink of personal chaos and social doom. The importance of clocks in *The Sound and the Fury* is well known, but look (as well) at the clock in Reba's whorehouse in Memphis, where Temple Drake has recently arrived: "She watched the final light condense into the clock face, and the dial change from a round orifice in the darkness to a disc suspended in nothingness, the original chaos, and change in turn to a crystal ball holding in its still and cryptic depths the ordered chaos of the intricate and shadowy world upon whose scarred flanks the old wounds whirl onward at dizzy speed into darkness lurking in new disasters."[17]

The most apt harbingers of futility, for Faulkner, are work shoes: brogans. "Beside his chair his brogans sit," says Darl of his father in *As I Lay Dying:* "They look as though they had been hacked with a blunt axe out of pig-iron." They epitomize the crudeness and sloppiness of Anse himself, especially to the brooding Darl. But to Joe Christmas, brogans are truly terrifying embodiments of his negritude, of the black abyss into which he is being drawn. In headlong flight from his pursuers, he stops in the cottonhouse not far from Joanna's house. "He paused there only long enough to lace up the brogans: the black shoes, the black shoes smelling of negro. They looked like they had been chopped out of iron ore with a dull axe. Looking down at the harsh, crude, clumsy shapelessness of them, he said 'Hah' through his teeth. It seemed to him that he could see himself being hunted by white men at last into the black abyss which had been waiting, trying, for thirty years to drown him and into which now and at last he had actually entered, bearing now upon his ankles the definite and ineradicable gauge of its upward moving." He could not escape the nemesis embedded in "the shoes, the black shoes smelling of negro: that mark on his ankles the gauge definite and ineradicable of the black tide creeping up his legs, moving from his feet upwards as death moves."[18]

So we are back with Faulkner where I, at least, first encountered him—staring into the abyss, encountering nothingness, as the philosopher

William Barrett memorably characterized him in his great history of existentialism, *Irrational Man* (1958). Given the importance of material things in Faulkner's symbolic universe, it is fitting that Faulkner imagined his alternative to the abyss as a specifically material shape—an urn, recalling of course Keats's Grecian Urn. And here I draw on David Minter's fine work and that of other predecessors.[19]

Minter cites a number of key references to vases and urns, which can be recast chronologically. In *Flags in the Dust* (1929), Horace Benbow returns from his assignment at the YMCA canteen in World War I with a glass-blowing set and makes "one almost perfect vase of clear amber" that he keeps "always on his night table," calls "by his sister's name," and addresses as "thou still unravished bride of quietude." In *Light in August* (1932), Lena Grove looks "like something moving forever and without progress across an urn" while Joe Christmas has a vision of urns cracked and spilling forth liquid putrefaction, and Gail Hightower as a young minister sees his future "intact and on all sides complete and inviolable, like a classic and serene vase." In the 1933 preface to *The Sound and the Fury*, Faulkner looked back on the creation of the character of Caddy: "I said to myself, now I can write. Now I can make myself a vase like that which the old Roman kept at his bedside and wore the rim slowly away with kissing it."[20]

The vase or urn is the crafted expression of aspiration, of longing. But of course the longing to create a perfect vessel is fated to fall short. "I suppose I knew all the time that I could never live forever inside of it," Faulkner wrote of his "Roman vase," *The Sound and the Fury*, in that same preface. Amid all the accumulation, manipulation, and creation of things, there is inevitable loss. Beneath the savage standardizations of consumer culture, there is a deeper, buried life. Horace Benbow saw it in the coeds' eyes on the train to Jefferson, when he was in pursuit of Temple Drake—the girls all had "that identical, cool, innocent, unabashed expression which he knew well in their eyes, above the savage identical paint upon their mouths; like music moving, like honey poured in sunlight, pagan and evanescent and serene, thinly evocative of all lost days and unabashed delights, in the sun."[21]

The Grecian Urn caught the core of unfulfilled yearning at the core of Faulkner's art—forever will she be fair but forever also out of reach. The awareness of inevitable loss, of frustration and defeat, is what makes Faulkner's tone so often elegiac. As he wrote Meta Carpenter, "what is valuable is what you have lost, since you never had the chance to wear out and so lose it shabbily." Faulkner's longing for lost things reenchanted the disenchanted world of modernity, endowing even the most banal objects with power and significance. Like his fellow Mississippian Eudora Welty, he knew that "when you go looking for what is lost, everything is a sign."[22]

Faulkner spent his life looking for lost things, and we are forever in his debt as a result, no matter how forgiving the terms of our installment plan.

NOTES

1. I discuss antimodern modernism in *No Place of Grace: Antimodernism and the Transformation of American Culture, 1880–1920* (New York: Pantheon, 1981) and producerism in *Fables of Abundance: A Cultural History of American Advertising* (New York: Basic Books, 1994).

2. *Selected Letters of William Faulkner*, ed. Joseph Blotner (New York: Vintage, 1978), 96.

3. William Faulkner, *The Wild Palms* (New York: Vintage, 1939), 114–15.

4. William Faulkner, *Intruder in the Dust*, in *William Faulkner: Novels 1942–1954* (New York: Library of America, 1994), 401, 402, 436.

5. William Faulkner, *Light in August*. The Corrected Text (1932; New York: Vintage, 1990), 4–5.

6. Ibid., 487.

7. *Intruder*, 402.

8. William Faulkner, *Requiem for a Nun*, in *William Faulkner: Novels 1942–1954*, 478. Faulkner on "an older light than ours," quoted in Frederick L. Gwynn and Joseph Blotner, eds., *Faulkner in the University* (New York: Vintage, 1965), 199.

9. William Faulkner, *As I Lay Dying*, in *William Faulkner: Novels 1930–1935* (New York: Library of America, 1985), 56.

10. Ibid., 158.

11. William Faulkner, *The Hamlet* (1940; New York: Vintage, 1991), 7; *Go Down, Moses* (1940; New York: Vintage, 1991), 70; *Intruder*, 294; *Sanctuary* (New York: Modern Library, 1931), 165.

12. *Sanctuary*, 226, 5; *Wild Palms*, 5; *Light in August*, 31.

13. *Light in August*, 191; *Intruder*, 108; *Wild Palms*, 177.

14. *Intruder*, 395.

15. *As I Lay Dying*, 43; *Go Down, Moses*, 85; *Light in August*, 469. On alchemists of the quotidian, see Lears, *Fables of Abundance*, chapter 12.

16. *Wild Palms*, 43.

17. *Sanctuary*, 180–81.

18. *As I Lay Dying*, 11; *Light in August*, 331, 339.

19. William Barrett, *Irrational Man* (New York: Anchor, 1958), 52–54; David Minter, *William Faulkner: His Life and Work* (Baltimore: Johns Hopkins University Press, 1980).

20. Minter, 85, 44, 99, 102, 130.

21. Ibid., 99; *Sanctuary*, 202.

22. Meta Carpenter Wilde and Orin Borsten, *A Loving Gentleman: The Love Story of William Faulkner and Meta Carpenter* (New York: Simon & Schuster), 311–12; Eudora Welty, "The Wide Net," in *The Collected Stories of Eudora Welty* (New York: Harcourt Brace, 1982), 179.

Contributors

Charles S. Aiken, professor of geography at the University of Tennessee, is the author of *The Cotton Plantation South since the Civil War* and a recently completed book-length study, "A Cosmos of My Own: William Faulkner's Geography."

Katherine R. Henninger is assistant professor of English at Louisiana State University, Baton Rouge. She has published essays on Zora Neale Hurston, Josephine Humphreys, and Faulkner, and is author of *Ordering the Facade: Photography in Contemporary Southern Women's Writing*.

T. J. Jackson Lears is Board of Governors Professor of History at Rutgers University and the editor in chief of *Raritan Quarterly Review*. He is the author of *No Place of Grace: Antimodernism and the Transformation of American Culture, 1880–1920*; *Fables of Abundance: A Cultural History of Advertising in America*; and *Something for Nothing: Luck in America*.

Miles Orvell, professor of English and American Studies at Temple University, is the author of *Invisible Parade: The Fiction of Flannery O'Connor*, *The Real Thing: Imitation and Authenticity in American Culture*, *After the Machine: Visual Arts and the Erasing of Cultural Boundaries*, *American Photography*, and *John Vachon's America: Photographs and Letters from the Depression to World War II*.

Kevin Railey, professor and chair of the Department of English at Buffalo State College, is the author of *Natural Aristocracy: History, Ideology, and the Production of William Faulkner* and essays on literature, theory, and education and pedagogy.

D. Matthew Ramsey is an assistant professor of American Literature and Film at Stephen F. Austin State University. He has published and presented several articles on Faulkner's connections to popular culture, queer theory, and film. He is currently working on essays on *Pirates of the Caribbean*, Faulkner's "Golden Land," and a book project entitled *Adapting the Postcolonial*.

Joseph R. Urgo, former professor and chair of the Department of English at the University of Mississippi, is dean of the faculty at Hamilton College. He is the author of *Faulkner's Apocrypha: "A Fable," Snopes, and the Spirit of Human Rebellion*; *Willa Cather and the Myth of American Migration*; *Novel Frames: Literature as Guide to Race, Sex, and History in America Culture*; and, most recently, *In the Age of Distraction*.

Jay Watson, associate professor of English at the University of Mississippi, is the author of *Forensic Fictions: The Lawyer Figure in Faulkner* and numerous essays on Faulkner, Freud, legal theory, Lillian Smith, and Erskine Caldwell. He was Fulbright Professor of English at the University of Turku and at Abo Akademi University, Finland, 2002–2003.

Patricia Yaeger, professor of English at the University of Michigan, is the author of *Honey-Mad Women: Emancipatory Strategies in Women's Writing*, *The Geography of Identity*, and *Dirt and Desire: Reconstructing Southern Women's Writing, 1930–1990*, and coeditor of *Refiguring the Father: New Feminist Readings of Patriarchy* and *Nationalisms and Sexualities*.

Index